CAROLINE LOCKHART: HER LIFE AND LEGACY

Caroline Lockhart
Her Life and Legacy

NECAH STEWART FURMAN

Introduction by Annette Kolodny

The Buffalo Bill Historical Center

CODY, WYOMING

The University of Washington Press

SEATTLE & LONDON

Library of Congress Cataloguing in Publication Data
Furman, Necah Stewart.
    Caroline Lockhart : her life and legacy / by Necah Stewart Furman.
       p.   cm.
    Includes bibliographical references (p.) and index.
    ISBN 0–295–97346–3. — ISBN 0–295–97347–1 (paper)
    1. Lockhart, Caroline, 1870–1962—Biography.   2. Women novelists, American—20th
century—Biography.   3. Women ranchers—Wyoming—Biography.   4. Ranch life—
Wyoming—Cody Region.   5. Cody Region (Wyo.)—Biography.   I. Title.
PS3523.O237Z67   1994
813'.52—dc20   93–44383
[B]   CIP

The paper used in this publication meets the minimum requirements of American National
Standard for Information Sciences—Permanence of Paper for Printed Library Materials, ANSI
Z39.48–1984.

*Choosing one's parents is the first major challenge in life.
I was fortunate.
In loving memory of my mother,
Lillah Jay Fairchild Stewart,
and my father,
Harold Davis Stewart.*

Contents

Illustrations

All photographs not otherwise credited have been provided courtesy of

THE WESTERN HISTORY RESEARCH CENTER

(CAROLINE LOCKHART COLLECTION)

UNIVERSITY OF WYOMING

LARAMIE, WYOMING

Prologue

The West is a territory of imagination, in a recurring drama of the
American character shaped by exigencies of place . . . . An exactly
defined region is less important, we would argue, than the perceptions
of the region, than the westering mind itself.

Arthur R. Huseboe and William Geyer,
"Herbert Krause and the Western Experience"

Today, more than a century after the United States Bureau of the Census
declared the frontier closed, people are still enthralled by that amorphous
region known as "the West."[1] Captivated by the image—if not the reality
of its legacy—journalists, dramatists, novelists, and historians have successfully mined the West for material, perpetuating the myths and stereotypes, both positive and negative, associated with the frontier phenomenon. Numbered among these writers was Caroline Cameron Lockhart.
Born in 1871, Lockhart became one of the first western women journalists and novelists to realize the value of a literature that would capture the
essence of a passing era, the spirit of a region, and its people.

From the vantage point of her upbringing as a Kansas ranch girl, her experiences as a journalist in the East, and her years as a novelist, newspaper
editor, and rancher in the West, Lockhart developed a growing consciousness of the transition taking place and of the conflicts between eastern
and western cultural values. Her books—compared favorably to those of
Owen Wister—reflected this awareness, championing as they did the region and culture of which she became so much a part.[2] Although the free
land was gone, the spirit remained, and Caroline Lockhart did her part to
preserve it.

For years, cowboys and Indians held top billing as the major characters
on the stage of public interest. The relatively recent feminist emphasis,
however, has contributed to studies of women in the West, both as individuals and as a social and political force. Despite the popular stereotypes
that emerged, few frontier women fit into narrow or specific patterns. The
true picture of the western woman was of course complex, with most women
encompassing various portraits.

Caroline Lockhart was such an individual—her complex personality resists easy categorization. Lockhart was not the Madonna victimized by male domination, nor was she a member of the Victorian Cult of True Womanhood, which decreed that women must be pious, pure, domestic, and submissive. Neither was she the Gentle Tamer, although a facet of her personality—paradoxically perhaps—yearned for a position in society and its accoutrements of home, husband, and family. Sexually liberated for the times, her penchant for flouting convention hindered her quest for married respectability. She had numerous liaisons and relationships throughout her life, but none that resulted in marriage.[3]

Above all, Lockhart was a writer with a point of view. She fought with her pen and her actions to preserve what she considered to be the best of an older and more primitive western society. To this end, she fought the encroachments of industrialization, eastern influence, and the sportsmen who came West to kill wild game for pleasure. An unrelenting crusader, she fought with vehemence and few holds barred for what she believed in or against the causes she opposed. She fought Prohibition because she thought it was a preposterous law and because she liked to drink. She fought ineptitude and quackery, whether in politics or the medical profession, although her motives were not always altruistic. She fought technology and much that it engendered because she saw it robbing the Old West of its primitive vitality and transforming its people in the process. She battled the town's "Better Element" because she could not condone their hypocrisy; yet, her diaries show the hypocrisy within herself. The many Lockhart Diaries—used as a therapeutic outlet for her innermost secrets—along with the testimony of many old-timers who still remember her, some with respect and some with dislike—revealed that she was a tough-minded, talented woman ahead of her time and often out of place.[4] Best described as "a diamond in the rough," Caroline Lockhart, through her novels and related journalistic writings, left a rich but largely forgotten literary legacy that contributed to the mythology of the West.

ACKNOWLEDGMENTS

Eloise Jensen Stock, wife of oilman Paul Stock of Cody, Wyoming, was the woman responsible for renewing interest in Caroline Lockhart's life and works. Charming and intelligent, Eloise Stock was herself a writer and teacher. Eloise befriended the novelist during her later years and ultimately decided that Lockhart's accomplishments and career were deserving of a biographical study. I would like to express my appreciation, in her memory, to the Stock Foundation, which provided the funding to carry out her wishes.

Professor Richard Etulain of the University of New Mexico first suggested that I become involved in this fascinating project. For this motivation, for providing me the hard-to-find *Old West and New,* and especially for his insightful reading of the manuscript, I am most grateful. A big thank-you also goes to the staff and management of the Buffalo Bill Historical Center, and particularly to senior curator Dr. Paul Fees, who provided both administrative assistance and unstinting moral support during the years required to bring the book to fruition.

Without the generosity of attorney David Dominick of Denver, Colorado, who provided access to the invaluable restricted collection of Lockhart materials housed at the American Heritage Center at the University of Wyoming in Laramie, the book would not have been written. Gene Gressley, director of the center, and his extremely helpful staff are to be complimented for their patience and their competent support during my research efforts there.

Among the primary source materials at the American Heritage Center, the Lockhart Diaries and autobiographical drafts enabled me to tell the story in a style otherwise impossible. Each of the three different drafts of various autobiographical materials—interspersed throughout different sections of the Lockhart Collection—despite minor literary and stylistic variations and inaccuracies in dates, contain basically the same content. All these materials are notable for the dialogue recorded verbatim by Lockhart, in detail and often in the dialect of those she encountered. When Lockhart attempted to destroy the most complete of these autobiographies, "Nothin'll Ever Happen to Me," a neighbor, Ann Harper, interceded to save the manuscript, which she then gave to David Dominick for his use. Although the Lockhart "Last Will and Testament" (Park County District Courthouse, Cody, Wyoming) indicates that the autobiography was sent to Lockhart's friend and editor, Francis Clark Smith in New York, there is no proof that this was done.

Caroline Lockhart's Diaries, written mostly in ledgers in journal format, proved to be even more valuable as a biographical tool, revealing as they do her innermost thoughts, loves, and hatreds, oftentimes with surprising candor. Interviews conducted with numerous residents of Cody, Wyoming, Lockhart's hometown, added to my understanding of this interesting woman. To those individuals who generously provided time and information, I am most grateful. Among them, local rancher and author Lucille Patrick Hicks was especially hospitable. Her book, *Caroline Lock-*

hart: Liberated Lady, 1870–1962, contains an interesting collection of excerpts from the Lockhart Diaries.[5] The originals of these were a rich and vivid resource. I remember well an enjoyable weekend spent discussing and analyzing Caroline Lockhart at the Patrick Ranch on the Southfork. I appreciate also the generosity of National Parks historian Mary Shivers Culpin, who provided a draft of her article on Lockhart and other valuable resource material.

Relatives of Caroline Lockhart—E. E. Andrews, Elizabeth Sutton, and Sylvia Crowder—as well as Lockhart friends such as Dorothea Nebel, have been extremely helpful in providing information otherwise unobtainable. Marian Sweeney, author of *Gold at Dixie Gulch;* Cort Conley, co-author of *River of No Return;* and Bill Painter of Millis, Massachusetts, provided me with photographs and with firsthand information on Lockhart's many relationships.

I am also grateful to many others who helped in the production and publication process—Joanne Pendall, who edited a portion of it; Lois Harmeson, my competent typist; Julidta Tarver and Gretchen Van Meter of the University of Washington Press, and Suzanne G. Tyler, director of publications for the Buffalo Bill Historical Center, who with great perseverance and understanding ushered the manuscript through the final stages. I would like to commend as well Christina K. Stopka, librarian/archivist, and Tina Hovekamp, assistant librarian at the Buffalo Bill Historical Center, and Lynn Houze and Jeanne Cook of the Park County Historical Society, who diligently assisted in efforts to verify dates and identify first names of the many regional characters referred to by Lockhart only by their initials. Our researchers went so far as to interview Cody old-timers, who told us that, in many instances, these individuals simply used initials as given names— nothing more.

And, finally, to members of my family—for your fortitude and the treasured times together: Thanks to all of you!

NECAH STEWART FURMAN
Tucson, Arizona

Introduction

It was with considerable personal satisfaction that Caroline Cameron Lockhart joined the old-timers to lead the opening parade of the annual Cody Stampede in 1952. More than a quarter century earlier, she had urged the "boosters" of Cody, Wyoming, to plan an "annual frontier event" that would showcase "exhibitions of cowboy skill" and thereby perpetuate "some of the Old West that we love." Her May 5, 1920, article in the Park County *Enterprise*, which she then edited, had had its intended effect.[1] July 4 and the annual Stampede came almost to be synonymous in Cody. Like the town's namesake and original promoter, Colonel William Frederick Cody—popularly known as "Buffalo Bill" from his touring Wild West shows—Lockhart had always regarded Cody, Wyoming, as a preserve of the frontier past: a place to which urbanites from the East and Middle West would flock as paying tourists. The visionary Cody had helped to found the town in 1896, locating it near the entrance to the Yellowstone country, designated a national park in 1872. Whereas Cody had arranged for a railroad spur to the town by 1901 and negotiated for federally supported dam and irrigation projects, by 1921 Lockhart was promoting the beneficial aspects of "dude ranching." In her novel *The Dude Wrangler*, published that same year, she not only recognized the changing conditions that had made tourism a staple of the region's economy; she also echoed the attractions of invigorating air, revitalizing scenery, and healthful activity which the guest ranches promised their "dude" clientele.

Together—he through his Wild West shows and the founding of the town that bore his name; she through her writing and community activities—Buffalo Bill Cody and Caroline Lockhart shrewdly catered to an early twentieth-century popular yearning to arrest time in the free-range era of the cattleman and the cowboy. Working close to nature, enjoying unfenced freedom and what Wallace Stegner has called "energetic individualism,"[2] the cowboy had come to symbolize what was left of a waning frontier. By the turn of the century, the image had become a commodity, variously merchandised through staged extravaganzas, pulp fiction, tourism, and—later—the movies.

Whereas the former army scout and buffalo hunter for the railroads sought to offer the fable whole and unblemished, the accomplished journalist was too honest not to report its harsher realities. Attracted to what Stegner has catalogued as characteristic of the cowboy hero—his "great physical competence, stoicism, determination, recklessness, endurance, toughness, rebelliousness, [and] resistance to control"[3]—and sharing many of those characteristics herself, Lockhart nonetheless wrote about the sometimes squalid working conditions of the poorly paid cowpuncher and about the presence of exploited immigrant laborers on the great federal dam projects. Although she may have gone West in search of the fable, and even homesteaded a claim in Montana in her later years, Lockhart also portrayed the complexities of a region undergoing rapid social and economic transitions.

Not that she started out to be either a regionalist or a western writer. Beginning her career in 1889, at the age of eighteen, as a news reporter for the Boston *Post,* and then moving on to the more prestigious Philadelphia *Bulletin* in 1900, Lockhart's journalistic pieces were marked by biting humor and a flair for physical adventure. On occasion, and often on her own initiative, she ventured into investigative journalism. But as a female reporter, she was never regularly assigned the great issues of the day—the massacre of 200 Sioux at Wounded Knee, South Dakota, in 1890; the adoption of women's suffrage by Colorado in 1893; the beginning of "Jim Crow" segregation following the Supreme Court ruling on *Plessy* v. *Ferguson* in 1896; or the United States' war with Spain over Cuba in 1898. Instead, with a few exceptions, she interviewed celebrities and socialites, detailed her tour of Europe in 1900, and generally produced the kinds of human interest features that won wide readership.

Three months in the New Mexico Territory in the spring of 1898 resulted in a story that revealed only her eastern-bred prejudices against Mexicans. Not until the publication of her short story, "A Girl in the Rockies," in *Lippincott's Monthly Magazine* of August 1902 did Lockhart begin to exhibit both a keen ear for colloquial western speech and an appreciation for the breathtaking beauties of western landscapes. Based on her tour of the Swift Current country of Montana earlier that year, "A Girl in the Rockies" gave notice of Lockhart's increasing interest in western locales.

The turning point, however, as Necah Stewart Furman's biography makes clear, was Lockhart's visit to Cody, Wyoming, in 1904, at the age of thirty-three, and her subsequent decision to move there permanently the next year. Already prominent as a journalist and short story writer, Lockhart would take from Cody much of the material required for her most serious literary efforts, her seven novels published between 1911 and 1933.

In 1904, when Lockhart first saw it, Cody still had the appearance of a rough frontier village. As Furman re-creates the scene, hitching racks for horses lined the wooden plank sidewalks and kerosene lamps lit the two blocks of the main street at night. Yet banks, schools, and office buildings were being erected with surprising rapidity. And the population seemed to be increasing daily. What appears to have intrigued Lockhart in all this was her sense of a community still trying to hold onto its frontier past— even in the face of inevitable change—and the panorama of characters she could encounter there. Ranchers and cowboys, sheepherders and retired army scouts, Indians and former Indian fighters all walked the streets alongside eastern-trained lawyers and bankers from Boston. A newly emerging genteel society was asserting itself, but the vaunted rugged individualism of an earlier age also made Cody a comfortable haven for lady doctors and female sheepherders, for suffrage lecturers and female card dealers, as well as for women like Lockhart, who lived an openly unconventional life.

What Lockhart gleaned from this panorama was an allegiance to a fable of an older West that permeated almost everything she wrote after 1904. In this, she was not original. As early as 1888, Theodore Roosevelt had introduced a distinctive note of nostalgia in his depiction of the cowboy. Roosevelt's autobiography and documentary history, *Ranch Life and the Hunting Trail*, illustrated by Frederic Remington, dwelt on the cowboy's rugged appearance, superior physique, and innate moral superiority; but Roosevelt had also acknowledged that the free-range era of the cattleman and cowboy was but a transient phase, destined to "pass away before the onward march of our people."[4] As population densities increased west of the Rockies and across the high plains, the United States Census Bureau declared the frontier officially closed in 1890. Taking note of that closure, Frederick Jackson Turner sounded an elegiac chord in his address to the annual meeting of the American Historical Association in Chicago in July 1893, attributing all that was good in the American character and in American democracy to "the existence of the frontier."[5] Within a decade of Turner's much-quoted address, writers like Zane Grey and Owen Wister had translated the historian's elegy and Roosevelt's nostalgia into best-selling fictions about cowboy life, their novels and short stories set mostly in the 1870s and 1880s. Where Lockhart differed from these contemporaries—to whom she was often compared—was in her willingness to balance the nostalgia with a gritty dose of the realities of change.

She most differed from her male contemporaries, however, in her introduction of strong female characters into the otherwise exclusively masculine domain of the bunkhouse and cattle drive. If Owen Wister's *The Virginian* (1902) glorified cowboy life as an escape from the gentle taming of women, Caroline Lockhart's *The Fighting Shepherdess* (1919) depicted a woman at ease in the saddle and at home on the range. Based on Lockhart's acquaintance with Lucy Morrison Moore, known widely as the "Sheep Queen of Wyoming," the heroine of the novel—like Wister's cowboys—flees the *civilizing* pretensions of the town for the emotional and economic independence of the open range. This image of a powerful female flourishing on a frontier landscape was relatively new in popular fiction, but the image gained force from the cumulative effect of works like Willa Cather's *O Pioneers!* (1913) and *My Antonia* (1918), Mary Austin's short stories—and now Lockhart's novels. Unlike Cather and Austin, however, Lockhart was drawn to the cowboy West. And although she would take liberties with the romantic stories of the lone cowboy, she could never altogether abandon the inherent romanticism of these stories' plot. None of her heroines would remain emotionally untethered. Like every one of Zane Grey's western women, the female protagonist of *The Fighting Shepherdess* finally marries a "dude" rancher from the East who has all along recognized her as "a diamond in the rough."

Such capitulations may explain, in part, why Lockhart's novels and short stories are so little known today. For, while Lockhart used the panorama of Cody to create a host of unusual characters—strong women among them—and while she developed keen ears for local speech and acute antennae for local social tensions, the rugged realism of her settings was too often undone by the melodramatic elements of her plot. In almost every novel, good and evil, each clearly identifiable, are pitted against each other as in a morality play, with the outcome never in doubt. And because she withdrew from challenging the generic assumptions of the cowboy fable, even her female characters fell short of becoming genuine innovations. Whether they intended to or not, Lockhart's virginal heroines exercised a moralizing influence over the rough cowboy heart and, in the end, they married appropriately. "Fallen women," however admirable, do not survive. In other words, Lockhart's powerful females were always exceptions, and they never escaped their romantic destiny.

Similarly, while Lockhart shared the sympathy of her predecessor, Helen Hunt Jackson, for the plight of the Indian, her depiction of indigenous culture was rarely rich in detail or understanding. *Me-Smith*, Lockhart's phenomenally successful first novel, published in 1911, clearly revealed injustices suffered by Native American characters at the hands of whites. But it never addressed the pandemic racial violence of the frontier West as had Jackson's historical account, *A Century of Dishonor* (1881), or her novel, *Ramona* (1884). Also unlike Jackson, Lockhart could not get over her aversion to Mexican Americans. In short, like so many easterners and midwesterners who had come to the West and Southwest in the early twentieth century, Lockhart brought with her all the blind spots and prejudices of her era.

By today's standards, Lockhart was an assemblage of contradictions. Never married, she was nonetheless unapologetically and openly sexually active—certainly with men, perhaps also with women. Yet none of her fictional heroines would be permitted such freedom, and the rare female character who challenged accepted sexual boundaries is offered either as villainous (as in *The Lady Doc*) or does not survive the story's last page. Always protective of her own economic independence and comfortable with the portrayal of strong independent women in her fiction, still Lockhart never campaigned on behalf of women's suffrage—even though many of the western states were among the first to grant women the vote. In an article published in the Park County *Enterprise* in 1920, she boldly declared that "nearly half of the cowpunchers of the early eighties were Harvard or Yale men, or young men from good eastern families," when, in fact, she knew from the old-timers who walked the Cody sidewalks that most cowpunchers were like her devoted lover Jesse: ill-educated, impoverished, generally unkempt, and permanently maimed from hard years on the open range. In what nowadays might be viewed as an early sensitivity to environmental concerns, Lockhart energetically opposed the extermination policies of the Montana Fish and Game Department. But while she tried to stop the wholesale slaughter of species like the bobcat, and while she editorialized against recreational hunting as editor of the *Enterprise*, she never had second thoughts about rodeo events that routinely injured the horses and steers used for "bronco-busting" and roping competitions. Nor, in her glorification of cowpunchers and sheepherders, did she ever appear to see the damage to the grasslands from years of overgrazing.

Precisely these contradictions, however, make Lockhart—both in her life and in her work—an apt emblem of the very transitions she tried to chronicle. The heroic qualities of a physically challenging existence lived close to nature appealed to an imagination always in flight from rapid technological change, urban blight, and the imposition of social restrictions of any kind. Little wonder that Lockhart identified powerfully with her cowboy heroes. As a result, she both catered to her readers' fascination with the disappearing frontier and, at the same time, helped to create its myth. And when three of her novels were made into movies, she also contributed to the early fable of the cowboy—and the West—on the silver screen.

Ever in pursuit of the fable and passionately identified with the life on the range she had so long written about, Lockhart, by 1926, at the age of fifty-five, became a rancher herself. On her Montana cattle ranch just west of the Big Horn River Canyon, she composed most of the manuscript that would become her last published novel, *Old West and New* (1933). As Necah Furman points out, the book was only moderately successful and did not fare well with critics. With 16 million people—one-third of the labor force—unemployed, the temper of the nation had changed. Escapist entertainments could be had more cheaply in movies such as *42nd Street, Gold Diggers of 1933,* or *Footlight Parade,* with their lavish production numbers centered around tunes like "We're in the Money." The grittier current reality had been depicted the year before in Erskine Caldwell's best-selling *Tobacco Road* (1932).

In fact, not even Lockhart could any longer write the fable whole. *Old West and New* was an awkwardly bifurcated text. Part One portrayed the West she had known at the turn of the century in Cody, when that town was just beginning to show the signs of rapid economic shifts. Part Two depicted the fully modernized West of filling stations and four-lane highways. Beyond offering graphic contrasts, the two parts simply did not work as a coherent whole. The heart of the story, after all, lay in the twenty-four years separating Parts One and Two, when the lives of the characters and their surrounding landscape underwent dramatic changes. But it was precisely this interval that Lockhart now found herself incapable of recording.

In the years following *Old West and New,* Lockhart struggled to compose both another novel and an autobiography, succeeding in neither. Her energies, instead, went into the Montana ranch. Deeply attached to the image of the resilient cowboy riding the open range, an image that she herself had helped to create, Lockhart had moved consciously from composing fiction to living within the western myth.

This may also help to explain why she could never compose her autobiography. Although importuned by friends and colleagues to record the story of her exceptional life, Lockhart produced only unconnected fragments, none of which were ever published. Useful as sources for reminiscences and remembered details—even if the dating and chronology are often unreliable—the autobiographical fragments are singularly unreflective. They do not reveal the meaning that she gave to her varied experiences nor the inner stories by which she lived. They are, at best, a journalist's *reportage.* At the point she was trying to compose the autobiography—during the Montana years—she had effectively become one of her own invented characters. On a daily basis, she was now inhabiting the roles she had once created for the characters in her novels. *She* became the heroine who tamed the drunken wildness of the male bunkhouse. And *she* enacted the hardy cowpuncher, testing her skills against the rigors of the aptly named Dryhead country. No longer did she merely report or describe ranch life. Instead, she had entered the world of her novels as daily experience. With fantasy and reality so powerfully fused, every day demanded the imaginative composing of what was now her own life. No energy remained to compose yet another written life story for others.

At the same time, Lockhart would have had few guides to making sense of a life that, in its own day, had been so unconventional. In the years following World War II and throughout the 1950s, gender roles became more rigid in the United States, with women attached to responsibilities as homemakers and men praised for their capacities as breadwinners. Sexuality was to be confined to heterosexual marriage only, and the powerful independent female was labeled as dangerous or, worse, deviant. Not until the advent of the Women's Liberation Movement of the late 1960s would Lockhart have had access to a vocabulary adequate to describe systemic discrimination in the newsprint business and an analytical framework sufficient to explain her lifelong discomfort with prescribed gender roles. But Lockhart died in 1962, at the age of ninety-one, familiar only with the more restrained suffrage movement of her younger years.

Thus, like so many women who went West before her, Lockhart left us sequential moments in her life, recorded in personal diaries. Indeed, the pioneer women about whom Lockhart wrote, and whom she greatly admired, rarely had the inclination or the capacity to compose coherent life narratives. The lives they were creating in the new West would not fit easily into available narrative structures. And in the relative isolation of a wagon train or homestead, with only infrequent access to adult company, these women often turned to the diary as both friend and companion. As a result, scholars of women's history in the West have come increasingly to depend upon the diary as the richest repository for excavating the truths of women's lives and for understanding women's decided impact on frontier culture.[6]

The most intimate sources for recovering Lockhart's story, therefore, are the personal diaries that she kept throughout her life. In these we can read the immediacy of the felt moment and glimpse revelations of inner conflict and painful disappointments. These were written for herself alone, and they are unquestionably our most trustworthy guide to Lockhart's interior world. Their pages contain candid assessments of herself and others, as well as detailed descriptions of her physical surroundings. Even so, because the personal diary is never static, capturing instead the ongoing experience, these texts may arrest a moment of time in words, but they do not offer the reflection and analysis that create a cohesive narrative.

Consequently, to compose *this* biographical narrative, Necah Stewart Furman has pieced together the autobiographical attempts, the personal diaries, the clues to be found in Lockhart's published writings, and the reminiscences of friends and family members. The result is the first serious study of Lockhart's life and work, set within the context of the changing West she sought to chronicle. Although all of Lockhart's novels have long been out of print, the reader will discover yet another woman who put her unique stamp on our popular conceptions of the waning frontier. With this biography, Lockhart at last assumes her proper place among such prominent contemporaries as Helen Hunt Jackson, Willa Cather, Mary Austin, Zane Grey, and Owen Wister. She, too, helped invent the West we all think we know.

ANNETTE KOLODNY
Tucson, Arizona

CAROLINE LOCKHART: HER LIFE AND LEGACY

Early Adventures

The sound of anything coming at you—a train, say, or the future—
has a higher pitch than the sound of the same thing going away.
Wallace Stegner, *Angle of Repose*

THE DOPPLER EFFECT

Amid the clicking noise of wheels on iron track and the roar of the engine,
the shrill sound of the train's whistle drifted back to her like the mythi-
cal siren's call. From her window, she could see a flat countryside tinged
with autumn and in the distance the snowcapped peaks of the Absarokas.
To the northwest, she caught an occasional glimpse of Beartooth Peaks,
the mountains that Chief Joseph of the Nez Perce had crossed in his great
escape. At times, the train crossed the Shoshone, or the great "Stinking
Water"—as the Indians called it—a clear, rippling river that belied its un-
attractive name. Beyond Carter Mountain, and barely visible, the Pallette
Peaks reached toward the sky. All a part of the Absaroka Range, the mountains created a majestic backdrop for the small western town situated across
the shallow river canyon.

In the year 1904, journalist Caroline Cameron Lockhart headed West.
Still a raw wilderness region at the turn of the century, the picturesque
town of Cody, Wyoming, was soon to become her new home.[1] Cody and its
environs would provide the setting for a career as colorful as the scenery and
the frontier characters that populated it. Talented and free-spirited, Lockhart would become one of them—first as a journalist and writer of short
stories; then as a top-selling western novelist; firebrand owner and editor of
a frontier newspaper; fervent crusader against Prohibition; promoter of the
memory of Buffalo Bill; and finally, as a successful ranchwoman who lived
the life about which she wrote.

GROWING UP IN THE MIDWEST: A KANSAS CHILDHOOD

The origins of Caroline's westering mind-set can be traced to a childhood spent near Eskridge, Kansas, as the daughter of successful farmer

3

and rancher Joseph Cameron Lockhart and his wife Sarah Woodruff. Of Scottish ancestry, the Lockharts had settled in Pennsylvania during the colonial period. After completing his education at a seminary in Kingston, eighteen-year-old Joseph Lockhart, the oldest child in the family, moved west to Polo, Illinois, where he became a merchant. When the Civil War intervened, Joseph in 1862 volunteered for a three-year stint with Company B of the Seventh Illinois Cavalry. Two of these years were spent as an aide to General William S. Rosecrans.

On 24 February 1871, his first daughter, Caroline "Caddie" Lockhart, was born in Eagle Point, Illinois. In 1874, Caroline's family, which would eventually include her older brother George and her younger siblings Robert and Grace, moved westward again to an area near Auburn, Kansas, a few miles west of Topeka. Later the family would move on to Burlingame and then to Eskridge.

Joseph Lockhart took advantage of the availability of virgin land, and before long the handsome cavalry officer became a rancher of some substance—the owner of over 120,000 acres of the famous blue-stem pasture land of Wabaunsee County. He would also eventually own considerable land in western Kansas and become a stockholder in the National Bank of Commerce of Hominy, Oklahoma.[2]

The Burlingame Ranch where Caroline spent her childhood was situated on the Santa Fe Trail. There she witnessed a transition era as the Atchison, Topeka and Santa Fe Railroad replaced the covered wagons and pack trains that transported homesteaders westward. The imprint of this frontier phenomenon remained with her.

In Kansas, the Lockhart children led a carefree childhood interspersed with the typical experiences of ranch life. Caroline learned to ride and by the age of five could curse with the best of the ranch hands. In desperation, her mother warned: "Caddie, if you don't stop that, God will send a bolt of lightning to strike you down—God is *always* watching!" This dire threat evoked to Caroline the image of "a large blue eye in the sky following . . . [her] every move."

To an intelligent and headstrong youngster, such a dictum represented a challenge to be tested. Hand in hand, Caroline and her brother George walked out into the yard and looked up apprehensively at a break in the clouds where they envisioned the large blue eye peering down at them. After some argument as to what swear words to use, the children made a choice and decided to recite them together. Drawing what they feared might be their last breath, they chorused: "Go to Hell, God-dammit!" But nothing happened. After a reasonable time, George said sullenly: "Tain't so! It's a big lie!" And another childhood illusion had passed.[3]

George, it seems, was Caroline's frequent companion in mischief. One of their favorite fantasies was of going to Mexico and to China "when they were big," but saving the money to get there looked hopeless. Then, an opportunity arose that made China and old Mexico seem possible. Joseph Cameron, according to Caroline, was a handsome man who was especially proud of his thick black hair and was distressed to find gray in it. Therefore, when Caroline proposed to him that she and George would jointly receive a penny for each gray hair they could find and show him, he accepted. Payment was to be "cash on the barrel head."

Joseph Cameron lay down on the sofa while Caroline and George explored for the few gray hairs among the black ones. The children did a "land office business" until they ran out of gray hairs, whereupon they conceived the idea of selling the same hairs twice. The thought of outsmarting "Papa" intrigued the youngsters and they giggled as they collected. But the consequences were not so funny. Caroline recalled what happened: "Something made him suspicious and he suddenly sat up. His black eyes bored into us as he accused us of fraud. He looked so angry and fierce that he scared the truth out of us." A lecture on the importance of integrity and square dealing in business was followed by a meaningful nod that sent the children toward the woodshed, where the frayed stub of a buggy whip waited for just such occasions. Needless to say, the children never got to Mexico on the penny proceeds of their enterprise.[4]

Caddie, who was tomboyish and athletic, liked to brag that she could outrun all the boys in her school. Growing up in the somewhat isolated western environment, she remained immune to the usual girlish fantasies "of a sentimental nature" until the age of thirteen, when she met a young boy by the name of Jim Baker. Tanned, barefoot, and ragged, Jim belonged to a party of horse traders camped down by the creek. Caroline liked Jim at once, and he reciprocated by showing her their "string" and explaining in cautious undertones the horse trader's secrets.

Such confidences inspired firm friendship, and Caroline decided that Jim should accompany her to prayer meeting. Although she personally regarded such church meetings as "a mild form of torture," she lied glibly to Jim, claiming that "tain't bad, and the preacher don't talk long." To make the ragged boy feel comfortable, Caroline even agreed to go barefoot. When the church bell sounded, she hid her shoes and stockings in the bushes and joined Jim on the Presbyterian church corner. Every head turned as Caddie and her "barefoot beau" walked down the aisle to take a front seat right under the preacher's nose.

The preacher's eyes twinkled and the audience tittered, but Caroline felt "brave & virtuous." She reasoned that she was doing her share to save sinners and, too, she liked sitting next to Jim Baker. Defiantly, the young-sters joined in the singing of "Throw out the Life Line" and "Jesus Loves Me." Rather than being upset by her daughter's behavior, Sarah Woodruff watched with amusement. As Caroline recalled, "There was that funny quirk at the corner of Mama's mouth—she had a grand sense of humor . . . and I took it without fighting back when, jumping up and down, George taunted: 'Caddie's got a feller! Caddie's got a feller!' " Caroline's first romance ended abruptly when the horse traders, with strong encourage-ment from the sheriff, soon left town.[5]

But the young girl's carefree days were numbered. Not long thereafter, Joseph Cameron, his face white and strained, had to tell his children that their mother was ill and might not get well. In later years, Caroline learned that Sarah Woodruff's attending physician had been a drug addict and that her mother's death was the result of an overdose of some opiate—a realization that would color her attitude toward doctors she suspected of quackery.[6]

Helpless without his "Sallie," Joseph Cameron lost control over his chil-dren, especially his headstrong daughter Caroline and son George. Grace, it seemed, was better able to conform to the traditional role expected of her. Caroline and her brother George, on the other hand, ran wild. In a civilizing attempt, Joseph Cameron hired several housekeepers, "each a little worse than the last," according to Caroline; but they all left in quick succession. Thinking that city life would have a beneficial influence, Joseph Cameron, for a while, housed the children at the Central House Hotel in Eskridge under the eagle eye of the landlady. Caroline, who would always enjoy new experiences, was thrilled with the idea of moving into town. George, however, balked when he learned that the proprietors took a dim view of plans to keep his pet coyote in his room.

The landlady, who wore a blond wig and painted her cheeks, got along famously with Caroline, although she was snubbed by the town's better ele-ment. The woman, remembered by Caroline as "one of the kindest women I ever knew," watched over her "like a hawk," fending off fresh drummers and befriending the girl. Nevertheless, the goodhearted woman had little control over Caddie's seemingly bottomless source of energy. "The climax came," Caroline said, "when Old Man Mercer brought George home by the ear, demanding payment for the cherries upon which he had gorged himself, and the town marshal told Papa he would have to do something drastic if I didn't stop riding my pony on the board sidewalk and running races down Main Street."[7]

This ultimatum, combined with the landlady's insistence that Caroline needed to go to a finishing school "back East," persuaded her father to take

George with him and to send her off to college. The close relationship she had with her brother during these early years was soon to end, never to be rekindled. With the exception of one visit to see her brother in Tucson, Arizona, there would be little or no contact between the two until a chance meeting at a celebration in Cody many years later.

Caroline first attended Bethany College in Kansas, and later the Moravian Seminary in Pennsylvania. Reputed at the time to be the second oldest boarding school for girls in the United States, the seminary was located in Bethlehem where her "Uncle Bob" lived. The idea was that Uncle Bob, Caddie's great-uncle and a widower, could keep an eye on her. Dressed in a homemade traveling ensemble that laced up the back, Caroline found herself traveling East to learn "to become a lady."[8]

EXILED IN THE EAST

Despite her initial excitement with this experience, Caroline's first impression of the Moravian Seminary was that it "looked like an outsized calaboose" and made her feel like "a convict sentenced to do a long stretch." Before long, however, she was creating her own excitement. On a dare she tried out the fire escape and was caught dangling in mid-air when the rope slipped off the rusty pulley. After being rescued by the yardman, she endured a session with the principal, who glared at her with what she described as "a fishy eye" and accused her of "disorganizing the school"—a statement Caroline took as a compliment.[9]

Still trying to improve the quality of life at the seminary, Caroline quickly learned that "even to *look* at a Lehigh University student was a major offense" and decided to capitalize on that knowledge at the first opportunity. Her chance came one evening when the students were celebrating a football victory. Knowing that the Lehigh college colors were brown and white, she had the bright idea of stuffing a pair of brown and white stockings, which she hung from a dormitory window on the third floor. A riotous mob of students soon gathered in the street, laughing and pointing to what appeared to be a pair of legs dangling from the window sill. Although Caroline was the prime suspect, no one could prove that she was the culprit.[10]

Despite her attempts to liven things up, by April 1889 eighteen-year-old Caroline Lockhart was tired of school. Her best friends—Edith Smith and Bessie S. Hale—had left the seminary for Easter vacation; Caroline missed them and was bored. Amid the funny cartoons with which she decorated her schoolbook was the revealing indictment: "It is sickening in here." Nevertheless, the slash marks and notes in a text on writing indicate that she took that particular course quite seriously. Acting was also in the back of her mind.[11]

The boarding-school experience, however, did little to smooth Caroline's rough edges. On one occasion, she was allowed time away from the seminary to visit her "Cousin Gussie," a proper Eastern lady who gave Caroline a tour of her portrait gallery of ancestors and patiently explained who they were. In return, Caroline entertained her cousin with accounts of her exploits in the little cow town on the old Santa Fe Trail. "If she suffered she did not show it," Caroline noted in her unpublished autobiography, "but when I finally ran down she asked what I meant to do when I finished school. I told her that I guessed I'd have to go back to Kansas and teach . . . so that I could help Papa pay taxes and keep us out of the poor house. It was an ordeal for us both," she concluded.[12]

In a candid self-appraisal, Caroline wondered why she had been invited: whether Cousin Gussie had heard of her escapades and was curious or, being a rich and lonely woman, had some plans for her future. "If it was the latter," Caroline added, "obviously she was disappointed in me and with reason." By her own admission, Caroline "was not a lovable character, being neither demonstrative nor affectionate, but crude, headstrong, and with a frightening vitality which very likely appalled her."[13] Although she never saw her aunt again, for Caroline "Cousin Gussie" remained the ideal of a truly great lady—a *grande dame*.

The honest self-analysis reflected in this autobiographical excerpt becomes all the more significant in light of Caroline's obvious admiration for her aunt's ladylike qualities. Throughout her life Caroline would be to a large degree a woman out of time, out of place. She would be torn between her innate free-spirited personality and her desire to fit the traditional lady's role. Caroline's days at the seminary did little, however, to achieve this objective. In later years, she admitted, "I learned to make Vassar fudge and worry the teachers, but not much else."[14]

In 1890 at the age of nineteen, Caroline's carefree time as a schoolgirl was shattered by the news of her father's decision to remarry. "The news was even a worse shock than my mother's death," she wrote; "I knew the woman [Katherine Reed] for she had been the family seamstress, and with a child's intuition I knew that she did not like me when she first came to our house to sew."[15] Sick at heart, Caroline had no one to talk to except Uncle Bob.

Arriving at the hotel where he stayed, she found the lobby crowded with impressive men carrying gold-headed canes and wearing tall silk hats and broadcloth frock coats. Many of them had come long distances in their private railroad cars to discuss a crisis in the affairs of Bethlehem Steel.

When it became apparent that Uncle Bob was much too busy to listen to her personal problems, she struck up a conversation with a Lehigh University student sitting nearby. Finding it difficult to converse comfortably on such short acquaintance, she suggested they adjourn to Uncle Bob's apartment for a drink. Remembering that her uncle always played host in this manner, and remembering, too, that her mother had warned that beer was "common" and that whisky "made fools of people," she filled drinking glasses with generous amounts of her uncle's finest Madeira. When the painful silences continued, Caroline suggested that they try another—and another—with the result that she made her way back to the seminary the next morning with a head as heavy as her heart.[16]

Forced to come to terms with her situation and realizing the mutual dislike that she and her stepmother felt for each other, Caroline decided that the only solution was to pursue her own interests. On the basis of her earlier experience, she knew that it would be impossible to return to Eskridge and succumb to the will of "Step"—as she referred to her father's new wife. She decided instead to try a career on the stage.

Although it is unclear how she carried out the deception, Caroline told her parents that she was going to finishing school and enrolled in Moses True Brown's School of Oratory. She was immediately impressed by the students' lack of talent, including her own. "My enthusiasm for a career as an elocutionist waned daily," she wrote.[17] Nevertheless, Caroline made her stage debut as a page in a production of the Grand Opera Company.

In this memorable performance as a boy, she was forced to wear one shoe too large and one too small. Stumbling and bumbling through the scene, Caroline experienced considerable pain, as did the audience; although they did enjoy a laugh when the well-shaped page plopped down on the edge of the throne and took off her shoe in the middle of one of Edouard de Reszke's most famous arias. The director, however, did not think it so funny and failed to ask her for a repeat performance. "Somehow," she later confided, "my enthusiasm to be another Sarah Bernhardt faded."[18]

Deciding that she could do a much better job of writing than acting, Caroline eventually converted the experience into a humorous article. Thus began a pattern and precept that would become the basis of her personal writing philosophy: "To write about something, one must first experience it."[19] And experience it Caroline was destined to do.

THE NELLIE BLY OF BOSTON

Disillusioned by her short-lived acting career, Caroline was determined to make her imprint. She might have persisted with her acting somewhat longer, but her father and stepmother showed their feelings by refusing to make it easy for her. She described herself as being "conspicuously shabby and hungry" and having difficulty making ends meet on the thirty-five dollar allotment they sent each month. Swallowing her pride, she wrote to her father asking for an increase, but in response she received a letter from her stepmother complaining of the high taxes and the cost of barbed wire. Caroline realized that the new stepmother controlled the pocket-book in her father's household and was not going to waste a penny on his errant daughter. Meanwhile, she existed in a chilly hall bedroom in a hotel located two miles from Beacon Street. Years later she wrote in her autobiography that she felt she was actually starving and that the roomers in the boardinghouse must have suspected, because the chambermaid one day "suddenly took me in her arms and held me close," saying, "Pore little girl, I wish I could do somethin' for you." "So I have found it always," she observed, "sympathy and understanding in the most unlikely people."[20]

From this time forward, Caroline's relationship with her father and other members of her family remained strained, characterized mainly by correspondence relating to finances and, later, by infrequent visits to see her sister in Oklahoma. To the young woman, it was clear that she must find some other way of achieving fame and fortune. The answer came to her, as she said, "out of a clear blue sky": Why couldn't she write for the newspaper? At the time everyone was talking about journalist Nellie Bly and her trip around the world. The prospect of a similar career appealed to Caroline's adventuresome spirit despite the scarcity of female reporters in Boston at the time. In 1889 being a news reporter was considered an unladylike occupation unless assignments were restricted to pieces about bringing up children, cooking, or other household matters.[21] Convention, however, would never stand in her way.

This first serious attempt to launch a career took courage for one so young, and Caroline recorded the event in great detail. A major problem, she soon realized, was appearance. "I eyed myself in the mirror and my heart sank within me," she said. "I was not yet seventeen and looked even younger." Her bright golden hair, which fell in a single braid down her back, presented a conspicuous problem. Thick and luxuriant, it would not fit comfortably under her sailor hat. Coping as best she could, Caroline set out to apply for her first job wearing a shirtwaist and what she termed "a weird-looking skirt made from a remnant."[22]

She decided to try the Boston *Post*. Disparagingly referred to as the "cab driver's Bible" and known to be in shaky financial condition, the *Post*, she reasoned, would be more likely to hire a young, inexperienced girl reporter. She found the offices of the *Post* housed in a two-story building "that had a list to the starboard." Once inside, she was directed to see the owner, a Mr. E. A. Grozier. Instead of the impressive personage she had visualized, Caroline saw a small, frail man sitting in an armchair with a light woolen blanket over his knees. He looked up at the girl with keen, searching blue eyes.

When she stated her business, the shadow of a smile passed over his face and he motioned her to sit down. Caroline positioned herself in a straight-backed chair. In her excitement, she hooked her heels over the front rung. The man noticed it; Caroline noticed that he noticed it, and she quickly put her feet on the floor.

" 'Have you had any experience?' " he asked.

" 'No, but I can learn if you will just give me a chance. I can do anything that men reporters can do!' " she asserted.

Again, the slight smile as Grozier studied her: "He continued to look at me until I felt that he knew what I had eaten for breakfast," she recalled. Then, just as she thought she was dismissed, he said: "You can see the Sunday editor, and if he has any assignment in mind for you, we'll see. You're [sic] salary will be $15.00 a week"—a sum that sounded fantastic to the aspiring reporter.[23]

Johnny Tincup, the Sunday editor, had bushy eyebrows and a beard to match, but he and Caroline were to get along splendidly. She made friends with her fellow reporters as well and soon learned that the *Post*'s stigma of being a "yellow sheet" comparable to Hearst's *Journal* in New York produced no inferiority complex among the paper's employees. Not to be outdone, and bolstered by her naturally venturesome spirit, Caroline attacked her new career with enthusiasm.

Her first assignment was to go to Austin and Stone's Dime Museum for a story about how the "freaks" lived. The objective was to find out what they were like as persons when not exhibiting their abnormalities for a livelihood. The manager liked the idea of free publicity and suggested that Caroline appear to be part of the show in order to gain the confidence of the show people. She agreed to recite a verse and planned to have dinner with them at six o'clock.

That evening Caroline recited an Ella Wheeler Wilcox poem to an almost empty house. "A thunderous silence" rewarded her efforts. Later, at the dining room table, she found herself seated next to the World's Fattest Fat Woman, who spilled out of a specially made chair to the left, while the World's Smallest Midget perched on a pile of catalogs and books to her right. The exceptional people paid little attention to the new girl because the Fat Woman and the Midget were involved in a fierce argument about "Love."

"Love is bunk!" shouted the Fat Woman, harpooning a slice of bread with a fork.

" 'Tain't" squeaked the Midget. "I seen it work myself." Across the table sat the Blue Man from India. "Do you take any stock in the sayin' 'Love at first sight?' " he asked, leaning over the table and looking pointedly at the guest.[24]

The following Monday when the Blue Man waited outside the *Post* offices to walk her home from work, Caroline didn't have the heart to refuse him. This experience with the "freaks" was the first of a series of incredible assignments that would soon earn her the reputation of being the Nellie Bly of Boston. That special assignment also earned her the "undying love" of the Blue Man from India.[25]

As indicated by her coverage of Austin and Stone's Dime Museum and its employees, Caroline's early newspaper stories show a natural penchant for capturing the dialect of whomever she might be interviewing. Furthermore, she inevitably used her talent for writing dialogue to reveal facets of character and personality. In this instance, a lack of extensive formal study of her craft was probably an asset. The ability to rely on her natural ear stood her in good stead. It is apparent, too, that she consciously studied the numerous individuals with whom her occupation brought her into contact—eccentrics such as Philadelphia Teddy, reputed to be "one of the best known hobos riding the rods and tapping on back doors."[26]

After each one of his transcontinental trips, Teddy made it a point to stop in at the *Post* and bring Caroline up to date on the news in police circles along his route, including the condition of their jails. She learned from Teddy, for example, that the worst jails were in Mexico and the best were in Ohio. When he needed "restin' up," Teddy claimed that he always tried to "get throwed in in Ohio," but some of the cops seemed to be getting wise to him. "And, I can't do nothin' to make them pick me up," the hobo added dejectedly.

On impulse, Caroline encouraged Teddy to get a job and even collected a presentable suit of clothes for him. The next day, after a bath, haircut, and shave, the hobo returned looking like a respectable working man. And before nightfall he arrived with the news that he had landed a job. A week or so later, feeling very proud of herself for having stirred the tramp's long-hidden pride and self-respect, Caroline was sitting at her desk in a self-congratulatory mood when in walked Teddy wearing his old hobo garb. " 'Tain't no use," he told her bluntly. "I quit. My boss coaxed me to stay, but like I told you, I kain't work. I hate work. I gotta hit the road or I'll go crazy." He placed the bundle of new clothes on her desk. "I couldn't tap on a back door an' ask fer a 'lump' lookin' like a banker," he explained. "Much obliged jest the same." And that was the last time she saw Teddy.[27]

Extraordinary people and adventures would continue to interest Caroline throughout most of her life. As a young reporter, she had plenty of opportunity for both. On one occasion, for example, the city editor borrowed her from Johnny Tincup for an interview with Colonel Robert J. Ingersoll, well-known public speaker on topics ranging from social reform and politics to sex, marriage, and morals. His controversial beliefs nearly always made Ingersoll front-page material, so Caroline was thrilled by the chance to interview him.

When she arrived at the Parker House for their meeting, the man who rose from behind the desk to greet her was the most impressive figure she had ever met. Tall, broad-shouldered, erect, and not especially handsome, he was nevertheless a "man of consequence." He had a generous mouth with rather thin lips and a rugged jaw that to Caroline "bespoke determination and courage above all else." "And was he surprised to see me," she added, "just a brat come to interview him!" As he looked at her with half-amused gray eyes, she stammered out her prepared questions:

"'Do you believe in capital punishment, Colonel Ingersoll?'" And so the interview proceeded.

Finally, Ingersoll interrupted: "'If you'll give me your questions,'" he said, "'I'll write the answers myself. How's that?'" Obviously experienced in being quoted and misquoted by the press, Ingersoll had figured out a way to eliminate a portion of the problem. Caroline agreed with his proposal, realizing that he probably recognized her for the amateur that she was.[28]

Caroline's experiences as a young reporter for the Boston *Post* included many "firsts" for women—from jumping off a four-story building to descending into Boston Harbor in a diving suit. Her natural yen for adventure combined with an extraordinary absence of fear would continually involve her in unusual and even dangerous experiences for one of her time and sex. Futhermore, as her employers soon realized, Caroline's stunts made good copy and sold newspapers. One of the most notable of these was her Boston Harbor diving exhibition.

On that occasion, people with "spyglasses" watched from windows and other onlookers gathered on shore as Caroline boarded a tugboat along with the president of the Towboat Company, the crew, and an experienced diver. Wearing bicycle bloomers, she was helped into a heavy rubber diving suit much too large for her. With twenty-five-pound weights strapped to her rubber diving sandals, and an iron breastplate and belt, she could hardly stand, much less walk, as the boat shoved off toward deeper water.

Everyone watched anxiously while the diver gave her final instructions before screwing the hermetically sealed helmet to the breastplate. Finally, she struggled clumsily over the edge and onto the iron ladder leading down into the water.

She forced herself to let go, and the light slowly faded as she descended into Boston Harbor. For an instant she felt panic and had difficulty breathing. After the initial fright and period of adjustment, however, she recalled that she "tripped along as if I were walking down Tremont Street." Twenty minutes later, she gave the signal to be raised. Grinning broadly, she stepped out of her diving suit, equipped with yet another unique experience upon which to base a good story.[29]

Eventually, as Caroline's articles earned her more notoriety, she was given a cubbyhole of an office across the narrow hall from the sports editor. Caroline and the editor soon became friends, and she had the opportunity to meet many of his visitors. Coming in from lunch in a bad temper one day, she stopped by to explain her problem. It seems that each day at noon when she walked down Washington Street, a "masher," as she referred to him, waited for her and made remarks as she passed. "Tomorrow," she said furiously, "I'm going to smack him!" Meanwhile, a young man sat tilted back on his chair, listening to the exchange. Sitting upright with a thump, he said quickly, "Don't do it. Tomorrow when you go out to eat, I'll walk behind you."

The next day, as planned, the young man walked two or three steps behind Caroline when she went out. The "masher" was waiting for her and made the usual rude remarks. Caroline recalled that he was "still twisting his mustache and smirking when a fist shot out and gave him such a smash on the jaw as laid him out cold in the doorway." Later she learned that her benefactor with the lethal punch was none other than John L. "Spike" Sullivan, the heavyweight boxing champion of the world.[30]

Many of her assignments were humorous, but nearly all had in common some element of danger—as when she got into a cage with a lion, which she remembered as having the "reddest mouth, the sharpest teeth, and the longest tongue of any lion who ever lived!"—and as on the occasion when the city wanted someone to test the fire department's safety nets. "You can bet your life you bounce when you hit," Caroline wrote after jumping from the fourth story.[31]

Yet, when Johnny Tincup urged her to ride as a participant in the Boston Horse Show and take the jumps, she was justifiably apprehensive. Although Caroline had grown up on a ranch, she was totally unaccustomed to riding sidesaddle or to jumping a horse. Nevertheless, her assignment to cover the horse show represented one of the city's outstanding social events and good newspaper material. At first she protested, pointing out that she had no horse, no saddle, and no riding habit. But Tincup had all the solutions.

Caroline was smart enough to take a dim view of the idea, but she had never refused an assignment yet, so she donned the borrowed habit—a handsome, well-tailored, black broadcloth that fit surprisingly well—and set off to make her own story. The fact that she did not have suitable tights to wear underneath concerned her, but she consoled herself with the thought that for the short time she would be in the ring, her white muslin "drawers" would do well enough.

When she arrived at the Horse Show in time for the special event, a beautiful, spirited horse was saddled and waiting. As the groom lifted her into the sidesaddle, she noted that none of the hurdles looked especially formidable except the last. Then the signal was given. At the last hurdle she leaned forward just as her mount gathered himself to jump. The horse, rearing backward, caught her under the chin with his head. Seeing that the blow almost caused her to black out, a groom snatched at the reins and led the horse out of the race. When Caroline dismounted a short distance from the track, she discovered to her consternation that the drawstring holding up her drawers had broken. Inch by inch, her bloomers slipped farther down until they hobbled her. With all the nonchalance she could muster, Caroline stepped out of them as the grooms turned their backs to laugh.[32]

Another assignment that proved perilous dealt with the Home for Intemperate Women. Caroline first heard of the place from a portly, dignified gentleman who occasionally shared her table at the small restaurant where she had dinner each night. One evening he mentioned that he lived next to "the Home" and that he felt an investigation of the place was warranted. "There is a high board fence with nails on top between this Home and my house," he said, "and the inmates are constantly trying to escape."

That was enough to interest Caroline and her editor. Research revealed that the institution was financed by charitable Bostonians for the purpose of reforming females arrested for drunkenness and other misdemeanors. Moreover, the Home professed not only to cure alcoholism but also to offer religious instruction "in a refined and godly atmosphere." "With friendly help and plenty of good books," the Home would teach clients "the error of their ways," or so the advertising went.

The problem, Caroline determined, was to figure out how to gain admittance. The next morning it rained, so she walked to the Home in a downpour, wearing a ragged skirt, an old shirtwaist, and a limp-brimmed sailor hat. She arrived soggy and disheveled, looking "the picture of bedraggled womanhood," as she described herself. At the door she found a girl handing out bundles of finished laundry and was invited in. Inside the dimly lit room sat an attractive woman of middle age who looked at her sharply and asked her to state her business. Shifting the bundle she was carrying and affecting a brassy voice, Caroline introduced herself as a Swedish workwoman by the name of Carrie Henderson. "I got de habit," she explained to the matron. "I can't keep no jobs. I heerd you could cure me."

"Carrie Henderson" was quickly accepted and soon found the place populated with more than a hundred tired and work-worn women ranging in age from seventeen to seventy. At dinner, she was served an unpalatable fare of boiled ox, dry potatoes, and a portion of turnips. She was then escorted to the basement and introduced to the largest laundry room she had ever seen. The next morning, after spending the night in a dormitory of unwashed women, those with "de habit" lined up in the hall, where the matron doled out doses of "the cure," a mixture that smelled "like horse liniment and tasted worse."

The time passed when Johnny Tincup was to get in touch with her, and Caroline began to be concerned. It turned out that when he first inquired, the matron claimed that Carrie had not been cured and that it would take at least three more months. The editor finally had to tell the woman that Caroline was not an alcoholic—that she was on his staff at the Boston *Post*—but the matron refused to believe him, pointing out that Carrie "is the toughest girl we've got!" It took a threat to bring the police before the editor obtained his reporter's release. Two weeks later, after the story was published, the Home for Intemperate Women had a new matron.[33]

By this time, Caroline was recognized as a local celebrity. As the first of her sex in Boston to do "all-around reporting," she began to receive assignments generally reserved for men. One of the more memorable of these came when the editor asked her to interview Robert Fitzsimmons, the challenger for James J. Corbett's world heavyweight title. Few people knew the former Australian blacksmith, so Caroline was to write an article on his background and what he was really like. With notepad and pencil in hand, she made her way to his cottage on Coney Island, then a popular seaside resort, where the boxer stayed during training.

Caroline and the fighter both stared when Fitzsimmons opened the door and she announced the purpose of her visit. "He stared," Caroline said, "because at that time no one had ever heard of a sportswriter in skirts." She stared, having visualized "a pugnacious-looking character with a jutting jaw." But Fitzsimmons had a calico apron tied around his waist and a smudge of flour on his face.

The prizefighter invited his guest to dinner and continued with his cooking. He was squatting at the oven when Caroline suddenly jumped up and let out a yell. A large lion had just sauntered into the room. " 'That's Nero,' " Fitzsimmons said casually. Nero and Caroline eyed one another until, bored, the lion yawned and ambled off into the parlor. After dinner, her host gave a boxing exhibition in the gym. The boxer and the girl reporter parted good friends, and the next time she saw Fitzsimmons he was the heavyweight champion of the world.[34]

Of all the celebrities she interviewed while on the staff of the Boston *Post*, by far the most significant, at least insofar as determining her destiny, was the famous army scout and showman, William F. "Buffalo Bill" Cody. That first meeting, not to mention his exciting Wild West show, remained vivid in her mind. What a sensation that show had created in the East! Even the Cabots and the Lodges had turned out to see it. And what a break it had been when the editor of the Boston *Post* had assigned her—a young reporter just out of pigtails—to interview the famous scout for the Sunday supplement. It was a great opportunity, and she had made the most of it, realizing that it might mean a raise in salary (and at thirty dollars a month, she needed it).

Caroline remembered the episode well and recorded the meeting word for word when writing her unpublished autobiography.[35] She had located Cody's private railroad car on a siding near old South Street Station. With trepidation, she rapped on the door; a voice from behind a red plush curtain invited her in.

" 'What do you want?'

'I'm from the Boston,' she announced brightly.

'Oh,' said the voice. 'Set down.' "

In the arena Buffalo Bill, wearing a wide-brimmed Stetson over flowing shoulder-length hair, cut a magnificent figure as he sat erect on his beautiful, prancing white horse. But when Lockhart met him that day, the "Last of the Great Scouts" was wearing a drab dressing gown, and his hair was tied in a straggly French twist with a knot on top. He held a water bottle full of ice against his head. His bare feet were thrust into a pair of oversized carpet slippers, and when he sat down, one of them dropped off. He regarded his shoes with interest.

" 'Do you like the East?' Caroline asked, making conversation. He pondered for some time before he replied.

'Well enough.'

'Warm, isn't it,' she added.

'Hot.'

'Do you mind our damp climate in Boston?' she asked with dogged vivacity. The Colonel wiggled his toes before he replied cautiously:

'Tain't like out West.' "[36]

Beginning to believe that as a reporter she was "a flop," Lockhart departed "with her tail feathers dragging." In desperation she went to the grounds where the riders stayed, with the objective of getting more information for her story. When Sunday came, she opened the paper in the dim hope that she might see a few paragraphs of the copy she had turned in. To her astonishment, the headline was splashed across the page in the *Post*'s largest type!

On Monday she received an added bonus when she learned that Buffalo Bill liked her story so much that he wanted her to go to the grounds and select a horse as his gift. There was one in particular that appealed to her. It stood with its head hanging down to its knees, looking sad and unloved. She hadn't the heart to pass it up for a better-looking one, although she noted that for some reason, the cowboys exchanged peculiar looks.

The Wild West show had been going for several days before she tried the horse, which piled her on the first jump. She learned too late that the one she had selected was the hardest to "sit" in the entire bunch.[37] Nevertheless, the whole experience made a lasting impression and renewed her interest in the West.

Partially because of her profession and partially because of her nature, even Caroline's vacations ended up being adventures. In the 1890s, Labrador for most people was just a name on a map; however, Robert Edwin Peary's explorations of Greenland in 1891–92 and further trips approaching the shores of the Polar Sea attracted public attention. Peary's well-publicized plans to reach the North Pole caught Caroline's interest as well, and it occurred to her that it might be rewarding to find out more about the unknown country firsthand. "Anything was better," she reasoned, "than spending a summer vacation on a hotel veranda with the 'rocking chair fleet!'"[38]

To accompany her on the trip, Caroline invited as her companion a frail, blonde young woman named Mabel H. Seymour, the sister of Robert G. Seymour, telegraph editor for the *Post*. A clergyman's daughter, Mabel had lived a narrow, conventional life, and as Caroline freely admitted, was her "opposite in every respect"; but they were good friends, nonetheless. After boarding a steamer at Halifax, Nova Scotia, the young women landed in Porto Basque on the southwestern tip of Newfoundland, where they waited for another steamer to take them north.

Until the passengers reached the Straits of Bell Isle, which lie between Labrador and Newfoundland, the days were uneventful. Once there, however, they learned what a rough sea could be like. The straits were covered with floating ice from a bad storm farther north, and the boat rolled and tossed until even some of the crew became ill. Their last stop at the "end of civilization" was a Moravian missionary station, where the northern lights made a gorgeous display in the sky above the tiny settlement of Eskimo huts and the small house of the missionaries.

The next part of their journey took them into uncharted waters traversed only by an occasional whaling or sealing vessel. The coastline had a grim beauty, bordered as it was by mineralized rocks and boulders that played havoc with the captain's compass. With the advantage of good luck and the captain's years of experience, the travelers reached their destination and dropped anchor in a small cove. A welcoming committee of Eskimos paddled out in kayaks and boarded the ship, where they helped themselves to fistfuls of blubber from a cask on deck. Mabel and Caroline soon became the center of attention as the Eskimo women noticed their long, narrow American-style shoes. In comparison with the Eskimo women's short, broad feet wrapped in soft moccasins, the bootlike styles of the American women looked strange and elicited many giggles and pointed remarks.

On the return trip, the travelers kept a sharp lookout for Admiral Peary's ship. A storm stirred up mountainous seas going through the Cabot Strait, forcing them to stop off at Cape Breton Island. There at the dock was the admiral's ship. Thinking that this might be an opportunity for a "scoop," Caroline approached one of the weatherbeaten crew members to see if the admiral would be willing to talk to a reporter from the States. When the explorer himself finally appeared, he was courteous, but final: He would be unable to tell her whether he had reached the North Pole because he had an agreement with the New York *Times* to give them the story first. Disappointed, Caroline gave up her plans.[39]

Caroline's earlier vacation from the *Post* had been even more exciting. Sometimes she hardly needed to plan her adventures; they simply seemed to happen. In this instance, she heard of a remote settlement called Naskeag Point on the Maine Coast and decided that it might be an interesting place to visit. The settlement, so small that it was not even on the map, consisted of fewer than a dozen families who had lived there for generations. Largely illiterate, the residents spoke a dialect peculiar to the region and made a meager living with their lobster traps. To Caroline, it sounded like an excellent place to learn to swim, row a boat, and gather local color.

Caroline arrived at Naskeag Point by boat and set out to find a place to board. At the first shanty, the head of the household informed her that they weren't "fixed to take furriners." Similar responses at other places made her feel the prospects for a vacation on the Maine Coast were rather bleak. Finally, however, she came to a small, unpainted house where the man, after a long, whispered consultation with his wife, decided to take her in for six dollars a week. Despite her status as a "furriner," Idy and

George, as the couple were known, treated her well. Idy stuffed her with excellent clam chowder, and George taught her to row, swim, dig clams, spear flounder, and set the heavy lobster traps.

Late one afternoon, Caroline decided to row to a small island some two miles off shore to pick wild strawberries. George, who was extremely knowledgeable about the sea winds and tides, suggested that she postpone her trip; but Caroline, headstrong as usual, ignored his advice and set off in a dinghy. By the time she had reached the island, a faint mist was hanging over Mt. Desert to the north, and after she had filled her bucket, it had become a thick fog. Knowing that she would have to beat the fog rolling in to the mainland, she shoved the dinghy into the water and rowed as hard as she could. But she had started too late; the wind died, and the fog closed in.

As darkness approached, the boat drifted slowly toward open sea. Sounds of surf breaking over rocks alerted her to a narrow ledge that rose between the bay and the ocean. The dinghy scraped up against it, and she knew she could save herself, for a time at least, by clinging to the rock. While the water of the outgoing tide swirled and foamed at her feet, she found footing and searched frantically for a hold in the large boulder projecting from the churning ocean. For hours she shivered in her wet clothing before hearing the welcome sound of a bell signaling an approaching search party. Through the fog she could see lights on the fishermen's boats. It had been four o'clock when first she left the mainland to gather strawberries. It was about the same hour the next morning when they pulled her out of the surf.[40]

Although Caroline generally chose to remember and record the more humorous or exciting aspects of these early years, the realities of such a life and their influence upon her character cannot be discounted. The death of her mother and her father's subsequent remarriage wounded her greatly and helped shape the course of her future. As a young woman on her own at a time when working outside the home was more the exception than the rule, she was forced to develop a toughness and independence of spirit that enabled her to survive.

Being a woman reporter at the turn of the century could not have been easy under the best of circumstances, and rather than representing the best, the Boston *Post*, according to Caroline's own description, had the stigma of being "a yellow rag." As a novice, Caroline was influenced by the general attitude of her fellow reporters. "We gloried in our shame," she said, "and worked the harder to scoop the respectable Boston *Herald* and lesser competitors. We believed like the soviets [Nazis] that the end justified the means and stopped at nothing short of burglary to get . . . what we went after. Ethics was just a word that didn't mean much—or anything." [41] Lockhart's chosen career obviously taught her many lessons, not all of which were positive.

Forced into an almost masculine role in society, her natural determination and daring dominated occasional inner desires to fulfill the more traditional role of wife and mother. Highly intelligent and strong-willed, she learned to capitalize on these basic attributes to succeed in her profession. Not until midlife would she question the path she had chosen. By then, Lockhart had to face the fact that she would probably remain single and childless. "I suppose I must resign myself to the future of a woman who is growing old without attachments," she wrote in her Diary. [42]

Having felt rejected by the first man in her life—her father—she took great pride in being able to handle problems by herself, without advice or help from others, especially during those early years. She was naturally competitive, but was more influenced by an *inner* drive toward excellence and superiority—a "need-to-show-them" attitude—that would become a compelling force in her life and work, whether writing or ranching. While a part of her may have wanted to become a refined *grande dame* like her aunt, the pattern had already been established—first by heritage and later by circumstance. Caroline Lockhart was destined to be a woman ahead of her time.

"SUZETTE" OF THE PHILADELPHIA *BULLETIN*

By 1900 Caroline had moved to Philadelphia where she boarded with Harry and Nina Peebles at 4836 Hazel Avenue. [43] She had moved up in the journalistic world as well, with a new position on the Philadelphia *Bulletin.* In retrospect, she admitted: "Exactly how I came to be there I am not quite sure; it has been so long ago," but she did recall that "the Philadelphia *Evening Bulletin* in its policies and management bore little resemblance to the Boston *Post* at that time." [44]

Whereas the *Post* was looked down upon, the *Bulletin* had practically no competition in the afternoon field, as indicated by its advertising logo: "Nearly Everyone Reads the *Bulletin.*" As a reporter on the *Post,* she had been accustomed to long working hours and fierce competition among the reporters. It was not unusual for representatives of the *Post* to have doors slammed in their faces, or for the most brash, as Caroline said, "to be given the boot." The city room buzzed with noise, excitement, and loud arguments.

In contrast, the atmosphere at the *Bulletin* seemed like a "Quaker meet-

ing house." At the *Post,* those who couldn't concentrate and type in bed-
lam, according to Caroline, were "merely out of luck." At the *Bulletin,*
however, the staff kept their voices to a "discreet pitch out of consideration
for those at work."[45] Even the assignments were staid and respectable—at
least in the beginning—and Caroline tried to adjust.

One of her first jobs was to interview Philadelphia socialite Miss Eva
Willing. Armed with "trivial questions" she set out to acquire what she
hoped would be "a pen-picture of Philadelphia's most exclusive grandame."
At the family's old-fashioned but handsome mansion on Walnut Street,
an English butler in livery opened the massive door and, after a somewhat
"undecided once-over," invited her into the tastefully furnished reception
room. When Caroline mentioned the purpose of her visit, the butler looked
startled. He was even more surprised to find that she didn't have a properly
engraved calling card, but he took her request upstairs with a backward
glance that looked "as if he half-wished he had locked up the silver."

The butler soon returned with a polite but firm note from a secretary
saying that "Miss Eva Willing would not be able to see a reporter from the
Bulletin." Whereupon Miss Caroline Lockhart had no choice but to leave.
She came away convinced that interviewing socialites was not her forte
and resolved never again even to make the attempt.[46]

The editor of the *Bulletin,* disappointed with her failure, hesitated to
give her another assignment, but Caroline came up with her own. Revert-
ing to her inimitable personal style, she proposed giving a reporter's view
of the city from the brim of William Penn's hat. To do so, she had to climb
the ladders inside the bronze statue and then crawl out on the brim. Stunts
such as this, and swimming the Delaware on a dare, added to her reputation
and increased the newspaper's circulation.

Under the pen name "Suzette," she wrote of her exploits and was given
her own column. Caroline won an avid following as *Bulletin* readers began
to anticipate what the liberated young woman would be up to next. A cigar
company, capitalizing on her fame, even named one of their cigars after
her—the "Suzette."[47]

Caroline's notoriety also gave her entree to such notables of the time
as politician William Jennings Bryan, financier Jay Cooke, and inven-
tor Frank Shuman, whose armored vehicle, "Land Super-Dreadnought,"
preceded the tank.[48] Since Cooke's attitude toward the press was well
known, Caroline's interview with the famed financier represented a journalistic coup.

Expecting to be "about as welcome as Typhoid Mary," as she termed it,
Caroline presented herself at Cooke's beautiful home in Ogontz, a fashionable suburb of Philadelphia. When the footman opened the door into

the spacious drawing room, however, she was pleasantly surprised to be welcomed by a tall man with snow-white hair and beard. The distinguished-looking gentleman, wearing a black broadcloth suit and a high pointed collar with an old-fashioned black silk cravat, was reserved yet gracious and appeared much younger than his eighty-two years. For a moment Cooke and the young woman reporter appraised each other, then "inexplicably," she said, "we both grinned." The interview proceeded as Cooke spoke freely of the crises he had faced; how he had been called upon by President Lincoln when the government needed funds to carry on the Civil War; and how he had weathered the failure of Jay Cooke and Company on Black Friday, 1873. Although considered by many to be unscrupulous in his business dealings, Cooke impressed Caroline as an honest and loyal American who had been "vilified and stigmatized" in the course of his business life. She also came away with an armful of red roses from his personal greenhouse.[49]

Because of her occupation and the strength of her personality, Caroline was destined to continue her adventurous and notable encounters. In 1900 she took a trip to Europe where she saw the actor Anton Lang enact the Christus in the Passion Play at Oberammergau, Germany; climbed in the Swiss Alps; and hunted wild game in Russia. In Paris, France, she renewed acquaintance with the great band leader and composer John Philip Sousa (although she does not explain where she knew him previously).

Sousa's new composition, "The Stars and Stripes Forever," was extraordinarily popular, and Caroline observed that "people stood on each other's feet just to look at him." Although her personal musical repertoire consisted of "Bury Me Not on the Lone Prairie," which she claimed to have learned from a hired hand back in Kansas, she and Sousa were soon talking about Wagner. Unaffected by his fame, the bandleader and Caroline got along well, and she came away with source material for another good interview for her paper.[50]

Not all of her Paris experiences were so positive, however, as she also had a penchant for getting herself into predicaments. On this same trip, for instance, her limited use of the French language in combination with her strong will resulted in a rather embarrassing appearance before a magistrate.

The problem started as a dispute with a coachman, who she thought tried to cheat her. The altercation attracted not only a laughing crowd but also a summons to court. During the proceedings, Caroline had difficulty understanding why the crowd "howled" every time she addressed the plaintiff as "cochon." Finally, she was "saved" by the appearance of a young American man who addressed "his Honor" on Caroline's behalf in perfect French. While the judge pursed his lips with amusement, the American told Caroline's side of the story, explaining that the young woman thought she was saying "coachman" and had not intentionally insulted the man by calling him a "pig." Subsequently, the case was dismissed, and the "cocher" drove off with his fare. Caroline's escapades in Europe, however, were limited by her pocketbook. When she returned to the Waldorf Astoria in New York, she had six cents to her name.[51]

Back in Philadelphia, Caroline took an active part in the life of the city. She counted among her friends the redoubtable Anna Jarvis, who would be remembered as the founder of Mother's Day. Around the turn of the century, when the Jarvis family first moved to Philadelphia, Anna was an attractive, intelligent woman who competently handled all the advertising for the Fidelity Mutual Life Insurance Company and cared for her blind sister, Elsinore. Feisty and strong-willed, Anna also became a standard bearer, launching campaigns against garbage collectors, garage owners, and the city engineers who she felt were responsible for the hazardous manholes in the streets. Caroline, who admired Anna's spunk and courage, used to take her out for dinner—occasions the reporter referred to as "rushing the growler." As she explained, "Anna was a great grumbler, always writing letters to the papers about politicians who ran the city" and calling the waiter's attention to the silver if it wasn't properly polished. Despite Anna's eccentricities, Caroline liked Miss Jarvis and considered her a "good old girl."

In 1905, the year after Caroline left Philadelphia, Anna's mother, Mrs. Anna Reeves Jarvis, passed away. On the second anniversary of her mother's death, at a memorial service at Grafton Church, Anna announced her crusade to honor "the world's 'neglected' mothers." With the passing years, Anna was increasingly distressed by the commercialization of Mother's Day and became more and more a recluse. She ventured forth only to seek satisfaction in the courts, or to force cancellation of conventions of "flower peddlers" or "confectioners" she felt were capitalizing on her idea.

Blind and penniless in her old age, Anna Jarvis was placed in the Marshall Square Sanitarium at Westchester where a committee of Philadelphians sponsored her care. Her nurse at the sanitarium wrote to Caroline that Miss Jarvis "often wished that 'Suzette' was there to help her get after the florists who were commercializing Mother's Day." Caroline kept informed of her friend's activities through the years and was distressed to learn of her "unhappy ending."[52]

Amid her busy life in Philadelphia and the escapades and interviews that provided material for her newspaper articles, Caroline began to write short stories for popular magazines. At the age of twenty-two, she published her first story, "The Greengrocery Man," in a Catholic journal sponsored by the House of the Angel Guardian. She tailored the story for her particular audience by presenting an extensive character sketch of an individual who, although honest with his customers, seemed to be absolutely devoid of what she termed "the milk of human kindness."

After describing the man's personality and actions, she told how, one cold day, the man failed to open his shop and how his body was finally discovered with "an old-fashioned picture of an old-fashioned child" clutched in his hand. "At last," she concluded, there was "a frozen look of tenderness on his still face." Almost as an afterthought (and sounding more like Caroline) she tacked on the moral of the story: "The world never missed him and the world never cared."[53]

Although this story represents an interesting exercise in character analysis, it is atypical and lacks the power and humor of Lockhart's later work. Before long, however, Caroline would be basing her short stories as well as her newspaper articles on personal experiences, with good results.

In "The Child of Nature," also noted by Caroline as being "one of her first stories," she seems to have found her own particular style and declares herself as a writer. The first paragraph is, in effect, Caroline expressing her own views: " 'This is a true story,' began the young woman who was known to be romantic. 'A clever lie is considered to be quite as effective as the truth in literature, I know, but, personally, I take more interest in a yarn labeled *fact*.' "[54]

The narrator continues by explaining that she had always wanted to be "a Child of Nature" in the Joaquin Miller style, and so decided to visit New Mexico, where she envisioned herself learning "flowery Spanish," being served "strange Mexican dishes," and enjoying the "wonderful hot springs along the Rio Grande." This setting came straight from Caroline's 1898 visit to New Mexico Territory with friend and editor Andrew MacKenzie, who wanted to take advantage of the hot springs there because of his ailments. True to her word, the story that she developed was indeed based upon fact.[55]

NEW MEXICO TERRITORY AND POINTS WEST

Caroline had met Andrew MacKenzie when he was editor of the Sunday edition of the Boston *Post*, and together they spent several months in Hillsboro, New Mexico Territory, in the spring of 1898. For a while the couple boarded at an old adobe hotel, then moved into an empty ranch house owned by a Mr. Hopewell of the Baldwin Ranch Company. Considerably older than Caroline's twenty-seven years, MacKenzie (or "Sweetie," as she sometimes called him) was in ill health. Their stay, which extended throughout April, May, and June, had been made less than pleasant by the unwelcome overtures of Mr. Hopewell, whom Caroline considered "uncouth and disrespectful." At first, as she confided in her Diary, she felt some "fascination" for the man, despite her loyalty to MacKenzie, but noted that Hopewell "lost his charm" after his disrespectful actions.[56]

In addition to Andrew's health and the landlord's overtures, Caroline worried about finances and found the "locals" most annoying. Being able to confide her concerns to her journal seemed to help. The unburdening of her innermost thoughts and worries to "Dear Diary"—a practice she termed "emptying her sack"—would continue to serve as a therapeutic outlet for Caroline off and on throughout most of her life. And, too, the detailed notes and dialogues she recorded served as good references for turning fact into fiction.

During the months in New Mexico, Andrew and Caroline both tried to produce some serious writing. *The Watchman* accepted a story by Andrew and one by Caroline called "A Wasted Photograph," for which they were each paid five dollars. But *McClure's* rejected her feature article, supposedly because of emphasis on news of the Spanish-American War. In her journal she resolved to put more effort into marketing, "for the summer slips away," she wrote, "and in the fall I shall need more money."

Feeling restless, Caroline and Andrew by mid-June considered moving to Hermosa or Kingston. Still worried about his health, Caroline—reflecting stereotypic prejudices not unusual for the time—confided to her Diary: "The heat affects him greatly and the Greasers are so damned annoying . . . the Mexicans are contemptible people. Thieves, liars, beggars, and traitors."[57] Disillusioned with the heat and the "locals," the two journalists returned to Boston soon thereafter. Although more humorous than the Diary observations, the later printed account of that summer in New Mexico, "A Child of Nature," published in *New Idea Women's Magazine* in 1904, is surprisingly similar. The characterization of the woman she hired as a cook, for example, shocks with its outspoken bias, especially in light of modern-day attitudes. Described as "a lady of Mongrel descent, half Mexican and half Apache," the woman—as Caroline explains—had been married to an Irishman, who "left her his name and a fine vocabulary of English swear words."[58]

The tale continues with a half-serious, half-humorous rendition of the effect of the wind and the dry southwestern climate:

> It [the trip] took us two days and that was when my lips cracked open. Everybody out there has cracked lips. The cracked lip belt is distinct, like the pie belt in New England. [The narrator interrupts herself.] Pardon me a moment

till I rub on a little cold-cream. I'm hoping these crevices will draw together in time.[59]

Ready to drop in her tracks from fatigue, the "Child of Nature" tried to persuade the Mexican teamster to put up the tent, but he "sulked and didn't want to put [it] up . . . til *mañana.*" When she insisted, the ridge pole fell down and cracked Mrs. Gallagher on the head. Mrs. Gallagher, Caroline recorded, "swore like a Pirate." In addition to having a colorful vocabulary, Mrs. Gallagher had interesting culinary techniques, such as

> always mixing a few cigarette ashes in with the dough when she made bread. . . . She baked bread in a bake kettle, and when she was ready to take it out she stabbed it to the heart with the same stick with which she poked the fire. A wood-rat galloped across my face one night, and drowned in a pail of water which we had brought up from the river to settle. Mrs. Gallagher made coffee from it as usual in the morning.[60]

Obviously, the passage of time had not changed Caroline's opinion of the Mexican help. Whereas in her Diary she had complained of their thieving nature, in the story she depicts them more graphically as sneaking around "like a pack of coyotes, waiting for a chance to steal." In slapstick style she brings the story to a conclusion:

> One morning I went to look at a prairie dog village, leaving Mrs. Gallagher in charge. She immediately disappeared and a burro came in and ate up our bacon. The Mexicans rushed in and took what was left. That night a storm came up and the tent blew down. In the morning I hired one of the thieves to take us back to Lake Valley.
>
> I ceased to be a Child of Nature right there, and I haven't had a return symptom.[61]

Caroline undoubtedly took literary license, but the story, compared with her earlier Diary entries, gives an accurate and only slightly fictionalized rendition of her feelings and experiences during that summer in New Mexico Territory. The major difference is that the concerns confided to her Diary are serious, whereas the story for public consumption is tempered with humor. This journalistic approach suggests a pattern that Caroline was to follow not only in her short stories and articles but also in her books. Her training as a newspaper reporter would have a lasting impact on her writing style—a style that would be regarded as humorous and entertaining, but offensive in its reality, especially to those about whom she wrote.

In the "civilized environs" of Philadelphia, Caroline began to produce stories on various topics. Those that moralized, such as "The Greengrocery Man," would eventually seem out of character, while others dealing with the more traditional and mundane simply lacked the power of stories based upon personal experience. "The Sign That Failed," for example, a story written for *Home and Art* magazine, falls in this latter category and tells of an attempt by Caroline and a friend called "Elizabeth" to set up housekeeping. In humorous detail, she records how they excitedly sign the papers making them homeowners, then begin to discover each other's idiosyncrasies and those of their neighbors. Caroline's major desire, it seems, is for "quiet, perfect quiet," while Elizabeth wants to be able to enjoy her own cooking, especially "fried tomatoes and cream sauce." After furnishing their new home with "furniture of every wood and style and epoch," they buy cooking utensils and a large galvanized-iron garbage can with a bouquet of blue roses painted on the side.[62]

Caroline, as keeper of this distinctive garbage can, develops a humorous rendition of experiences centered around household chores and the mutilation of the beautiful can either by "jealous neighbors" or by a "perverted milkman," who kicks it the length of the alley each morning exactly at 4:00 a.m. Nevertheless, the two young women manage to cope with each other and the neighbors until a deluge of solicitors start ringing the doorbell at all hours of the day and night.

In an effort to ward off this intrusion into their privacy, Caroline posts a lengthy notice to peddlers and agents. At this point the story goes from the humorous to the ludicrous. The sign, rather than keeping people away, attracts a crowd of interested neighbors and passersby, who "surge against the front door" and ring the bell before they leave.[63]

The story is entertaining and is based more than likely upon a semblance of fact, but little is outstanding about it. It does reveal the author's developing talents as a humorist and it probably contributed toward the monthly payments on the house she wrote about. Far better were her action stories, which were based upon real-life adventures in much the same manner as her news articles.

Lockhart published one such story, "A Girl in the Rockies," in *Lippincott's Monthly Magazine* in 1902. Under the pseudonym "Suzette," she told of a hair-raising adventure on the Blackfoot Reservation in Montana. This story is significant not only because it is well written but also because it reveals her character and attitudes, especially when studied in combination and in comparison with her autobiographical account of the same adventure.[64]

Starting out on one of her unusual vacations, Lockhart boarded the train

in Philadelphia and, after what seemed to be "endless days and nights of
flat prairie with few stops," she stepped down on the cinders at Blackfoot.
Although there was nothing in sight remotely resembling a hotel, she did
see a government store across the street with Indians in colorful blankets
going in and out. She also saw a "spry old man in a woolen shirt and ragged
overalls" tying his team to the hitching rack. When she approached the
old man, he was somewhat hesitant until he determined that she wasn't
a "floozie." Eventually, however, he agreed to serve as her guide to see the
scenery in the Swift Current country. This accidental meeting with Sourdough Sam led to what she termed "one of the most terrifying adventures
of my life." [65]

Sam, whose picture would hang for years in her front living room in
Cody, Wyoming, appointed himself as her chaperone as well as her guide.
Any individual who used language that he considered "too salty" around
his charge quickly heard from him. Despite Sam's seventy-odd years, Caroline recalled that "he went over the boulders and climbed the tallest peaks
with the agility of a mountain goat." [66]

Convinced that she just had to see a particularly spectacular lake, Caroline persuaded Sam—against his better judgment—to take her over the
treacherous MacDonald (Swift Current) Pass, a route reputed to be so dangerous that even the Indians were leery of it. In the fictionalized account of
this adventure, written for *Lippincott's*, Sourdough Sam (Old Man MacNeil
in the story) tells the girl: "It's a hell of a trail and you couldn't nowise
make it."

"But I'm determined to go."

The old man looked skeptical.

"No woman ever went over that trail," he said. "It's the roughest in this
country."

But the girl doesn't take *no* for an answer. "Now, listen," she says, "I'm
bound to go. . . . If you won't take me, someone else will, and I mean
to win my bet from Big Steve." [67] So Caroline's heroine, patterned after
herself, sets out to accomplish a feat that would scare most men or women.

In the actual climb, Caroline's horse got away from her and left her
stranded on the mountainside. Sourdough Sam, around the bend ahead
of her, was unaware of what had happened. Caroline, left clinging to the
side of the mountain, grabbed at bushes and tufts of grass to keep herself
from slipping. In her autobiography, she tells of her predicament in more
exciting terms than she would later write it for publication:

> I couldn't go ahead, I couldn't go back, so with arms and legs outstretched
> I laid flat on my face and waited. . . . I felt nauseated and I remembered

wondering why fear should make me sick at my stomach. Sourdough Sam
estimated later that there was less than six feet between me and eternity
when he threw me a rope and hauled me off the shale. When he saw my loose
horse he guessed what had happened and snatched off his saddle rope, and
literally tumbled down the mountain to reach me before it was too late.[68]

It was this episode that she converted into the focal point of the fictionalized version. In the story, she is more explicit with geographic details,
which were fresher in her mind in 1902 when the story was published than
in later years when she was writing her autobiography. In the short story she
indicates that her objective had been to go to Swift Current, a new mining camp along the Rockies, then over the pass into the MacDonald Lake
Country. Also in the short story, and in contrast to the autobiographical
account, she takes advantage of literary license to interject her views on
feminine capability and eastern influence.

The girl in the Rockies, for example, is portrayed as a particularly daring
and capable sort (a hardly exaggerated version of "Suzette"), who makes
the first leg of the venture to Swift Current all by herself. Before she starts
out, however, she stops overnight at a primitive boardinghouse, where
she wagers with the stage driver (who doesn't think much of easterners
or women) that she can make it. After getting directions from Joe Kipp,
"a prosperous half-breed," the girl sets off on a trek that involves fording
streams, fighting flies, and conversing with a band of Indians.[69]

During the course of her ride, she rhapsodizes over the "cool morning
air," sweet with "the fragrance of wild roses," and the prairie below "like
a gay carpet woven in gaudy colors of red, yellow, and blue." She misses
the right trail, but by nightfall reaches the home of the Witzels, who have
a house described by Caroline as looking like the home of "any eastern
family in moderate circumstances." Caroline then dismisses them rhetori-
cally, saying: "The girls had been graduated from Oberlin College, and the
family, though pleasant, were of a type too familiar to be interesting."[70] Her
autobiographical account makes no mention of such a family; therefore,
it appears they have been placed in the fictionalized version to give the
author opportunity to express her personal opinion of eastern middle-class
provincialism.

In contrast, she does go into considerable detail in her autobiography
about being invited by Jennie Lamont, a "half-breed" girl who has been to
boarding school, to accompany her on a visit home to see her grandmother.
Assuming that "grandma" lived in a house of sorts, Caroline writes that
she was "startled" to be led into an authentic Indian encampment of lodges

centered around a big canvas tent. She described their welcome by "an old woman who came out of a tepee making strange clucking sounds as she hobbled toward us. There was no embrace, no kiss, only the light in her sunken eyes showed her pleasure: 'This is my Grama Mountain Chicken,' Jennie said happily." [71]

That night they rolled themselves in their blankets and slept "head to foot around the tent," and the next day the Indians prepared a feast, the main course of which Caroline described as being "long, white strips of something I never had seen in a butcher shop." "It was unseasoned," she recorded, "but not too bad and I ate it to the last inch." From then on, she resolved to "take it as a personal insult if anybody used the derogatory term 'gut-stripper' in . . . her presence." [72]

Why Caroline chose to moralize about the influence of eastern lifestyles in her printed version, when she could have included the story of her visit to the Indian camp, is not readily apparent; but she obviously found the primitive abode of her friend more interesting. She was also much impressed by the plight of the Native American—an empathy that would continue throughout her lifetime and one that she shared with authors of the time, such as Mary Austin and, somewhat later, Mari Sandoz.

In her autobiography, for example, she tells of her meeting with Jennie's "Uncle Four Horns," described by Caroline as "tall, arrow-straight, with strong features and great natural dignity . . . a proud and commanding figure." When she tried to make conversation she says, "He did not unbend quickly. . . . It was only when I spoke of his people that he showed interest. . . . He spoke without bitterness but with a hopeless resignation that cut me to the heart." She then quotes what, in effect, amounts to a soliloquy in which the uncle expounds on the plight of the Indian. Impressed by the Indian's "pain," "despair," and "utter hopelessness," she noted that tears blurred her eyes as she wrote. [73] When considered in its entirety, the Montana vacation and the story she wrote based upon it signify a renewal of her interest in the West and an innate appreciation for the standards of courage and self-reliance demanded by the primitivism of the region.

She continued to exhibit her feelings for the Native American in later works as well. In other stories, such as "The Spirit That Talked from a Box" and its sequel "In the White Man's Way," the "Red Man" gets revenge for past injustices. Even the publisher's advertising for the later story reflected popular sentiment. Touted as a story telling "how an Indian learned to revenge himself with instruments of torture more subtle and painful than the scalping knife and the stake," the story reveals the pro-Indian attitude prevalent around the turn of the century. Not unlike other prominent authors and artists, Caroline's stance exhibits the cumulative influence of the humanitarian reform movements of the 1880s, the impact of Helen Hunt Jackson's A Century for Dishonor, and the trend toward the establishment of Indian rights associations.[74]

Caroline's re-exposure to the West was significant not only because it influenced her choice of subject matter but also because she found within it a sense of place. From 1902 on, most of her short stories and all of her novels would be western in orientation, whether they were character sketches, situation comedies, or action tales. In the West, she discovered a rich source of colorful and contrasting personalities, varied and beautiful terrain, and a strong kinship with a spirit she felt was worth preserving.

The Swift Current country would provide her with material from which to write still another short story for Lippincott's. In this tale, entitled "The Pin-Head," some of the same characters, such as Bacon-Rind Dick, are reintroduced. Set in a small mining camp in Swift Current canyon, the story revolves around the petty but intense feuds of its isolated inhabitants; yet, when fire threatens the lives of a family, erstwhile enemies rally to their assistance. Written after Caroline's return West, the story differentiates quite clearly between life in such a community and life in the East. "It is difficult," she says, "for persons whose lives are broad and interests many to enter understandingly into the atmosphere of a small and isolated colony . . . its threadbare topics of conversation, and its paucity of ideas." "On the other hand," she continues, "the world off there to the East . . . off there where the Great Northern starts, where miners are entombed by the hundreds, where there are riots and cowardly murders, burglaries, social and political wars, that world where these things happen, is, to the small and isolated communities, like a myth."[75]

Caroline was naturally gifted with a good ear for dialect. This story in particular reveals her growing fund of western dialogue and euphemisms, which she used to maximum effect. In "The Pin-Head," for example, Dad Walker, a member of the Swift Current community, identifies DeWolfe as "the skunk who dens in the shack across the street." DeWolfe, in turn, speaks of Edgar Harrison as "the wood pussy who lives down there by the bridge"; while Edgar, from his rocking chair by the window, talks about "the pole-kitties up the street."[76]

At the climax of the story, Dad Walker accuses his neighbor of thievery. "Harrison, you are a petty larceny thief. You stole my airtights [canned goods], and I'm goin' to lick you."

"Back up, pardner," Bacon-Rind (Richard Watkins) warns. He then admits that he is the real culprit and states his case. Dad Walker learns that Watkins is in love with his niece and accepts his explanation, saying:

Well, then, Richard Watkins, . . . I can't give you jools or a furnished house, but you got my blessin' and them eight airtights, for any pinhead that's smart enough to get away with a girl and my grub right under my nose—why, I feel that it's comin' to him.[77]

Time and again, Caroline's stories and novels would reflect the fact that she liked writing about human interaction in small communities and about strong women who could cope "in a man's world." Just as she was able to meet the challenges of providing for herself and functioning successfully in her chosen profession, she enjoyed writing about women in the same mold—whether it was about herself as "Suzette" in the Rockies; Bronco Bess, who broke and sold horses for a living; Poker Nell, who dealt cards in her husband's saloon; or the Sheep Queen of Wyoming.

The short story featuring Bronco Bess, for example, incorporates two favorite Lockhart themes—the strong, capable woman of the West, and small-town morality. In this tale titled "The Woman Who Gave No Quarter," also published by *Lippincott's*, Caroline tells of Bess's ostracism by the town's "better element," her love for her daughter, and her ultimate fate. Especially well written, "The Woman" is unusual for Lockhart because of its lack of humor and a poignancy that brings tears to the eyes.[78]

In the story Mrs. Atkinson, the pillar of local society (who had worked as a dressmaker back East for a dollar a day), tells the new professor in town that Bronco Bess is "one of our local characters." She explains snobbishly: "We don't call on her at all, because, . . . as you know, it wouldn't be possible to recognize her socially."[79] Caroline analyzes her character further:

Only the rare women of her sex could understand the heart of Bronco Bess. Her physical courage was the courage of a lioness; her nature was that of the Indian in its craving for outdoor life. The occupations of women fretted her, their petty interests bored her. They could not understand her, so they ostracized her, and with the meanness of small natures, 'dealt her misery.'[80]

As the plot evolves, the reader learns that the new professor was Bess's husband, who had spent her inheritance and then deserted her and their little daughter. In the meantime, the professor has recognized Bronco Bess and is terrified that she will tell his "wife" the true story and ruin his reputation. Bess, however, decides to bide her time. When the young daughter, a student in the professor's school, wins her cowardly father's heart and the right to attend the Honor Scholar's Picnic, the professor's "wife" takes it upon herself to write a note to Bess saying that local society had determined that it "would very much simplify matters" if the child would remain at home.[81]

Her maternal instincts riled, Bess demands a meeting with the contrite professor, arranges for the child to go as his special guest, and accompanies the picnic wagon on horseback. The professor sits on the buckboard, clutching Bess's daughter (and his) in his lap. Then the crisis comes when, on the steep descent, the brakes on the wagon fail and it looks "like sure death" for all that Bess loves. Heroically, she races her horse ahead of the careering wagon and literally drags it to a stop; but her horse slips and falls, crushing Bronco Bess beneath the saddle. Lying in a crumpled heap in the mud, she looks up to see the professor's face above her own:

"A strange smile softened and beautified the face of Bear Tooth's woman outcast," Caroline wrote. Then Bess's face hardened—"It was her moment of vindication." " 'I have never taken quarter,' she said at last, 'but—I'll give it. Take her [the child],' she continued slowly, 'and treat her—as though she were your own.' "[82]

In "A Treasure of the Humble," Caroline deals again with small-town morality. In this tale, the society women of Prouty, a typical Cody-type town, pay little attention to the plight of a single woman "on hard times" until they learn that she is boarding a man in the house. But in the tradition of the West—and Caroline Lockhart—the woman is saved by the love of a good man.[83]

A similar moral code makes up the plot of "The Qualities of Leadership." In this story, Miss Cowley, a member of an old and conservative family back East, decides to marry the pastor, Mr. Bethly, and go West where she fully expects (because of her background) to become a leader of local society. The story evolves as the former Miss Cowley makes one mistake after another, but her biggest failing (like that of the women of Prouty) is lack of a kind and understanding heart. When she refuses to help her servant girl, who is "in the family way," she is put to shame by Mrs. Rippletoe, who tells the pastor's wife:

You'd like to run the church societies and things, generally, but you haven't got the makin's of a leader in spite of the social trainin' I've heard you mention so frequent. All the social trainin' I ever got was shootin' biscuits in a Harvey's Eatin' House, but I've noticed that it takes more than social trainin' to be a leader. It takes kindness of heart, along with courage, whether it's in a city or Upper Sage Creek. You're done for in this community. I'm meaner than sin when I get started.[84]

Thus Caroline's rough but soft-hearted woman wins out over the small town social climber. How much of this reaction was a result of her own somewhat anomalous position on the fringes of "good society" is hard to determine; however, it seems at the very least to have added a dimension to her understanding of human nature. Like Mrs. Rippletoe, Caroline Lockhart had the courage and strength of conviction to be a weighty adversary.

In her later short stories, published after the move West, friends (and enemies) frequently found themselves used as characters, as in the situation comedy called "His Own Medicine."[85] In this vignette Caroline reverts to her traditionally humorous style, depicting the town barkeep as the local expert on women and the confidant of every man who patronizes his bar. She tells how the various townsmen—from Helm of the River Lumber Company to Cummings, the proprietor of the Iowa Notion Store—all come to the barkeep for advice on how to handle their wives or attract the object of their affections. But the real problem begins when a "bunch of she tourists from New York" stop by the bar on their way to Yellowstone Park. Caroline sets the scene accordingly:

" 'I've always been perfectly wild to go into a bar; I'd like to put my foot on the brass rail and say "Two, please—no water," chirps one of the young women.' "

The barkeep, recognizing a familiar voice, suddenly pales and tries to make his escape—unsuccessfully. Then a small woman in a walking skirt and an alpine hat enters and spies the barkeep (her long lost Gustave) trying to skulk off. Caroline tells what happens:

" 'So-o-o!' The long-drawn word reeked with satisfaction. 'This is where you are, is it!' The wiry figure stiffened for battle. 'Liar! . . . Coward! . . . Scoundrel! . . . to desert me!' "[86]

While the onlookers expectantly wait for the barkeep's tough reply, he wilts before their eyes. " 'Get up!' she cried, advancing upon the cringing form. 'Get up! I'll see you upstairs!' "[87] Once again Caroline's wily women show their muster.

In similar style, "The Tango Lizard," advertised as "a story rich in humor and its delineation of human nature," contrasts the ranch woman, Mrs. Savage, who stands six feet two inches "in her carpet slippers," with Miss La Fay, a flapper who is "thin and graceful, with ankles like an antelope."[88] While Mrs. Savage, whose husband had drowned, built up "the best paying horse ranch in the state," Miss Le Fay "lived for clothes and shows" and danced her life away.[89] In this manner, Lockhart effectively and humorously delineates between a woman of the West and a woman of the East. Her preference for strong men as well as strong women is apparent both in her novels and in her short stories. Typically, the rough but tough cowboys win out over the soft "dudes," and Western manners and mores win out over those Eastern.

Between short stories and adventures, Caroline, as "Suzette" of Philadelphia *Bulletin* fame, continued her reporting assignments, which included covering the "embalmed beef scandal" during the Spanish-American War, and a day-by-day account of one of the nation's most sensational counterfeiting cases. Then, in 1904, the *Bulletin* assigned her to return once again to Montana to do a feature story on the Blackfoot Indians.[90] Occurring as it did when Caroline was reanalyzing her career goals, this assignment came at an important time in her life. Having established herself as a newspaper woman and short story writer of some repute, she began to think seriously of trying to write full-length novels. After fifteen years as a reporter, Caroline was ready for a change; and the way led West.

The Novelist

Go, therefore, and do that which is within you to do; take no heed of
gestures which beckon you aside; ask of no man permission to perform.
                    Frederic Van Rensselaer Day, *The Magic Story*

THE TURNING POINT

When Caroline Lockhart first arrived in Cody in 1904, she was much impressed with the Wyoming countryside, and Cody was equally impressed
with her. The arrival of the good-looking young journalist, already well
established as a popular short story writer and reporter, was a newsworthy
event. "Miss Lockhart," a reporter enthusiastically announced, "has re-
cently resigned from the staff of the Philadelphia *Bulletin* and *Press* and . . .
is in Cody for several weeks stay." The writer also indicated that Miss
Lockhart, a contributor to *Century* and *Lippincott*, was now interested in
"general literary work" and would be visiting with former newspaper editor
Andrew MacKenzie.[1] The "several weeks stay," however, was destined to
extend to the better part of a lifetime as Caroline quickly felt a kinship
with the western spirit of the place.

As the Burlington Railroad brought her closer to her destination, Caroline Lockhart felt a familiar twinge of excitement. She typically enjoyed
new experiences, and she was eager to see Andrew again. Andrew Mac-
Kenzie's illness and decision to try the warm springs and high altitude of
Cody, Wyoming, had come at an opportune time—if illness is ever opportune. With the assignment on the Blackfoot Indians behind her, she
had decided to extend her visit to Wyoming, especially when she learned
that Andrew had gone West for his health and had taken up residence
at Irma Flats outside Cody. Caroline and Andrew had known each other
since he was editor of the Sunday edition of the Boston *Post*. She held
fond memories of the months they had spent together in Hillsboro, New
Mexico Territory, in the spring of 1898 and looked forward to seeing him
again. Now six years later, she was visiting Andrew in a similarly isolated
western locale.[2]

As Caroline Lockhart stepped off the train that day in October 1904, her fine figure and gold-burnished hair caught the sun and the approving glances of onlookers. Buxom but small waisted with a generous, almost sensual mouth, she made a fashionable and pretty picture. Still a young woman at age thirty-three, Lockhart had the intelligent eyes of one who makes her living observing people and places. Waiting to take her into town was a four-horse stage driven by Fred Johnson. In the distance across the sagebrush flat, she saw the small village of Cody, Wyoming.[3]

Founded in 1896 by William Frederick "Buffalo Bill" Cody, George T. Beck, and other directors of the Shoshone Land and Water Company, the town had been in existence just eight years when Caroline Lockhart first arrived. Originally established in 1895 as "Cody Town" or "Cody City" near the northeast corner of Cedar Mountain, south of the river above De Maris Hot Springs, the town had been resituated in part to prevent the railroad from monopolizing all the real estate. Subsequently, in February of 1896, Cody, Beck, and surveyor Charles Hayden located another site several miles east. The new location had easy access to the river, a passable ford, and was still conveniently close to the entrance to the beautiful Yellowstone country.

The visionary Cody, quick to see the assets of the area, had made arrangements for the Chicago, Burlington & Quincy Railroad to build a spur within one and a half miles of the townsite by 1901. However, his plans to divert water from the Shoshone to irrigate 60,000 acres of land in the vicinity met with federal opposition. When Caroline arrived in 1904, the town's newspapers, the Cody *Enterprise* and the Wyoming *Stockgrower*, were heatedly debating whether the Colonel should relinquish the Cody-Salsbury Segregation to the federal government.

Caroline, with her journalist's ear for such things, realized that basic to the debate was the recurring issue of state versus federal rights. And in this case, it appeared that federal rights would win. The losers would be the owners of the fine old ranches whose lands would be inundated by the proposed dam at the head of the Shoshone River (Stinking Water) canyon. Losers, too, would be the people of Cody, who had already invested $1,000 in a road to Yellowstone—a road that would soon be under water as well.

Six months after Caroline's arrival, Colonel Cody would succumb to government pressure and sign over his relinquishment, contingent upon some $2¼ million in federal funds being poured into the project. According to the agreement, the Wiley-Guernsey Company was also obligated to invest $2 million. This trade-off of "Western Independence for Federal

Aid," according to the *Stockgrower*, supposedly would "make the city of Cody, the center of a garden of the fertile tracts."

In the fall of 1904, however, Cody hardly resembled a garden spot. It was the typical frontier town with board sidewalks, hitching racks, kerosene lamps on the two blocks of main street, stores with false fronts, and thirteen saloons for the few hundred inhabitants. Yet there were signs of progress. On the corner of 4th (now 12th) and Sheridan, sat Colonel Cody's grand Irma Hotel, an impressive structure built of native sandstone. In addition to the usual service rooms, the hotel boasted fifty guest rooms and an elegant dining hall.

Other places of accommodation included the De Maris Hot Springs Resort, the large two-story Cliff House Hotel west of Cody, erected by Charles De Maris to house those who came to benefit from the medicinal properties of the springs. There was also the Hart Mountain Inn, owned by "Badland Dave" McFall, where one could room and board for two dollars a day.

The Cody Lumber Company and its supplier, the Hud Darrah sawmill on Carter Mountain, attempted to meet demands for new construction, which included plans for a new national bank building and a four-room school. Dr. James L. Bradbury had just completed his new office building, made of eye-catching red and white stone. There were two bakeries (Dibble's and Lenninger's), Cummings Drug Store, Richards's Taxidermy, Atherton's Horseshoeing Shop, and the Brundage Hardware, among others.[4]

From Caroline's perspective, however, the town's biggest asset was its panorama of interesting people. The owner of the Ladies' Emporium, for example, was Nellie Bruce, otherwise known as "Poker Nell." Nell, who wore a diamond embedded in her front tooth, had been a card dealer in her husband's saloon. There was also Etta Feeley, the "madam" from Red Lodge, who set up her establishment on the outskirts of town.

In addition to shopkeepers and the inevitable influx of "dudes" from the East, cowboys and Indians, miners, sheepherders, homesteaders, and an occasional outlaw all passed through Cody. Many decided to stay—making Cody an oasis of an older civilization, a place locked in time and space. Here the spirit of the Old West struggled to retain its strength and integrity, despite the efforts of certain elements to force the yoke of progress and urbanization upon its character.

Feeling that the Old was better than the New, the young reporter was destined to become a part of this internal struggle between the forces of urban progress and advocates of an older and rapidly passing frontier era. The struggle would persist to color the political and social character of the town and the writing of Caroline Lockhart.

The western spirit of Cody captured Caroline's professional interest and appealed to her crusading nature. As a self-reliant, individualistic young woman, she appreciated those virtues in others. Despite her years as an expatriate in the East, Caroline's midwestern heritage and rural upbringing contributed to her appreciation of the frontier environment.

In the fall of 1904, Cody was indeed the typical frontier cow town. Tumbleweeds rolled down Main Street to lodge against the steps leading into Nick Noble's Black Diamond Saloon, cowboys tied their horses to hitching posts in front of clapboard buildings, and Indians wrapped in multicolored blankets paraded along dusty streets. Essentially, Cody represented a cultural fault, almost as observable as a geological one.[5]

After years of exposure to the elements, the inhabitants of the town, especially those past the prime of life, looked as weathered as the false store fronts and board sidewalks. Caroline took note of the dust devil that whirled its way toward the edge of town and the crisp chill to the air that hinted at a bitter winter to come. Above all else, there was a timeless quality to the place.

Lockhart's visit to Cody in 1904 represented a turning point in her life and career. Despite her relative youth—thirty-three—she had a rich backlog of personal experience and an understanding from which to focus in on the universality of provincial lifestyles. Pragmatically, she saw the town as a creative source—a wellspring of local color that would provide raw material for her literary efforts. Cody, she decided, would be a "fruitful place" in which to realize her writing ambitions.

In this respect, Caroline Lockhart was in step with literary fashion: Local colorism, with its emphasis on dialects, the picturesque, and the romantic, had retained its popularity from the 1860s through the turn of the century. With almost scientific detachment, she admitted: "Cody here is my workshop. I go East to play and enjoy it twice as much as though I lived there all the time."[6]

This reference to Cody as her "workshop" is significant, revealing as it does her overriding attitude toward the town. The term helps to explain Lockhart's actions and eventual position within the community as well as her treatment of its residents and, conversely, their reaction to her. Intellectually, Lockhart decided to use Cody as a literary laboratory, its residents as subjects for research, and her pen as a prod to test the caliber and responses of the town's various characters. She then published her conclusions in a style so picaresque and humorous that the identities of those she wrote about, or what she had discovered, were scarcely concealed.

Underscorings, slash marks, and occasional notations in the books and pamphlets that she used to study her craft reveal personal and professional philosophies. One such paragraph read:

> The spirit of observation, as applied to the world in general, outer and inner, is practically identical with what is called . . . the scientific spirit in the larger sense, with all the enthusiasm, the sense of values, the accuracy, the verifying caution, that characterize the born observer.[7]

The observation of human nature she deemed extremely important and, subsequently, became very good at it. In this respect, her reporting background stood her in good stead and refined her powers of observation. The journalistic approach also provided her with an effective formula for writing. Heavy slash marks in a book on the short story by J. Berg Essenwein reveal her interest in the following precept:

> A short-story should have for its structure a plot, a bit of life, an incident such as you would find in a brief newspaper paragraph. . . . He [Richard Harding Davis] takes the substance of just such a paragraph, and, with that for the meat of his story, weaves around it details, description and dialogue, until a complete story is the result.[8]

The influence of this precept, reinforced by her training on the staff of the Boston *Post* and the Philadelphia *Bulletin*, is readily apparent both in her short stories and in her novels.

Although Caroline Lockhart's decision to stay in Cody seems to have been primarily an intellectual one, on an emotional level she admitted that she "liked the country with its picturesque and friendly folk." "The mountains and the sagebrush plains, the stimulating air and the amusing episodes of the town," she said, "appealed to her." In addition to being picturesque, the town was deceptively calm, which was also an asset from Caroline's point of view. In later years, when questioned as to why she chose to live in Cody, she referred to a book called *The Truth About an Author* by Arnold Bennett. Bennett, she explained, wrote about what she had determined herself "by groping and experimenting—that the best results come out of monotony." "One's mind is most active in dullness and allows concentration," she claimed, adding—not quite truthfully—"Excitement isn't necessary to my existence. I've been bored in Paris for that matter."[9]

It is true that Caroline became bored easily. It is also true that she needed calm to put pen to paper, but contrary to her denial of needing excitement, she did require activity to satisfy her addiction to adventure. In this respect, Lockhart's actions spoke louder than her words. As her life in Cody, and elsewhere, testified, her modus operandi was to create her own excitement—with her pen or her personal actions, if necessary. Throughout her lifetime, she would continue to be lured by new experiences and adventure—even if she had to create them as figments of her literary imagination or stir them up with her own controversial stands.

In essence, the West provided her a suitable backdrop. Always a bit of an actress with a flair for the dramatic, Caroline used the West, exemplified by Cody, as a stage upon which she could play her part with liberal abandon—whether the audience approved or not.

Her decision made, she adopted Cody as her hometown and purchased the house and lot at 1126 Rumsey Avenue. Eventually she would also buy the house and lot to the west for use as a rental property.[10] The small white house on Rumsey became Lockhart's permanent residence, despite time spent in Denver and on the Dryhead in Montana during later years.

Not long after her arrival, she discovered that there existed in Cody an internal struggle, the winners of which would have the right to determine the town's character. Was it going to be turned over to the "scissorbills" infiltrating from the East, or would the advocates of an older era survive? The scissorbills, as Caroline called them, were considered by the old-timers to be encroachers who sought to create an urban oasis in the West. In addition to the Dudes versus the Old-timers, the community contained subfactions—Wets against Drys, Methodists against Episcopalians, Sheepherders against Ranchers. An astute and intelligent observer, Caroline quickly analyzed the internal workings of her sociological workshop and began to interject her own personal views and strong personality. Having decided that Cody epitomized an era that was rapidly passing and worth preserving, she did her best to postpone the inevitable.[11]

Although calm on the surface, the town was continually agitated by opposing forces. As she soon discovered, the lawlessness of the frontier environment erupted periodically to disturb the town's tranquility. One such occasion occurred shortly after her arrival. On 1 November 1904, the sleepy atmosphere of Cody, Wyoming, was shattered by violence. It was midafternoon and the guests of the Irma Hotel sat on the wide veranda watching a dog fight in the dusty street. They paid little attention to the two horsemen who rode casually into town, then went into the bank where Charles Hensley, the assistant cashier, worked at his books behind the teller's grill.

"Hands up everybody, quick!" yelled one of the men.

Ira O. Middaugh, the cashier, happened to be in a private office with a man named Luce, president of a bank in Logan, Iowa. Hearing the commotion, Mr. Luce hurriedly hid himself in the safe (where he nearly suffocated). Mr. Middaugh, however, quickly slammed the door separating the office from the main room. Unable to break down the door, one of the outlaws ran out of the bank and around to the side.

Immediately in back of the bank building in his private office, Judge Wall sat talking with lumberman Hud Darrah. Two bullets crashed through the glass door announcing the holdup in progress. The shots brought the other outlaw dashing into the street, where Middaugh lunged at him, grabbing his wrist. In the ensuing melee, Middaugh was shot and killed.

By now, the townspeople realized that a holdup was taking place in broad daylight and quickly organized a posse. But the bank robbers had headed toward Thermopolis—a town frequented by members of the notorious Hole-in-the-Wall gang and a known haven for outlaws. The robbers found fresh mounts there and disappeared into the Badlands near the Owl Creek Mountains.[12]

It is this episode that Caroline used to introduce her readers to Cody, Wyoming. No longer on the staff of the *Bulletin,* she continued from time to time to treat her avid Eastern audience to a glimpse of the "real" West. As "Suzette," she covered the Cody holdup as if she were on the scene, giving a shot-by-shot description of the event and depicting for the first time many of the Codyites whom she would use again and again as characters in her stories and books.

The article, entitled "Suzette Tells of Manhunt and Holdup in Cody," tells the reading public not only of Judge Wall but also of Mrs. Wall, who, along with her husband, grabs a Colt revolver to shoot at the robbers; of Chamberlin, the dentist who arrives on the scene to take a few shots; of "the little woman doctor," Frances Lane, who comes scurrying through the crossfire, "ducking bullets like a sage hen" to reach Middaugh; of Dick Roth, saloon keeper, "whose place is held up so regularly that he worries when they don't come"; and of "Old Man" Jerry Ryan, "perched high on a scaffold against a new building . . . like a turkey buzzard in a dead tree."[13]

In a humorous style that was to become characteristically "Caroline," she skillfully described the actions of the townspeople during the holdup, revealing to her readers the makeup of many of the town's better-known citizens. "The clerk of the Irma," for example, "leaped nimbly over the office desk and leaped nimbly back," while the "stately and reserved" Englishman, Captain Corfield, who "came out to see what the West was like," hid behind the safe but said that he "was merely guarding it." In comparison, Dr. D. Frank Powell, formerly Buffalo Bill's scouting companion who was then managing Colonel Cody's interests in the Big Horn Basin, "saw the

holdup from the windows of his room on the second floor of the Irma."
Despite being seriously ill, he grabbed his revolvers ("neither of which happened to have a cylinder in it") and ran out on the veranda, brandishing
them about.[14]

Then there was " 'Dad' Pierce, the fearless Colonel of the Forest Rang-
ers," who hid behind the radiator, and Charles W. "Sandy" Dibble, "the
fiery baker who lived next to Roth's saloon." "Dibble," Caroline reported,
"wiped his doughy fingers on the door jamb and reached under the counter
for his gun; but his wife, proving to be the better man of the two, took it
from him and sat on it until the trouble was over." Dr. Louis Howe and
Mr. Brown finally managed to run out of the bank "like two jackrabbits";
while Jacob Schwoob, the young mayor, excitedly shouted, "Five hundred
dollars, boys, dead or alive!" George T. Beck, son of "Senator" Beck of
Kentucky, upped the ante: "Two hundred and fifty more!" "Suzette" concluded her action-packed article, saying: "A reward of $2,750 is offered for
their capture, dead or alive, but the Codyites will have to ride faster and
shoot truer than they do at present to get it."[15]

One might have thought that, as a newcomer, Lockhart would have
been a bit easier on her neighbors, but this was merely a hint of what was
to come. Cody's residents were destined to see themselves time and again
in various literary guises. From the beginning of her sojourn there, she was
blatantly honest in her characterizations. Her word pictures, painted in a
most realistic and entertaining style, were bound to irritate. And although
the townspeople may have disagreed, outsiders considered her novels and
short stories to be—as one individual termed it—"accurate, if humorous
depictions of the town's characters and their idiosyncrasies, which gave an
added tinge of red to the town's composite 21-inch 'neck.' "[16]

To Caroline, however, her goals and profession came before her subject's
sensitivities. Taking to heart the advice of Frederic Van Rensselaer Day,
whose words she underscored, Caroline would "do that which . . . [was]
within her to do" and "ask of no man [or woman] permission to perform."[17]

Not all of her vignettes were barbed, however. Some, such as her tales
of Mine Alpert Heimer and his friend, the Old Cattleman of Southfork,
were simply amusing and consequently became very popular. Depicted in
newspaper articles to the *Stockgrower*, Mine Alpert Heimer was 'a literary
creation patterned after the bartender at the Irma Hotel. Alpert, however,
soon opened his own saloon—the Manhattan—in the Shoshone bank
building. The new saloon increased the total number of such establish-
ments to eight in the block and fourteen in the town. "With a population
of 1,800 souls as arid as the soil about them," according to Caroline, this
was "none too many."[18]

Along with Alpert, Caroline created the Old Cattleman, based upon a real-life character by the name of Sam Aldrich. In her articles for the *Stockgrower,* she refined her talent for western dialect and her special brand of humor. Her chronicles of the activities of these two not only amused Basin readers far and wide but also provided her with a means to express her opinions on community affairs, ranging from the new sewer system to the electric sign owned by the Cody Trading Company.

Lockhart has Mine Alpert, for example, attempting to explain the town's newest addition to the Old Cattleman:

> 'Mine Alpert' lowered his voice to a whisper. "Cody's got a mass-sewer."
>
> "You been eatin' larkspur?" demanded the Old Cattleman suspiciously.
>
> "Fella, you're locoed! Only the last time I was in town everybody was kicking because Council wouldn't vote money for a sewage system. You can't tell me that Cody's got a sewer in ten days time."
>
> "The dumbness of you people what lives out of town hurts me," declared 'Mine Alpert' in disgust. "A mass-sewer is a man!"[19]

People were not always disturbed by the notoriety Caroline accorded them. The bartender, for example, capitalized on the free publicity by signing his advertising "Mine Alpert Heimer."[20]

Although Caroline spent the majority of her time writing vignettes for newspapers and articles for magazines during this period, her major objective was to produce novels about the West. Cody proved to be the perfect setting. With its remnants of frontier lawlessness, social rivalries, elements of change, and unique characters, the town—thinly disguised in her novels as "Prouty" or "Crowheart"—added spice to her life and to her writing. The higher level of creative energy generated by her move West resulted in the most productive period of her life.

ME-SMITH

The first decade of the twentieth century was a time of transition for the Big Horn Basin and for Caroline Lockhart. Colonel Cody continued to promote the area, going so far as to enlist the aid of his former hunting companion, President Theodore Roosevelt, in his campaign to complete the Northside Canal. Cody also opened two roadside hotels—the Wapiti Inn and the Pahaska Tepee—along the government road to the National Park. Even then, Buffalo Bill was being recognized as "the unselfish benefactor of Big Horn Country," but others were also promoting the region.

George Beck initiated his own campaign to bring electricity to town and made a successful bid for a franchise to set up an electric light plant. In the canyon, preliminary work for construction of the Shoshone Dam began in 1904. Beleaguered with contractors who defaulted and a tight labor situation, the project proceeded in stops and starts.

In addition to Caroline Lockhart, other new members of the community included "Kid" Nichols, "champion wrestler of Iowa and other states," and James W. Hook, who purchased the *Enterprise* from Colonel J. H. Peake.[21] The arrival of the first gasoline-powered buggy in 1905 marked still another milestone in the life of the town and prompted Caroline to write about the event in the Philadelphia *North American.*

The automobile, owned by Frank Stannard, an electrician in the employ of George Beck, was a unique machine without gears or chains. A rope belt from a pulley on the engine drive-shaft to another on the rear axle propelled the newfangled invention. Its trial run gave Caroline license to comment not only on the machine itself but also to philosophize on it as a portent of other "dastardly" changes to come. Speaking as the Old Cattleman, she says to Mine Alpert:

> "I just met something I take for an autymobile as I was coming up the street, and my cayuse clum a telegraph pole; it took thirty minutes coaxin' with a pair of spurs to get him down. . . . Did that man who brought that machine here have any gredge agin' the town?"
> "None that I know of," Mine Alpert replied, "he's just come."[22]

The automobile, the colorful pair concluded, was simply "a sign of the times." Speaking of two old-timers that had passed on—Two Dog Jack and Sour Dough Sam—the bartender continued mournfully: "T'would a broke their hearts to a seen what the old town is coming to. . . . T'want half a dozen years ago that we used to ride into Red's place of a Sabbath afternoon four abreast, and shoot holes in the ceilin' in . . . innocent glee." Now, they noted, "females with high foreheads and purposes is gallopin' from house to house with petitions to close up the dance halls and stop the gamblin." The saloons, they "feared" would be next. "Time has never been the same," they moaned, "since Buffalo Bill went on the water wagon and Nolan's restaurant began puttin' table cloths over the ilecloth. That was the beginning of the beginning of the end." "Next," they predicted, "it will be finger bowls and dress soots."[23]

Again, this type of writing followed one of Caroline's basic beliefs: "All fiction is a good story based upon fact," she scribbled in the margin of one of her books on writing, and committed the precept to practice.[24]

The automobile, as her story skillfully and not so subtly noted, was not the only news of the day. The town ladies were, in reality, campaigning to close the gambling and dance halls. By siding with the men against the town ladies, she undoubtedly weakened her own social standing in the community; yet, she was generally well-accepted—at least at the outset. Caroline Lockhart was, after all, a celebrity. Along with Buffalo Bill Cody, she was the town's major claim to fame.

Despite such civilized advancements as electric lights, gasoline-powered buggies, and efforts at reform, Cody still reveled in its westerness. In 1907, much to Caroline's appreciation, members of Redmen's Lodge dressed up like painted Sioux Indians and chased Buffalo Bill's Deadwood Stage down Main Street. Their purpose was to advertise the big dance being held that night at Redman Hall. Similar rough and rowdy Fourth of July celebrations served as precursors to the permanent institution that would be known as the Cody Stampede.

Caroline, meanwhile, took mental notes, worked on her first novel, and contributed copy to the Philadelphia *Bulletin*, the Philadelphia *North American*, and the Denver *News*. When the town fire of 1907 put Mine Alpert, the bartender, out of business, she used the event as a suitable time to close out her bartender series and concentrate on her novels.[25]

In the interim, Caroline established herself as part of the community. Although the specific reasons are not documented—perhaps because his health improved—her friend and lover, Andrew MacKenzie, went his own way. But she soon cultivated new friends, among them Dr. Frances Lane, who had tried to help Middaugh during the 1904 bank robbery; the wife of the town founder, Augusta Sorenson "Daisy" Beck; mayor Jacob Schwoob; and wealthy easterners Dwight and Elizabeth Armour ("Lizzie") Hollister, Maude and John P. "Willie" Altberger, Russell and Edith Crane, and Alta Booth Dunn. Although Caroline was not the type to enter into the activities of the local ladies' club or the informal coffee-klatches, photographs in her scrapbooks indicate that she did enjoy parties and such outdoor pastimes as riding horseback with Dr. Lane and other friends.[26] Circumstances, however, would alter Caroline's relationships with some of these early acquaintances.

Never one to be without male companionship for long, Caroline soon found a replacement for MacKenzie. Another friend from the East, the handsome Harry Thurston, had also made the journey West where he became the Forest Supervisor for the area and, eventually, owner of the first Ford agency in town. But Caroline's relationship with Thurston was cut short when in 1906 he married Josephine Goodman, daughter of Julia Cody Goodman.[27] Caroline, in the meantime, renewed acquaintance with another friend whom she, more than likely, had met in the East—John R.

Painter, a married man who held mining interests in the Sunlight Basin area north of Cody.[28]

Despite the new friendships, male and female, it is apparent that Caroline spent most of her time writing. During the seven-year period following her arrival in 1904, she published at least a dozen short stories for well-known magazines of the time (and probably others that have not been preserved); wrote an indeterminate number of vignettes and articles for various newspapers; worked on two novels; and saw her first full-length book, *Me-Smith*, into print.

Me-Smith—touted as a true western in the mode of Owen Wister—brought her immediate national recognition. Her publishers claimed that readers of the book, advertised as "a story with red blood in it," would hear "the cry of the coyote" and experience "the deadly thirst for revenge as it exists in the wronged Indian toward the white man, the thrill of the gaming table, and the gentleness of pure, true love." Of the major character her publishers said: "Smith is one type of Western 'Bad Man,' an unusually powerful and appealing character who grips and holds the reader through all his deeds, whether good or bad."[29] Patterned after real life Wyoming outlaw James Smith, otherwise known as "The Squaw Man," the character is indeed a memorable antihero; however, Lockhart conjures up no false sympathy on behalf of the cattle thief and murderer, who refers to himself vaingloriously as "Me-Smith."[30]

The two major female characters, tomboyish sixteen-year-old Susie MacDonald and refined schoolmarm Dora Marshall, vie for top billing as the heroine. Susie, depicted as a courageous and defiant young westerner who wears her hair in a single, blond-streaked braid, resembles Caroline in her early years. Smart as well as saucy, she recognizes Smith for what he is—a thief and a killer.

The schoolmarm, portrayed as a "provincial from a small mid-western town," has high ideals and aspirations of influencing the badman to turn from his "life of crime." A subordinate but integral character in the plot is Susie's mother, an Indian woman called Prairie Flower, who becomes part of a love triangle featuring Smith and Dora. The incorrigible Smith not only professes love for Prairie Flower in the hope of stealing her money, but he also shoots an Indian in the back to get his blanket, and lowest of low—he abuses a horse.

It is left to the Indians to conjure up a fitting end for such a person. With a hint of symbolism, Lockhart has them slowly drop the outlaw into a den of rattlesnakes. And, yet, even an "*evil* westerner" must make a final show of strength and courage: "Tell her, you damned Injuns—Tell the Schoolmarm I died game, Me-Smith!"[31]

The book, enthusiastically received by the reviewers as well as the reading public, catapulted Lockhart into the category of Western Novelist. The New York *Times* said: "The author has humor and dramatic force, an infallible ear for local vernacular and a keen eye for types. As a delineation of western life at once realistic and picturesque, it compares favorably with Mr. Wister's 'The Virginian.'" The Chicago *Daily News* raved: "The strongest, most consistent story of the West which has appeared in years, and in many points excels *The Virginian.* It marks the author as the possessor of unquestioned literary genius." The Philadelphia *Public Ledger* also compared Lockhart to Wister: "Not since publication of *The Virginian* has so powerful a cowboy story been told." Reviews of the book continued to be overwhelmingly positive. The Indianapolis *News* called it "a big novel"; the Chicago *Record-Herald* termed it a "gripping, vigorous story"; and *The World Today* said that it was "a remarkable book in its strength of portrayal and its directness of development." "It cannot be read without being remembered," the reviewer concluded. Readers in general agreed; by May 1911, the book was in its fifth printing.[32]

Years later, the book was remembered by author Albert Payson Terhune (of *Lassie* fame) who admitted to Miss Lockhart:

> Not only do I remember most clearly and pleasantly your visits to the Evening World Office [sic], but I have vivid memories of *Me-Smith.* A powerfully compelling book and with a most unique hero, Smith's character stays fresh in my recollection after all this gap of time. And the climax scene, on the ledge, with the rattlesnakes, is something not to be forgotten.[33]

Whereas Wister had his Virginian, and Bertha Muzzey Bower her Chip of the Flying U, Caroline Lockhart had, by contrast, the memorable Me-Smith, western antihero.[34] And therein lies the key to the success of this first novel. By giving a slightly different twist to the basic formula Western, Caroline had discovered an approach that separated her book from the stack and caught the public eye.

Her decision to make the "bad man" the major character is personally revealing, showing as it does her almost eccentric adherence to painting her literary portraits with broad strokes of reality. As a reborn westerner who had been an expatriate in the East, she had developed a perspective with a difference. She saw and appreciated the West for what it was—both good and bad, replete with cruelty, moral volatility, and violence as well as honesty, freedom, and beauty.

Despite this perspective, Me-Smith and the characters that followed do not reveal complex social or psychological insights on the part of their cre-

ator. By selecting the antihero as her main character, Caroline Lockhart
had simply taken a different slant and thereby captured audience interest.
The Me-Smith character per se was not unique—merely his casting in the
"hero" or central role. The badman Me-Smith—like the Virginian—remains a representative, although archetypal literary figure. Even Wister
had his Trampas.

For Lockhart, this first novel represented a tremendous success that provided entrée to the eastern marketplace. Her publishers, the J. B. Lippincott Company, were so pleased with the book's acceptance that they ultimately printed four of a total of seven Lockhart novels. With Me-Smith
off to the press, Caroline could devote her attention to an issue that had
been troubling her for some time, namely, the numerous problems and
personalities associated with construction of the Shoshone dam.

THE LADY DOC

In 1907 the engineer on the Shoshone dam project, W. C. Cole, recorded in his diary that work on the tunnel through Rattlesnake Mountain
was proceeding fourteen months behind schedule. The project had been
plagued by spring storms that brought snow and freezing temperatures and
"hung-over" workmen, who could not resist the tempting libations offered
by the numerous saloons. There also had been problems associated with
the fact that many of the laborers were immigrants. Ethnic tensions were
inevitable. Moreover, the Bureau of Reclamation officials had to contend
with the usual number of injuries and accidents resulting from such dangerous work and the lack of safety codes. Taking advantage of the situation,
local doctors Frances Lane and James T. Bradbury contracted with the
government to provide medical care for the laborers.[35]

Caroline Lockhart noted these developments with interest. Her instincts
as an investigative reporter were sharpened by a growing estrangement from
Frances Lane. The initial cause for the dislike between the two women became a choice subject of local conversation and varied according to whom
one listened. Most people, however, seemed to believe that both women
had become interested in mining man John R. Painter. As Cody attorney
Ernest J. Goppert, Sr., recalled: "Both of them fell in love with Painter, a
married man." Goppert also believed that part of the problem originated
from the fact that "Dr. Lane was too much 'in' with the 'ins' here in Cody,"
which he felt was a source of irritation to Caroline. "Caroline," he said,
"led too public a life to live like she was doing" [and not be criticized],

while "Dr. Lane didn't live with a man all the time [hence her acceptance by the "better element"]." [36]

On the other hand, there was speculation that Caroline and Frances Lane had once been interested in each other, or in a mutual female friend. In that event, there is the possibility that Caroline's association with John Painter represented a cruel rebuff to the lady doctor. In Caroline's case, there is little to substantiate such charges; there was no doubt that she enjoyed male companionship. Frances Lane, however, eventually took as her living companion suffragette Marjorie Ross. A small, attractive woman, Ross had come to Cody on a lecture tour and decided to stay on with Dr. Lane.

In contrast to Marjorie Ross and Caroline herself, the Lady Doc was described by Lockhart and others as

a singular-looking person who affected mannish dress and ways, putting her foot on the brass rail in bars and calling upon all and sundry to buy her a drink. She was not ill-looking [and was] intelligent and exceptionally shrewd in business. [37]

This description, found in the author's unpublished autobiography and substantiated by photographs and the testimony of Cody old-timers, appears to be accurate. Portraits of Frances Lane show a plain, unsmiling woman dressed severely. Although the photographs reveal a serious nature, they give no indication of the strength of her personality. Codyites, however, recall Dr. Lane as being "formidable." Dick Frost claimed that, "[When I was] a youngster, she frightened me. I felt she had a heart for most anything." Ray Prante held the same impression and described her as "a tall, unkempt woman who 'strided' when she walked and wore a pork pie hat tilted at a rakish angle." [38]

Caroline, although much more feminine and attractive in appearance than Lane, also had a strong personality and a sometimes overbearing strength of character. The similarity of the two women probably accounted, at least partially, for their inevitable conflict. Each protected her own territory and each developed her own following. Dr. Lane did have her supporters—especially among those whom Caroline managed to offend with her caustic wit and pointed pen, or with her liberated ways. Certain members of the community held the doctor in such high esteem that they eventually proposed naming a street in her honor.

According to Lockhart's reminiscences, the controversy originated when she first became suspicious of Dr. Lane's true motivations in signing a government contract to care for the laborers on the dam. From the doctor herself, Caroline first heard the news. As stated in the agreement, a fee of one dollar per month was to be deducted from the men's paychecks to pay for the physician's services.

Subsequently, Frances Lane and her partner, James Bradbury, bought a small house and furnished it with hospital beds and equipment. "It was the Lady Doc's proud and frequent boast," Caroline charged, "that she was making money hand over fist." [39] Although Caroline admitted that she was not the "squeamish" type, she was shocked to hear Dr. Lane brag about her coup. The novelist's training as a reporter motivated her to look into the activities of the two physicians.

When an epidemic among the workmen was followed by several deaths, Caroline confronted her former friend: "Doc, doesn't it bother you to lose so many patients?" she asked pointedly. At the time, Caroline recalled, Frances Lane was sitting with her chair tilted back and her hat pushed up on her forehead. She thrust out her arm and a clenched fist: "Christ!" she replied. "Those roughnecks don't mean any more to me than squashin' a fly!" [40]

From that time on, Caroline viewed the Lady Doc in a new light. Although this episode could have been conjured up by the novelist to add credence to her case, there was usually a strong element of truth in situations about which she wrote.

To Caroline's disappointment, the townspeople showed little interest in the workmen or the quality of care they were receiving from the Lane-Bradbury Clinic. But the workmen cared; they discussed the situation with bitterness in talk around the local saloons. Some even refused treatment at the "Butcher Shop," as they referred to the clinic. [41]

Caroline's inquiries revealed that numerous instances of questionable care and treatment justified the men's concerns. An Italian workman, Marko Ferko, who had been seriously injured in an explosion in the canyon, was a case in point. Bradbury examined the man at the site, hastily wrapped the broken leg, and announced that the man's thumb, also badly injured, would have to be amputated; but Ferko's cousin protested. The two men then placed the laborer on the bottom of a coal wagon and drove him to the Lane-Bradbury Clinic.

At the hospital the cousin sat by Ferko's bed all night, the next day, and until ten o'clock the following evening. During this period the patient received no care for his broken leg, nor was he provided with food.

Six days later, the cousin returned and found that the man's leg still had not been set, although Bradbury claimed that he had taken care of it.

On the following visit, however, the doctor informed Ferko's cousin that it would have to be amputated and pulled back the covers to reveal a leg that was badly twisted and discolored. According to the cousin's affidavit:

> I tell Bradbury the leg never was set. He call me every bad name and tell me if Marko not let him cut off leg the next day, he throw him out of the hospital.
>
> I tell him he not have throw him out because I *take* him out. The lady doctor was standing there and she say: 'The damned dago is goin' to die anyhow. You take him out of here—and quick!'[42]

This testimony was enough to spur Caroline to action. In her autobiographical account, she wrote: "It would take time and work, I realized, but I felt it would be well worth it if I could call public attention to a situation like this." Whatever her motivations—and they were probably mixed—Caroline was "on the warpath."

When she learned that the cousin had transferred Marko to the care of doctors Louis Howe and Frank Waples, she enlisted the aid of an interpreter and went over to the Waples hospital, where she obtained a sworn statement from the patient substantiating the lack of proper treatment.[43]

On 12 November 1907 Lockhart obtained another affidavit from one Charles Raines, who was sworn and deposed by Justice of the Peace William H. Brundage. Raines had entered the Lane-Bradbury Clinic on 23 October 1906 with typhoid fever. During the month he was in the hospital, he claimed to have received no more than four doses of medicine. Nothing had been done to reduce his fever; he was not given even cold sponges nor ice packs. In addition to negligent treatment, however, Raines charged Bradbury and Lane with fraud.

As Raines reported his story, in the same room with him was a man referred to only as "Pitts," also suffering from typhoid fever. "He was sicker than I," Raines said, "and they told me to wait on him, which I did. The man was sick for approximately eight days, and during the last few days he was totally unconscious." While Pitts lay unconscious, according to Raines, a nurse came into the room, touched the hand of the unconscious man with a pencil, and proceeded to endorse his government check. Dr. Lane then endorsed the check as well. Pitts died only hours later.

In similar manner, according to the man's testimony, Lane attempted to force Raines to sign over his last month's pay check also. "Whether the check was mailed to me from Corbett, and she opened the letter, or whether it was given to her by the paymaster, or some other official, I do not know," he said. "I only know that she had my check without my knowledge or consent." "She was crazy mad when I would not sign," he added. "I never saw such a devilish look on a woman's face." [44]

After his release from the Lane-Bradbury Clinic, Raines hired a team from the Buffalo Bill barns and went to the De Maris Hot Springs to finish recuperating. He testified that when he later went to the first National and the Shoshone Banks, he learned that Bradbury had been there while he was in the hospital, inquiring about Raines's account. "Afterward," he said, "I met Bradbury on the street and he put out his hand to shake hands with me. 'No, sir,' I says, 'You are no friend of mine.' . . . He has not spoken to me since." [45]

Raines's story did not end with the attempt at fraud. Despite the lack of medical attention, Bradbury tried to charge the man extra for what he termed "unnecessary trouble." Raines refused to pay. The workman concluded his testimony by offering to contribute fifty dollars toward investigation of the Lane-Bradbury hospital, adding, "There are plenty more who only want the chance to do the same." [46]

The deposition of John Oleson, sworn before Notary Fred C. Barnett 12 November 1907, supported the charges of negligent care and reported how the doctors had amputated the arm of Billy Dunn, with whom he shared the same hospital room. Oleson testified that the doctors were unable to stop the flow of blood, which resulted in the man's death. [47]

Raynald McDonal had a similar horror story. He told how he had been driving a four-horse wagon when he fell under the wheels while trying to reach for the brake. With his leg so badly broken that bones came through the skin, he was placed in the back of a wagon and taken to the Lane-Bradbury hospital. At the clinic the doctors wanted to amputate—a favored procedure—but the patient refused. Instead, McDonal said:

> Bradbury put on a plaster bandage so thin that it wouldn't keep the leg in place and it grew crooked, with the foot turning in. Then they put me on the operating table and broke the leg over again. Besides this, they slashed and sliced my leg with a knife more times than I can remember while I was in bed and without giving me anything to put me to sleep. I tried not to holler but sometimes I did and Bradbury would tell me to "Shut up." He handled my leg as if it were a stick of wood. He was rougher than Lane; but one time Carl Hammitt, the sheriff, came to see me and Lane cut a part of the plaster bandage away to show him the leg. She cut the bandages with a big pair of scissors and while she was explaining the condition of the leg to him she kept tapping on the bare bone with those scissors. The sweat was standing

out on me and Carl said: "Don't that hurt?" "Well, I guess it hurts!" I said, and then she stopped.[48]

McDonal, whose hospital stay extended from 16 May to 23 October, was later moved to the hospital annex, where the flies, he said, "swarmed so that we could hardly see each other." John Oleson had been a patient while McDonal was there. McDonal recalled that "Oleson was weak when they put him in there and he used to lie on the bed and fight flies until he was played out." With one exception, McDonal claimed, "Every man amongst them said they'd rather crawl off and die than go back."

Ironically, McDonal may have been the exception. After consulting another doctor, who told him that his leg would have to be broken and reset, McDonal returned to the Lane-Bradbury Clinic. "I went to these doctors after I got out," he explained, "because I guess the doctors here are all alike and these two understand about my leg from the beginning."[49]

Another laborer, J. T. Keyes, seriously injured his arm in a cave-in. Keyes testified that he thought the doctor was simply going to set his arm. Bradbury gave him chloroform, however, and when he awoke, his arm had been amputated above the elbow. Although Dr. Lane appeared to be the major target of Caroline's investigative activities, affidavits such as Keyes's implicated Bradbury to an even greater degree.[50]

Nevertheless, research into the doctors' medical training showed Bradbury's background to be more credible than his partner's. According to Lockhart, James T. Bradbury had been an iron-molder in Kewanee, Illinois, until he was thirty years old, at which time he enrolled at Chicago Medical College. After graduation, he became a general practitioner and, at the time of his contract with the government, had been in practice for approximately six years.

A framed diploma hanging in the office of the Lady Doc showed her to be a graduate of Hering College, also in Chicago. However, Lockhart learned from a member of the American Medical Association in the East that Hering College was not recognized by the national association "because it was considered a diploma mill."[51]

Records of the American Medical Association (AMA) substantiate this charge. Hering Medical College, founded in 1892, was listed as a "homeopathic" institution which practiced a method of treatment frowned upon by the majority of the medical profession. In 1902, Hering College was absorbed by another small college, and by 1917 the parent institution had disappeared as well.

The *Flexner Report* of 1912 resulted in the establishment of an accreditation system for American medical schools; therefore, Hering College could not have been officially accredited before its absorption, and there is no verification in the AMA directories that it was accredited thereafter. The evidence suggests that Hering College, like other homeopathic institutions of the time, was "hounded out of existence"—to use Lockhart's terminology. On the other hand, Bradbury's alma mater, now the Chicago School of Medicine, was listed as being fully accredited.[52]

Lockhart's investigations revealed other related and equally shady activities taking place in Cody at the same time. She found, for example, that "business had picked up" for Cody gravediggers and undertakers after the spring of 1906. Claude Humphrey, who ran the "undertaking department of the Cody Trading Company," was described, tongue-in-cheek, by Lockhart as "an undertaker whose enthusiasm for his calling is well known." Claude supposedly "whistled while he worked," and "when his services were needed," he responded "in high spirits and with such alacrity that it . . . was a matter of considerable comment in the town."[53] Local humorists liked to tell how Dr. Ainsworth, the county coroner, went to hold an inquest upon the body of a man who had come to a violent end, and met Claude en route to the graveyard with the corpse.[54]

Claude's insensitivity was such that it irritated even Frances Lane, who complained that the undertaker's practice of allowing the corpse's bare feet to stick out of the grocery delivery wagon offended the neighbors. As a result, Claude was fired, but he took the burial records with him.

When Caroline went to the undertaker's home to ask for a record of the burials he had made, Claude simply grinned: "I ain't a-goin' to get none of my friends in trouble," he said. "I ain't a-goin' to git in trouble myself."

"How," Caroline asked, "could a burial record get anybody in trouble?" But Claude evaded the issue and kept his records.

In addition to the undertaker, Caroline also interviewed the local gravedigger, A. Walls Connell. Connell, a shrewd little Irishman with deep-set blue eyes twinkling under the wide brim of a cowboy hat, talked freely.

"Prior to the spring of 1906," he said, "there was not much doing in the grave-digging line, but then business picked up." He explained that, after that time, he began digging graves for the patients from the Lane-Bradbury Clinic. The interview continued:

Did I dig graves for the Lane-Bradbury hospital? Did I dig graves; say, I didn't do nothing else! I dug nineteen graves in two weeks. I dug three graves in one day. They came so fast for awhile that I couldn't plant em' in a nice row as I aimed to do. . . . I kept a record of every grave I dug and I've got the name of the feller that's in it. The undertaking place won't know, and the hospital won't tell, so I'll just take the trouble to keep this thing straight.[55]

Caroline asked Connell how the corpses were buried—in coffins or boxes. Connell replied that the poor ones were often "rolled . . . in a blanket, put . . . in a box, chucked . . . in the bottom of a wagon, and sent to the graveyard lickety-split." "They buried one feller in his undershirt," he added—"a dirty one at that."

Connell concluded, saying:

> I haven't any particular gretch against the Doctors. I don't know Lane much but you have to collect money from Bradbury with tweezers. He owed me $5.00 for digging a grave, for months. He said he couldn't give it to me until he got it out of the government. During that summer I dug about forty-one graves, and thirty-six or seven of them were for the Lane-Bradbury hospital.[56]

As part of her investigation, Caroline also talked to the deputy sheriff of the county, Carl Hammitt. Hammitt, known as "a man of few words and unquestioned veracity," was highly respected for his personal courage by the old-timers in the community. When questioned about the Lane-Bradbury Clinic, Hammitt admitted that he knew "a good many things about this hospital, things which I know to be true but . . . cannot prove. . . . I know that men have told me that they have laid in this hospital begging for water, for food, for other attentions which they should have had."

Asked to provide specifics, Hammitt told of two typhoid patients staying at Brun's lodging house who were entitled to "free" service under the clinic contract, but who "begged as for their lives" when he wanted to take them there. He also mentioned the case of Bessie Felty, a trained nurse who had worked in the hospital for ten months. Bessie claimed that "she knew enough on these two doctors to send them over the road," but she had to "leave the country" when they claimed she was insane.

Lockhart also asked the sheriff about the Billy Dunn affair and quoted him as saying: "I believe that Billy Dunn, who was shot on the Fourth of July by Harry Jordan, died in this hospital of neglect." Hammitt explained that Dunn had been employed on the works at Corbett, an irrigation ditch project, but the hospital refused to treat him because he had not been injured while at work. Consequently, his fellow workers raised ninety dollars to pay the medical bills; but "this money," Hammitt said, "was taken from under his [Dunn's] pillow, whether with or without his consent I do not know." Hammitt said that Bradbury admitted that he had taken sixty dollars of it "for hospital care," but the sheriff never learned what had happened to the remainder. Billy Dunn bled to death after the doctors amputated his arm.[57]

Although Sheriff Hammitt appeared to be aware of such goings-on, for lack of adequate proof, or perhaps for personal political considerations, he chose to do nothing about them. But Caroline Lockhart was not one to give up so easily. Her investigation completed, and armed with the affidavits necessary to prevent Lane and Bradbury from filing suit against her, Caroline launched an all-out campaign to expose the two physicians.

Copies of these signed affidavits, preserved by attorney David Dominick, along with her autobiographical notes, seemed to substantiate her suspicion that all was not well at the Lane-Bradbury Clinic. Dominick noted in a brief comment written on the edge of his manuscript that "Caroline did do a little editing of these affidavits—all of which suited the case she was pushing, but none of which seemed to alter the original content too much."[58] It is probable that Caroline made the alterations after she began to realize that the only way she would be able to get action on the problem would be to write up the testimonies in story format for the newspapers.

As a first attempt, she contacted the Denver *News,* but they rejected her story as too controversial. In retrospect, she acknowledged that she should have sent it to the Denver *Post,* whose management, she felt, would have had the courage to publish it.[59]

The controversy surrounding the Lane-Bradbury Clinic divided the town into two camps. Leading the opposition was the Lady Doc's companion, Marjorie Ross. That faction, Caroline said, viewed her as "a malicious, vindictive outsider, resentful of some fancied slight and jealous of the lady doctor's popularity, charm, and good looks."[60]

There were those, however, who sided with Lockhart. One of these individuals (and possibly Caroline herself) wrote a letter to the Billings *Gazette,* sparking outside interest in the case. As a result, the paper published an exposé of the situation, but local pressure soon forced the reporter to retract his story.[61]

Carrying her case a step further, in February of 1908 as the investigative reporter "Suzette," she wrote a letter to John E. Wilkie, chief of the Secret Service in Washington, D.C., asking for his assistance in the matter. Wilkie, who had become acquainted with Lockhart during the trial of a celebrated counterfeiting case in Philadelphia, sent a friendly reply:

> Your special delivery letter reached me this morning, and I beg to confirm my wire to you as follows: 'Will be very glad to see the story and will do every-

thing possible here to get action.' I await the receipt of your story and the accompanying affidavits with interest, and if such a condition is disclosed, as is suggested by your letter, I will make every effort to interest the President and the Secretary of the Interior, with a view to bringing about a change.[62]

Wilkie prudently concluded by asking for a brief statement explaining her motive for taking up the fight against the contracting physicians. This would place him in a position, he said, "to meet any suggestions or criticisms that might be urged against your bona fides in this matter."[63]

Unfortunately for Caroline, there is no evidence that this attempt at censure through government intervention was any more successful than her efforts through the newspapers. The correspondence with Wilkie, however, does lend credence to the seriousness of her intent, just as the affidavits—even if somewhat diluted by literary alterations—support Caroline's contentions that Doctors Lane and Bradbury were guilty of negligent care, criminal malpractice, and possibly fraud. It is apparent also that the Bureau of Reclamation and local officials were remiss in not conducting an investigation themselves. In all fairness, of course, and as attorney David Dominick points out in his study of the controversy, quality medical care in frontier communities at that time was the exception rather than the rule. Furthermore, at such an early stage of urban development, there were few, if any, civic regulations to guide the actions of town officials.[64]

After trying unsuccessfully to rouse civic or governmental intervention in the case, and without other recourse, Caroline resorted to launching a personal attack using the weapons she knew best—her trusty Remington Rand typewriter and her literary talents. The result was her most controversial novel, blatantly titled *The Lady Doc*. Later, when interviewed by T. A. Larson for his history of Wyoming, Lockhart admitted: "I drew as accurate a picture of Cody as I could and stay out of jail."[65]

Published in 1912, also by J. B. Lippincott, *The Lady Doc* was lauded by the Chicago *Tribune* as a "compelling book—one so absorbing that hours slip by unnoticed until the end is reached."[66] Needless to say, residents of Cody—especially Frances Lane, depicted as a small-town quack whose major character traits are jealousy, hate, greed, and dishonesty—also found the book compelling. As the book's major villainess, the Lady Doc destroys lives and love affairs with callous insensitivity. Lockhart, with a literary bravado unusual for the time, hints at a lesbian relationship between the Lady Doc ("Emma Harpe") and the book's heroine, the pretty young waitress ("Essie Tisdale"), who was patterned after another real-life Codyite. Before long, other townspeople identified themselves in the book's thinly disguised characters, which is exactly what Caroline intended. To make sure that there was no question, according to Codyite Francis Hayden, "Miss Lockhart gave out a list with the reprint of the book telling people who was who." [67]

Other easily recognized characters included "Mrs. Percy Parrott," a pointed caricature of the wife of the president of Cody's Shoshone Bank, Mrs. Sammie Parks; and a crusading newspaperman "Sylvanus Starr," in reality, John K. Calkins, editor of the local *Stockgrower and Farmer.* The local businessman of the book and the Lady Doc's fellow collaborator, "Andy P. Symes," was none other than George T. Beck. Caroline's portrayal of Beck, as well as that of his wife, the book's "Augusta Kunkel," earned the author their fervent dislike.

Even close friends and associates failed to escape Caroline's scrutiny. The "Dago Duke" of *The Lady Doc* was Bill Miller de Colonna, local war hero and artist, with whom Caroline had a close relationship. This fact, however, did not deter her from depicting his human frailties. Like the cartoonist who often accentuates his subject's most homely physical traits, Lockhart accentuated her characters' personal foibles, sketching unmercifully accurate, if sometimes exaggerated, word portraits of the town's residents.

As one reviewer observed of *The Lady Doc:* "It is doubtful if any modern male writer would have been able or willing to present so unchivalrous a view of even one member of the gentler sex. Not since Balzac's 'Ma Cousine Bette' has there been so consistent a picture of a repulsive woman." The reviewer went on to point out what he considered to be the book's artistic flaw—the fact that Lockhart had included within an ordinary western story a character demanding "a more subtle setting and treatment." "But," he continued, "the genuine courage required to set forth such a character at all must be admitted. For the type is unfortunately real enough. . . . Evidently Miss Lockhart is one of the few American writers of fiction who are not afraid to depict life as they find it." [68]

Not always were her character portraits unfavorable, however. Those she saw as having the redeeming traits of honesty, kindness, and courage fared rather well. The good-hearted owner of the boardinghouse, "Mrs. Hank Terriberry," for example, is shown as a kind person who has concern for others. Patterned after Hattie McFall, who with her husband "Badland" Dave McFall, owned Cody's Hart Mountain Inn, the Terriberry character in the book celebrates the salt-of-the-earth pioneer who settled the West. Minor characters such as "Faro Nell" (see "Poker Nell" of Cody) and the station agent "W. J. Kissick" also received favorable treatment as truly representative westerners unsullied by eastern airs and evil influences.

In the story line, the Lady Doc's career as the town's female villain is brought to an end by a wealthy, educated man from the East, "Edouard Dubois" (alias Charles De Maris), who exposes the Lady Doc and marries the erstwhile waitress, Essie Tisdale. Essie is eventually discovered to have a genteel background suitable to her elevated station in life; and the townspeople, finally recognizing the Lady Doc for the fraud that she is, run her out of town in the caboose of a sheep train—the epitome of western insult.[69]

In actuality, Frances Lane continued to practice in Cody, and Caroline Lockhart—now thoroughly disliked by a facet of the community—proceeded with her next novel. In the meantime, the book continued to have repercussions both within and outside the local area. The controversy, magnified as it was by small-town mores, created a social schism that forever relegated Lockhart to the outer fringes of "acceptable" Cody society. As a woman ahead of her time, her choice of a sexually liberated lifestyle undoubtedly compounded the problem. Indication of the personal price she paid, as well as her developing view of American literature, is revealed in an excerpt from a 1914 issue of the Philadelphia *Bulletin*. Here she gives her rationale for progressing from short-story writing to the next stage of her career as a novelist. She also reveals the bitterness and hurt resulting from the Lady Doc experience.

After a reference to "the plethoric output of silly drivel by authors of the 'perfect lady type,'" she commented upon the many American novelists, who, she said "are interested in producing books that sell rather than books that interpret life." Referring to her own development as a writer, she admitted that she gave up writing short stories because of editorial restrictions. "To produce sincere work," Lockhart maintained that

> a writer must follow his or her ideals, not those of an arbitrary editor. With the novel one has somewhat more freedom than with short stories. The latter must be made according to the accepted pattern to receive attention. Editors are afraid of anything new, and the mediocre writer content to produce marketable wares is much more likely to achieve early success than the serious student whose aim is to create works of art. I believe that editors are mistaken. They judge the calibre of the public mind by the letters they receive from persons who have time to write to magazines. Let us have done with absurd ultra-puritanism.[70]

Continuing, she commented specifically upon public response to *The Lady Doc* from outside the community: "I was abused in some quarters for . . . *The Lady Doc*," she admitted, "and many women physicians wrote informing me that my characterization of one of their fraternity was hopelessly untrue and unjust. I can only say that I make the truth of my books conform to the truth of life as I see it out in Wyoming." [71]

During the 1950s, undaunted by threats of libel suits, book-burnings in Cody's back alleys, and the novel's banishment from local libraries, the indomitable Caroline got the last word by reissuing the book. "Sort of wanted a new fur coat," she chuckled, "but I decided I would get more fun out of this." At that time, only nine people protested its publication in writing, while 1,500 supposedly signed a petition in favor of its reissuance. [72]

Today, decades after *The Lady Doc* was published, residents of Cody still talk of the infamous book in an opinionated manner. Some sources claim that Caroline found it necessary to move to Denver upon publication of the book, but records of the Denver *Post* show that she did not take up residence in Denver until 1918, six years after *The Lady Doc* had been published. [73]

Until 1918, her jaunts away from Cody consisted of business trips to the East to confer with publishers, or what might best be termed "working vacations" to the Sunlight Basin and Salmon River country in Idaho, and one trip to South America. Shortly after *The Lady Doc*, published in September 1912, appeared in Cody, Caroline did leave town to take a particularly adventuresome vacation that involved shooting the rapids of the Salmon River Canyon in Idaho. But she returned, although, as she later wrote: "They [the Cody people] didn't think I would . . . but I showed 'em." "That woman [Dr. Lane] knew I had the goods on her. I could prove every word of what I had said in the book, and she knew it." [74]

On these trips to the Sunlight Basin "to gather atmosphere" for a new writing project, and later to the Salmon River country, she was the guest of John R. Painter. [75] If there was any substance to the contention of townspeople that the controversy resulted from competition between the Lady Doc and Caroline for the affections of Painter, the fact that she was his guest—both before and after publication of the book—suggests that she had won the battle, or at least, had won the man.

THE FULL OF THE MOON

During the years 1906–12, the Lady Doc controversy occupied a considerable amount of Caroline's time, but it was by no means the sole focus of her boundless energy. While researching one book and arranging publication of another, she began writing what was to be the most introspective of all her novels. *The Full of the Moon,* copyrighted in 1913 and published just two years after *The Lady Doc,* represents the nearest thing to a published autobiography that Caroline would produce. That she chose to look inward at this juncture is not only a natural outgrowth of the personal trauma associated with the Lady Doc affair but also the result of a very human need to justify the actions she had taken and to better understand herself.

Years previously she had made a drastic change in lifestyle; she had opted for the wide-open spaces of the West over the increasingly urbanized East, and she had decided to become a novelist. In reaching this objective, Caroline had proven herself, although at some personal cost. Diary entries made during her forties reveal that she was torn between her desire to continue a liberated lifestyle and her desire for the more traditional but constraining position that marriage afforded. She ponders her situation, reflecting on "the dark hours" and wondering if there could be any happiness in store for her, "just one more discontented spinster." [76]

The conflict she was experiencing, between her desire for career success and marriage, meant that real happiness eluded her and led to inner doubts. It was a time, she felt, for introspection and self-appraisal. And from the purely pragmatic viewpoint, the type of novel she was planning would not interfere with her other research efforts; it would be relatively easy to produce, based as it was upon her own life and character. Thus, for Caroline, The Full of the Moon represented a personal catharsis. For the reader, the novel would provide a mind's-eye view of how the author regarded herself.

Like the young Caroline Lockhart of Philadelphia days, the heroine of the book is an independent young woman called Nan Galbraith. Caroline's description of Nan could well have been composed while the writer was sitting in front of her mirror: "Brown hair streaked with sunny tints . . . Nan was not beautiful, this Golden Girl, . . . but she was unmistakably a lady," albeit with "an unusually high spirit, vivacity, and keen interest in life." Although there are those who would disagree with Caroline's portrayal of her alter ego as "a lady," she continued to regard herself as such throughout her life. Being a "lady," in Caroline's opinion, had everything to do with inner attitude, with being a "personage." It had little to do with sexual mores. [77]

Despite the danger inherent in making such literary analogies, the autobiographical similarities in The Full of the Moon are too obvious not to have credence. Furthermore, Lockhart's penchant for basing her fiction on thinly disguised fact occurs too often not to be acknowledged as her own particular literary eccentricity, derived from her training as a news reporter and from an apparent psychological need to write for personal therapy as evidenced by the way she used her confidential Diaries. In her Diaries she bared her innermost thoughts—about herself and others. The recording of such impressions—so private in nature that she eventually tried to burn them—provided her a therapeutic outlet for emotions that many people feel but keep carefully hidden. In similar vein, *The Full of the Moon* is an adulterated example of the use of her craft to maintain personal equilibrium.

The heroine in *The Full of the Moon*, therefore, not only resembles Caroline physically but she also has the same attitudes toward life. For example, Nan's family expects her to teach Sunday school and marry the socially acceptable Robert "Bob" Ellison, but she rebels. "I am not sure that I am going to be married *at all*," she announces, adding, "I'm going to have my fling." When her father asks her to explain just what she means by "fling," Nan says hesitantly: "I want to go out West—by myself—and have adventures and be independent and . . . and meet a different kind of people from those I've ever known."[78]

Caroline continues the dialogue, using her personal experiences to develop the girl's character, and in so doing provides a mirror to her inner self. Nan's mother, Mrs. Galbraith, receives with consternation the news that her daughter wants to "go West." She warns her that she "will be the first of our family to bring a blush to our cheeks," whereupon Nan (in another episode from Caroline's own life) reminds her coldly:

"You blushed when Grandfather Maitlock married the sempstress."[79]

When Mrs. Galbraith replies that she is expected to observe "conventions," Nan, speaking for Caroline, retorts:

"Conventions—conventions! . . . I've heard nothing else all my life. I can't do anything I want to or know the people I want to or be what I want to because I'm Nan Galbraith and must observe the conventions. I'm—I'm stunted—that's what I am!"[80]

With the consent of her understanding father, however, Nan gets her wish and is permitted to "go West," where she hopes to find, "when she finally marries," an "active man, a man who is doing something in the world, making his own way."[81]

Borrowing again from her vacation experience with Andrew MacKenzie, Caroline sets the stage for her novel in the little town of Hopedale, New Mexico, close to the Mexican border. Upon her arrival, the heroine encounters Sour Dough Sam, one of Caroline's favorite real-life characters, and one she continued to use in a number of her novels and short stories. In Hopedale, the reader is also reintroduced to Mrs. Gallagher, the memorable Mexican cook of the short story "A Child of Nature." Unlike Bertha M. Bower, who used one central character (Chip of the Flying U) for a series of novels, Lockhart's style was to use repeatedly several minor characters, such as Sam and Mrs. Gallagher, to add what she identified as "western color."

In comparison with the character in the short story, the Mrs. Gallagher of the novel is depicted in a more favorable light. Although portrayed as Nan's benefactress, the character is undoubtedly the same Mrs. Gallagher—again described by Lockhart as "a mongrel lady with an Apache mother, a Mexican father, and somewhere in the States, an Irish husband named Gallagher." Obviously, between her visits to New Mexico in 1898 and publication of The Full of the Moon sixteen years later, she had not changed her attitude toward the "Greasers," as she called them. "Like all inferior races," she wrote, "the low-caste Mexicans invariably mistake generosity for weakness."[82]

The border setting for The Full of the Moon afforded Caroline the opportunity not only to reiterate her personal prejudice but also to employ ethnic conflict as an important part of the plot. By graphically describing Mexican attitudes toward Gringos, as well as the attitude of Gringos toward Mexicans, she hints at the root of animosity between the two and indicates that such prejudices were often mutual. As reviewers duly acknowledged, the book "throws much light . . . upon the Mexicans and their attitudes toward Americans."[83]

In the novel, the Mexican horseman Ignacio Bojarques is the personification of hostility as he uses a local festival—a celebration of "the victory of Spain over the pigs of Americans" to ride down the heroine with his horse. Described as "a devil when roused . . . with proud blood in his veins," Bojarques twirls his mustache in truly villainous fashion and tosses his head: "Pigs of Americans—bah!" he snarls. Such scenes, a bit raw even by today's standards, motivated a reviewer for the Boston Globe to say of The Full of the Moon: "It is a book of strong contrasts and the life of the West is portrayed with picturesque frankness."[84]

Balancing the derogatory portrayal of Mexican people in general, Caroline has Nan showing special concern and care for a deserving Mexican child. The seeming paradox is in character for a person of Lockhart's complexity. While her writing reveals a distinct distaste for Mexicans as an ethnic group, she nonetheless could develop individual friendships among them. Despite her biases, she did have favored acquaintances other than Anglos. Native Americans, for example, were frequent guests in her home in Cody, and the wife of Chief Plenty Coups was her close personal friend— one of the few women she claimed to have ever really "loved." In her autobiographical manuscript she wrote:

I can safely say that I could count the women I have really loved on the fingers of one hand. There are many I have liked, but love is something else. Perhaps, strictly, the number should be three, namely, my grandmother, a girl-friend of many years, and an old Indian woman called Other Buffalo. It is not that I am allergic to members of my own sex but simply for the reason that from the nature of my work and interests, my associates have always been men.[85]

Other Buffalo, the last and youngest wife of Crow Chief Plenty Coups, was a Mandan and, therefore, not on good terms with the other wives. Caroline empathized with her position just as Nan Galbraith in *The Full of the Moon* seemed to empathize with the Mexican child.

Typically, and in keeping with the western formula, Caroline took literary delight in putting in his place the wealthy individual who misuses power. Consequently, the reader finds the renegade Mexican, Bojarques, overshadowed as the major villain of the plot by the prosperous rancher, Hank Spicer. Spicer, who at first opportunity makes sexual advances toward Nan, is obviously patterned after the lecherous Mr. Hopewell of Caroline's New Mexico experience.[86] Heartless, corrupt, and a defiler of women, Spicer is the stereotypical western villain.

In contrast, the hero Ben Evans is the typical cowboy in appearance and actions, although he is not without human frailties. The women characters, as in *Me-Smith*, represent two contrasting types—the refined but independent easterner, who appreciates western values and western men (Nan Galbraith), and the native western girl, unpolished but courageous and astute (Edie Blakely). Despite their differences in backgrounds, Caroline characterizes both women in what she probably felt to be a favorable light. Nan, after all, was patterned after her own rebellious self.

In light of today's standards, a daughter who decided to go off to another state or even abroad to pursue her own interests would probably be considered enterprising. In 1900, however, the same daughter might well have been viewed as incorrigible, unladylike, and a source of heartache to her family. A reviewer of the time considered Caroline's heroine in just such a light. "Our heroine has the joy of sending 'gleefully' home a cryptic telegram, which aged the family by years," she writes. "The story holds as fine a young hero as one could meet on a summer's day. . . . But as for the young lady who holds centre stage, she is the kind of person whom, as Richard Watson Gilder once said, 'one gets up in the night to hate,' and it is disconcerting to perceive that she finds favor in the eyes of her creator."[87]

Nan found favor in the eyes of her creator because Caroline had treated her own family in similar manner, and under the circumstances considered herself the victim of an uncaring father. There is no indication that Caroline felt any twinges of guilt for the estrangement from her family; to her way of thinking, her father's remarriage made it impossible for her to return home. This reality, combined with an inner drive to "make something of herself" resulted in the atypical life she chose to lead. Yet, it was this very difference, this departure from tradition, that made her a woman misunderstood and sometimes disliked—a person out of time, out of place.

Nonetheless, as the storyline continues: Nan and Edie, Lockhart's female representatives of the cultural conflict between East and West, vie for the affection of the cowboy hero. The West and Ben Evans soon cast a hypnotic spell on Nan (as it had on Caroline), and the eastern girl dreads the day when her father will demand her return to more "civilized environs." The day arrives as Mr. Galbraith, in a surprise move, sends Nan's former beau, Bob Ellison, to bring her home.

Through his staging, Ellison is placed in a "testing situation"—a characteristic scenario in literature universally and in the western novel in particular—reminiscent of Walter van Tilburg Clark's *The Track of the Cat*. As a condition of life, every man and every generation must face the symbolic "cat."[88] Some lose and some win. In *The Full of the Moon*, Ellison wins as Lockhart has the easterner make a dramatic entrance at the town "baile" just in time to get the drop on a gang of Mexicans, who are holding Nan, her cowboy, and other gringos at gunpoint.[89] For pure romantic escapism, as well as a touch of symbolism, such a scene can't be beaten; and under the artifice of the theatrical moment, East is once again measured against West in the form of the Dude versus the Cowboy.

Caroline explains the difference between the two and the special attraction of the westerner to a girl from the East:

> [Bob's] trained self-repression, his instinctive good manners and breeding, were in constant contrast to [Ben's] the cowboy's raw selfishness—the self-ishness of a child who has not seen enough of the world to recognize the claims of others.
>
> Yet Ben was the embodiment of the spirit of the cowboy, an incarnation of the sand and brawn and grit of the far West, and, as such he made a mighty appeal to the primitive in the girl, to her youth, imagination, and markedly romantic nature.[90]

In this manner, Lockhart, like Owen Wister in *The Virginian*, symbolically unites the best qualities of two culturally divergent regions. Yet, when Spicer unjustly charges Ben Evans with rustling, it is once again the dude from the East who wins the cowboy's freedom in court and, ultimately, Nan's heart.

Throughout the novel, Caroline interjects strong personal feelings and actual autobiographical episodes and experiences. As it did for Nan, the "full of the moon" seems to have had over Caroline a perpetual sway. And as Nan was initially attracted to Ben Evans, so would Caroline continually engage in affairs of the heart with cowboy types—from ranch hands Ned Paul and Lou Erickson to Pinkie Gist, rodeo cowboy; to wrangler Dave Good and friend of her later years, Vernon Spencer. Yet, if Caroline could have conquered her inner demons, if she could have had all things her way, she (like Nan) would have chosen to marry a polished intellectual who was also a physically active and successful outdoorsman—a man like the dude Bob Ellison, who had proved himself worthy, or possibly a man like John Painter.

THE MAN FROM THE BITTER ROOTS

John R. "Jack" Painter was a mining man. Handsome and slender, he sported a heavy, dark mustache that added an aura of intrigue to his tanned face. "J.R.," as he was also called, was the type of man Caroline Lockhart preferred—intelligent and polished, yet an outdoorsman. He was also married.

By 1895, Painter had moved his wife Evelina and his three children—Mary, Marguerite, and William—from Philadelphia to the Sunlight Basin (Big Horn City) area north of Cody. For the next five years, J.R. divided his time between managing his music store in Philadelphia and establishing himself as a mining man in the West.[91]

To lessen the cultural shock of their new environment, Evelina Painter brought with her a tutor for the children. In addition, they frequently took extended trips back East. On these jaunts the family traveled in style in private railroad cars, courtesy of financier and railroad developer Henry Villard. J.R. also made lengthy trips to Buffalo, New York, to raise money for mining activities, and to Grangeville, Idaho, to see his attorney. J.R. may well have met the vivacious Caroline Lockhart on one of these business trips, or even earlier during the time he lived in Philadelphia.[92]

Caroline's move West in 1904 made it possible for her to continue, or renew (as the case might have been) her affair with Painter—much to the chagrin of his wife and, perhaps, Frances Lane. Never one to be overly concerned with convention, Caroline consistently disregarded the advice of well-meaning friends where "affairs of the heart" were concerned. Her good friend and editor, Anna Howe, was forthright in warning her about going with "every Tom, Dick, and Harry," as she termed it; but Caroline insisted on continuing such relationships, even though, as she admitted: "I've been getting the devil and am in hot water."[93] As if to fill a void created by the lack of familial support, or as a result of what she considered to be her father's rejection, she seemed compelled to substitute an ongoing parade of lovers in order to maintain her self-esteem.

Caroline had two reasons for continuing the relationship with J.R. Painter: First, she was infatuated with him. In later years, she wrote that Jack reminded her of another friend and lover, the banker Andrew Ross; but Andrew, she felt, lacked Jack's "brilliancy and humor."[94] Second, and pragmatically, in the relationship with J.R., she saw potential for another novel.

J.R., on the other hand, seemed unable to resist the colorful Caroline. As a token of his affection, he bought her a beautiful diamond and amethyst ring that she wore throughout her lifetime. During one of his wife's trips to take the children to Philadelphia for schooling, J.R.—at the risk of jeopardizing his marriage—invited Caroline to join him at the Sunlight Basin ranch.[95]

Monroe Wagoman, a former employee who worked on the ranch, recalled that after Mrs. Painter returned to Sunlight and learned of Caroline's extended stay, she made life so miserable for J.R. "that he pulled up stakes and moved on." J.R. left the ranch to his wife, who later sold it and moved to Cody, where she died in 1925. Recollections of relatives indicate that there was no formal divorce for at least six years after their separation. By 1918, however, this situation had changed and Painter apparently obtained a divorce. Estranged from his wife, J.R. in 1907–8 was investigating mining possibilities in the Salmon River country in Idaho.[96]

The Salmon River country had a primitive beauty. Next to the Snake and short stretches of rapids in the upper Colorado, the river itself was reputed to be "the wickedest water in the West." Rising in the Sawtooth Range, the Salmon River, also known as the fabled "River of No Return," flowed some three hundred miles to empty into the Snake on the border between Oregon and Idaho. Tributaries of the Snake fed some of the wildest parts of Idaho. Largely uninhabited, the two hundred miles between Salmon City and White Bird served for years as an isolated refuge for deer and mountain sheep. Eventually, however, civilization encroached; ranches and small towns began to spring up as people mined the banks of the Salmon, cultivated the silt of bordering sand bars, and felled logs from trees to build homes. By the turn of the century, the little town of Dixie Gulch had become the river's major supply point, post office, and port of debarkation for river traffic.

With the well-known Captain Harry Guleke, Painter explored the Salmon River country and found the picturesque Jersey Creek Bar to his liking. By 1908, Painter had purchased the land from Edward Oscar Eakin and homesteaded additional acreage on which he ran a small herd of cattle and planted an orchard. "Painter Bar," as it came to be known, was situated on a bend of the Salmon River at the mouth of Jersey Creek.[97] Across the river, J.R. started another mining operation. The Painter mine, called "The Surprise," was reputed to have been "very rich." A former employee recalled one particular shipment of ore to Belfry "worth $22,000," a respectable sum for the time.[98]

On the north side of the creek, J.R. built a beautiful hunting lodge. Considered elegant for such a backwater location, the lodge had a handsome stone fireplace, a trophy room, and French windows. Furnished with Navajo rugs, redwood furniture, and appropriate curtains and drapes, the lodge became a popular vacation spot for Painter's well-to-do friends from the East. Paying guests also enjoyed good hunting and the social graces of their host, who dressed for dinner and set his table with crystal and fine silver.[99] Getting furniture and appointments to such a remote area proved to be a task in itself. The lodge furnishings as well as equipment for the mine had to be brought downriver on scows and barges. By 1912, however, the lodge and the Salmon River mining venture were well established.

Caroline, in the interim, had published her first two books, Me-Smith (1911) and The Lady Doc (1912), and was putting the finishing touches on her third, The Full of the Moon, which she would have ready for publication in 1914. She also began gathering material for her next novel. Shortly after the first of the year (1911), she had the opportunity to join J.R. once again, this time for a hair-raising adventure riding the rapids of the Salmon River—an experience that provided her with material for an article in Outing Magazine and for her new novel featuring J.R. as "the Man from the Bitter Roots."[100]

As general manager of the Salmon River Mining Company, J.R. planned to send over ninety thousand pounds of machinery on barges through the rapids. The flat-bottomed scows were clumsy but durable crafts, sturdy enough—the crew hoped—to survive the white water and rocks of the rapids. While waiting for the barges to be constructed and the sweeps to be adjusted with careful precision, Caroline listened to tales of the river. The natives seemed particularly impressed by the Pine Creek Rapids, three miles below Shoup. As one old-timer confided:

> I'll tell you about me, mum. I have fit Injuns; and I ain't afraid of a gun, er a knife, er pizen, er grub in the Bismark Restauraw but you couldn't get me down that river 'thout tyin' and gaggin' me. And the Pine Creek Rapids— you go through like a bat out of hell, mum.[101]

Caroline found the old-timer's assessment to be no exaggeration.

The navigator in charge of the venture was Captain Guleke, renowned on the river for his expertise and record of success. "A moose of a man," according to Caroline's description, Guleke was to handle the head sweep on the pilot boat. Captain David Sandilands, a wiry Scotsman, took the hind sweep in the second barge, and a man named Cummings handled the third. Caroline was to ride with Guleke.

With the equipment on board and securely tied, she stowed herself in the stern along with the baler. The crewmen cast off the ropes, and the steermen gripped their sweeps. The first sixty miles were uneventful—swift water, but nothing disturbing. Caroline began to think that the dangers had been overstated.

By noon of the second day, however, Guleke and Sandilands suddenly became quite serious and announced that they were approaching the Pine Creek Rapids. The crew dug out life preservers and moved the cargo to give the baler room to work. The river's path narrowed and the mountain cliffs rose sharply from the water's edge. Caroline described the feeling of danger that faced them:

> There was something creepy, ominous, in the quietness with which we glided from the stiller water of the eddy into the channel. Nobody spoke; it was silent as a graveyard, save for the occasional lap of a ripple against the barge. . . . Then the current caught us like some wild thing. Faster and faster we moved.[102]

Hearing something like thunder back in the hills, she turned to look at the captain.

"Hear 'em roar?" he asked.

"Roar! It sounded like Niagra [sic] Falls." And as far as she could see, there was nothing but spray and foam, with white water churning against the mass of rocks. "For an instant," she wrote, "the barge poised on the edge of a precipice with half its length in mid-air before it dropped into a curve of water that was like the hollow of a great green shell. The sheet of water that broke over us seemed to shut out the sun. When the boat came up like a clumsey [sic] Newfoundland, the water was swishing through the machinery and we were drenched to the skin."[103]

Once past the Pine Creek Rapids, the venturesome crew had to face other rapids nearly as bad: the Growler; the Big Mallard, where one of the men had lost his brother; and the Whiplash, where Sandiland's boat hit a rock at the head of the Lemhi Bar and threatened to capsize. Caroline recorded that the barge struck with a splintering crash, but the big flywheel in the bottom saved it from sinking. Just as it seemed that the passengers would have to go overboard, a wave lifted them off the rock. A crew member threw his body over the sweep to hold it down, while the captain directed the barge toward the nearest landing. The machinery was unloaded, the boat repaired, and the equipment replaced on board.[104]

It had been a memorable adventure for Caroline and another opportunity to prove to herself that she was more courageous than most men, another chance to earn recognition of a sort. As always, something compelled her to do it; yet, like those with less courage and perhaps more sense—she *had* been afraid. In the article for *Outing Magazine*, she wrote:

> I died so frequently shooting the rapids of the Salmon River . . . that the grave no longer holds any terrors for me. Even the distinction of being one of the first two women ever to attempt this hazardous trip was no solace to me at times when I was less than a foot from my Everlasting punishment, and at such moments glory seemed a puny thing indeed.[105]

But those moments of fear did not last long; Caroline continued to feel the need for glory and recognition.

With the new mining equipment in place, Painter's Surprise Mine was ready for business. Local mining man Bill Jackson constructed "a water-powered two-stamp mill at the mouth of Little Five Mile Creek," and Bill Hart and Clyde Painter (no relation) packed the ore in. The system worked efficiently, and the ore proved to be rich. The mining operation suffered setbacks, however. German investors, interested in gold mining in the area, attempted to enlarge their holdings. According to old-timers, these foreign investors were not above using force to persuade local owners to sell. Painter, like the hero in Caroline's novel, had mining equipment damaged or destroyed by a neighbor of German origin.[106]

After her exciting trip down the rapids, Caroline returned to spend the following summer and fall of 1912 with J.R. on the Salmon River. She made note of all the crises her lover had faced and worked them into the plot of her novel, published in 1915, which she titled *The Man from the Bitter Roots*. True to form, Caroline's major characters in the book are easily recognized. The hero, Bruce Burt, is a courageous mining man, and the heroine, Helen Dunbar, is a reporter for a newspaper. In what appears to have been an appeal to anti-German or even anti-Semitic prejudices of the World War I era, Lockhart has her protagonists battle a crooked financier (Sprudell), a German saboteur (Smaltz), and the rapids of the Salmon River to find love in the Bitter Roots.[107]

Full of action and adventure, the book inspired a reviewer of the foreign edition to refer to the novel as "an exciting book, whose conflicts and struggles are at the point of overpowering the reader." To Caroline, who had experienced some of the episodes firsthand, it probably seemed little more than fiction-based-on-fact. The reviewer conceded that her characterizations reminded him "of an excellent gallery of mining men" reminiscent of Bret Harte and Jack London.[108] The book is also reminiscent of Wister's characterization of the Virginian, for the Man from the Bitter Roots, like the Virginian, shows that intriguing blend of eastern culture with western virility—a facet of J.R.'s personality that Caroline greatly appreciated.

Caroline ended her visit to the Salmon River country in November 1912 and, according to the local newspaper, planned to go to Philadelphia before returning to Cody. J.R. accompanied her as far as Elk City.[109] She was still living in Cody at this time but made frequent trips to the East to negotiate with publishers and to have her manuscripts edited and typed. (During this period, she was concerned with finding a publisher for The Full of the Moon.) The following summer, in July 1913, Caroline was once again in Elk City en route to Salmon River country to visit J.R. and complete The Man from the Bitter Roots.[110]

By December, her novel finished, she was back in Cody and packing her trunk for a well-earned vacation to Honduras, where she planned to do a final edit on the manuscript. Her good friend, Mrs. Charles "Nellie" De Maris, whose family operated the local spa, accompanied her as far as Denver, where she planned to stop and visit friends.[111]

From Denver, Caroline proceeded to St. Louis, Missouri, and points south to New Orleans. It is possible that she planned to meet J.R. in South America; however, his grandson, Bill Painter, thinks that J.R. went to Nicaragua rather than Honduras because of a contract he had secured through Senator Borah of Idaho to provide cement for construction of the Nicaraguan Canal. Painter, who is writing a biography of his grandfather, admits that, "for several reasons, I now wonder if such a contract or trip really happened. I'm still working on this. It is possible, I suppose, that the Nicaragua story was invented . . . as a coverup of a trip with C. L."[112]

Whether in the company of J.R. or alone, Caroline Lockhart arrived in La Cieba, Honduras (or Nicaragua, as the case may be) sometime shortly after the New Year in 1914. In her autobiography she writes: "I had just finished the manuscript of a book (The Man from the Bitter Roots) which had been accepted by the J. B. Lippincott Co. but whanted [sic] to go over it once before submitting it. And what better place than the little town of La Cieba on the coast of Honduras."[113]

From New Orleans, La Cieba was only an overnight trip away by boat. After a rather rough crossing on the old Vicarro line, the small boat arrived at La Cieba. On the wharf, she spied a tall, rangy American described in her autobiography as having a triangular face "like a child's drawing of a cat." The man, who wore a broad-brimmed Panama hat and a seersucker suit, advised her that the Grand Hotel de Paris was the best the small town could offer. Her new acquaintance arranged for her steamer trunk to be sent to the hotel and walked her over himself.

The "best" that La Cieba could offer was none too luxurious. The focal point of the room was a single bed covered by a canopy of mosquito netting. Off to the side, a waxy, fly-specked mirror hung above a bureau with a missing caster replaced by a Gideon Bible. A small picture of the Virgin Mary, also fly-specked, decorated one of the plaster walls. Despite the spartan accommodations, Caroline found herself fascinated by the other guests and their unusual backgrounds. The man who had helped her with her luggage was a veterinarian on the run for the murder of a man in Dallas, Texas. Another interesting acquaintance, a tight-lipped young man called "Malone," had organized his own revolution in La Cieba, installed his own president, and essentially ran the little town.

The tropical heat was oppressive and the flies annoying, but Caroline plunked away industriously on her typewriter. When she became ill with the dread *calentura* (fever), the veterinarian gave her horse-size doses of some medication, and within two weeks she felt well enough to complete the revisions to her manuscript.

To celebrate, she decided to take a two-day boat trip to visit an old, historic town a few miles down the coast. The excursion party had gone some distance when they saw what appeared to be smoke drifting out over the Gulf from the direction of La Cieba. After the party of sightseers arrived at their destination, they learned that La Cieba had burned to the edges of the jungle during the night. Upon her return, she heard that the explosion of an acetylene tank near the hotel had caused the fire. The little town's ancient fire engines proved to be inoperable, and the strong headwinds from the Gulf had ignited the frame buildings "like shavings soaked in kerosene." At intervals Caroline heard shots and was told that the soldiers from the fort had orders to shoot looters on sight. She found the Grand Hotel de Paris reduced to a heap of smoking rubble and with it the steamer trunk containing her manuscript, clothes, and money. The nearest cable station was in Puerta Cortes, which meant that she had to wait for the next boat before she could send an S.O.S. to the States.

Strangely enough, when Caroline returned, she granted an interview to a reporter from the Philadelphia *Bulletin* that gave a totally different version of her South American adventure. In the interview, titled "Suzette Loses Novel in the Ocean," not only do the circumstances surrounding the loss

Caroline labeled this portrait "Papa and his Prodigal."
Courtesy of Elizabeth Sutton.

Caroline Lockhart.

Caroline as a schoolgirl in the East. Her father sent her first to the
Moravian Female Seminary in Bethlehem, Pennsylvania,
which she likened to "being put in the calaboose."

Caroline attended Bethany College in Topeka, Kansas.

In Boston, Caroline enrolled at the Moses True Brown School of Oratory,
but soon gave up her acting aspirations.

Caroline in a diving suit for one of her daredevil escapades.
She dived into Boston Harbor "to be able to write about the experience."

Camping out with friends on the Newfoundland trip.

Caroline with one of her early beaus, "Captain Sammy"
of the Newfoundland Parliament and Department of Steamboats Line.

To the consternation of the more conservative element,
Caroline was quite liberated for her era.

The writer at work.

Lavicy Moore, daughter of "The Sheep Queen of Wyoming."

Caroline and the Sheep Queen's daughter.

"Getting atmosphere," as Caroline termed it, meant serving as cook and
bottle washer for Chief Baconrind and family to get her story
on the oil-rich Osage Indians.

Caroline Lockhart (*center*) and Cody friends go for a ride (*circa 1900*). Frances Lane is at far left.

Caroline Lockhart and the town's founding father, William F. "Buffalo Bill" Cody. *Courtesy of Buffalo Bill Historical Center.*

Dr. Frances M. Lane, the "Lady Doc" of Caroline's novel, was a respected member of Cody society and Caroline's favorite enemy.

John R. Painter, a mining man and a major love interest in Caroline's life. *Courtesy of Bill Painter.*

John R. Painter on the Salmon River.

Caroline's manuscript, "The Man from the Bitter Roots,"
supposedly burned in this fire at La Ceiba, Honduras.

Ready for the Cody Stampede. Caroline was
one of the Stampede's founders and was its association's first president.

From a postcard with the caption: "Caroline Lockhart, author of
The Fighting Shepherdess and *The Dude Wrangler*. Cody Stampede, 1921."
Courtesy of Buffalo Bill Historical Center, Cody, Wyoming.

Caroline Lockhart, riding high at the Cody Stampede, circa 1934.
Courtesy of Buffalo Bill Historical Center, Cody, Wyoming.

Vehemently anti-Prohibition,
Caroline stands behind the beautiful mahogany bar in her home.

Caroline holds open bar for her free-spirited friends.

Caroline with her pet bobcat "Wampie."

"Whiffy," Caroline's pet skunk, gets the drop on Dave Good.

View from the L/♥ Ranch in Montana

Old-timers Caroline Lockhart (*left*), Vern Spencer, and
Orilla Downing Hollister lead the Stampede parade, circa 1960.
Photograph by Jack Richard.

of the manuscript differ, but her destination, rather than being Honduras, is given as Nicaragua. This version, therefore, supports the possibility that J. R. Painter met her in South America, since he is thought to have held a contract with the Nicaraguan government.

The article, subtitled "Caroline Lockhart Mourns Manuscripts Representing Two Years' Hard Work in Her Trip to the Nicaraguan Coast," tells how her book, along with her baggage, went to the bottom of the ocean when a small boat transporting them from the steamship to the coast capsized. "It wasn't the weighty import of the manuscript that sank the boat," Caroline quipped, "but I have a notion that my rifle and boxes of cartridges were partly responsible." [114]

Which version of the South American episode is the accurate one is impossible to determine; but the manuscript was lost, and Caroline had no recourse but to rewrite the novel from memory. *The Man from the Bitter Roots*, published in October 1915, was made into a movie starring actor William Farnham. Dedicated to her editor and good friend, Anna Howe, wife of Dr. Louis Howe, "with all gratitude and affection," the book reveals yet another facet of Caroline's adventurous and liberated life. [115]

Her close relationship with the real-life hero of the book, John R. (J.R.) Painter, continued until near the end of his life. Although occupied with her career, her various lovers, and later, her ranch on the Dryhead, she maintained contact with J.R. through the years and periodically lent him money during hard times.

Despite her own continual money worries and feelings of financial insecurity, Caroline generously loaned money throughout her life to various people, including her housekeeper, an eccentric acquaintance, and her lovers. Not infrequently she took whiskey and cigarettes to "down and out" cowboys in the "calaboose," and on at least one occasion she arranged for a load of hay to be delivered to a woman referred to as the "Goat Lady of Meeteetse." Highly educated, the woman had become a recluse and lived in a modest house surrounded by books, goats, and cats. With the assistance of her friends, Harvey and Dorothea Nebel, Caroline delivered the hay to the "goat lady," who insisted on preparing lunch for the visitors. When the smell of animals encouraged the Nebels to decline, Caroline accused them of being "chicken." Dorothea Nebel recalls that on other occasions, she helped deliver bread that Caroline had baked for sick friends or a bottle of whiskey for a friend dying of cancer to help her cope with the pain. "Unknown to people," Dorothea said, "Caroline befriended many down-and-outers." [116]

In the course of one month, Caroline recorded loans of $25 to her housekeeper and $100 each to two different men friends. "My impecunious lovers . . ." she confided to her Diary. "Wish I could get one once that wasn't perpetually hard up." [117]

Of all these lovers, in J.R. Painter she came closest to finding the rare combination of eastern gentleman and courageous westerner that she so admired. Why she refused to marry him, probably even Caroline didn't know. It was not because he failed to ask. "A letter from Jack," she wrote in August 1918, "saying everything but the garden had gone to hell on the river. That he . . . meant to marry me if I would but permit." [118]

But Caroline wouldn't permit—perhaps because of the difference in their ages (J.R. was ten years older), perhaps because of his financial instability, or more likely, because she seemed to require the attentions of not one but several men. And, in the interim, she had met Orvier B. (O.B.) Mann, who would supplant J.R. as "the love of her life." Although she recorded in 1918 that her heart ached for Jack because of his problems, she was by this time carrying on relationships simultaneously with four men: gentleman rancher O.B. Mann, cowboy Jesse Mitchell, banker Andrew Ross, and J.R. [119] It was not in Caroline's character to be monogamous, although she did yearn periodically for the respectability that marriage provided.

Not long after Caroline apparently refused J.R.'s proposal of marriage, he advertised for a housekeeper. The woman he selected, Ellen Galbraith Jones, worked in that capacity for eighteen years, during which time Caroline and J.R. remained in contact. Finally, one year before his death in 1937, Painter married Ellen Jones. For Caroline, the news came as a shock and brought back memories of her father's marriage to the family seamstress. On 2 February 1937, she wrote: "Just got a letter and am shocked and angry as all hell. Jack has gone and married the cook. Not that I would have married him but it doesn't seem square since he pretended to love me to the last." [120]

Throughout her life Caroline vacillated on the subject of marriage. Her personal magnetism and appeal to the opposite sex were beyond dispute, but her receptive moods never quite matched those of her lovers. "There never was a man, save Harry Thurston, the pinhead," she wrote, not quite truthfully, "who would not have stuck to me had I retained my interest." [121] Underneath it all, Caroline yearned to reach the goal she set for herself: "to be the best known woman not only in Wyoming but in the West." [122]

Marriage didn't figure into her plans, but writing did. And by 1917 she had in mind another good subject for a novel—a woman she would refer to initially as the daughter of "Jezebel of the Sand Coulee" and later as "the Fighting Shepherdess."

THE FIGHTING SHEPHERDESS

By nature of her training and profession, Caroline Lockhart was attracted to unusual personalities, particularly those who reflected yet another aspect of the kaleidoscopic western culture. One such individual was a woman known as "The Sheep Queen of Wyoming." "Of all the extraordinary characters I have met in my unconventional life," the author wrote, "none stands out more clearly." [123]

The Sheep Queen, otherwise known as Lucy Morrison Moore, owned twenty bands of sheep, managed her own outfit, and was worth approximately a million dollars. Upon inquiry, Caroline learned that this remarkable woman had last been seen on Copper Mountain, where she was said to be "feudin' with the cattlemen over range." "Never know what that old sister will do next," the informant volunteered. "She's tough, really tough, but you gotta hand it to her. She's got guts. She don't ask nothin' from nobody in a fight." [124] Sensing a good novel, Caroline set out on a one-hundred-fifty-mile ride on horseback to find this rugged individualist and induce her to tell the story of her life.

Late one afternoon after many days in the saddle, she smelled the distinctive odor of sheep and saw them scattered over the foothills. She rode down a coulee until she came to a flat where sheepwagons encircled a large tent. Half a dozen dogs announced her arrival with their barking, and a woman climbed agilely out of a wagon and watched, unsmiling, as she rode up.

The woman, according to Caroline's description, appeared to be about sixty, with a "fresh, healthy complexion and short iron-gray hair so tightly frizzed that it looked like a nest some industrious bird had built." The author noted also that she was "short and plump but not too stout" and "her features though not masculine showed firmness and determination in every line." Fully expecting her to look mannish and be wearing a shirt and levis, her visitor was surprised to see that although the woman was barefoot, she wore a clean apron over a gingham "wrapper."

The Sheep Queen waited for her guest to speak. When Caroline told her that her job was writing, and that she had come to learn how a woman could manage such a big outfit and make a success of it, a quick gleam in the woman's sharp blue eyes reflected her pride and willingness to talk.

"Get off," she said peremptorily. "You can help Lavicy herd bucks." [125] Jerking her thumb at the sheepwagon inside the circle, she indicated that Caroline would be expected to share a bunk there with her daughter. The Sheep Queen then yelled at a wrangler called "Slim" to come and put up the horses and climbed back into her wagon.

When the dinner bell rang, announcing the evening meal, Caroline found three sheepherders already at the long table in the big tent. There was little conversation, but the Sheep Queen was obviously upset by news a herder had just reported. To ward off raids by coyotes or an occasional wolf, she had ordered her men to plant crossed stakes, draped with men's shirts, around the range. The scarecrow effect and flapping sleeves scared off the "varmints," but the wind eventually blew away the shirts. To solve the problem, she had placed an order from her "Sheepherder's Bible" (the Montgomery Ward catalog) for dozens of men's long-tailed night shirts, which she painted with a big black "M" for the Morrison brand. To her exasperation, however, the sheepherder brought news that "every cowboy on the range was now wearing a new shirt with the tail cut off and marked by a large M on the chest!" [126]

To get a feel for the work and the people, Caroline joined into the activities of the camp, including the nasty chore of "dipping." Lockhart found the Sheep Queen's daughter to be a bit of a chore also, but she chose to tolerate the young woman to get her story. "Lavicy," as she was called, was "an Amazon of a woman" and "a moose for strength," according to Caroline. That first night, she noted that Lavicy took the news that Caroline was to share her quarters as a matter of course and merely informed her that she was to sleep at the back of the bunk.

Shortly before dark, Lavicy returned to the wagon, explaining that she had been down in the corral "rassling sheep." Her face streaked with dust and sweat, she was a sight to behold in her sheep-rassling costume: a wide-brimmed Stetson pushed to the back of her head, a filmy white lace blouse that hung in shreds about a well-endowed body, a divided skirt, pink stockings with the toes out and a pair of incredibly dirty pink satin slippers. She treated her guest with something slightly less than total disdain:

> "What do you work at? Hash?" she asked as she splashed at the tin wash-basin.
>
> "Sometimes I write for a newspaper!" Caroline responded.
>
> Lavicy was unimpressed. "That's nothin," she said finally, "I write songs. I wrote one called 'The Cowboy's Indian Bride.' Like as not you've heard of it."
>
> "No doubt," Caroline said graciously.
>
> Lavicy changed the subject abruptly. "Do you snore? I'm a light sleeper an' snorin' keeps me awake. I git up as soon as it's light so I gotta have my rest. If you git to trashin' around, we'll split the bed an' I'll take my half of the soogans and sleep on the ground!" [127]

Forewarned, Caroline crawled to the back of the bunk and made herself as small as possible. To her amusement and dismay, Lavicy's head no sooner touched the pillow than she was sound asleep and flapping the canvas with her reverberating snores.

Caroline came to know Lavicy well during the following weeks and recorded in vivid detail how they climbed the steep, rocky hills of Copper Mountain and herded the bands of sheep. It turned out that the girl was basically good-natured, and she and Caroline got along rather well. Lavicy knew her sheep, but "her ignorance of the outside world was exceeded only by her conceit, which was colossal," Caroline observed. Because of her mother's wealth, the girl acted superior, although her world actually was circumscribed by mail-order catalogs and problems with cattlemen. Toward the latter, Caroline said, "she and her mother were as merciless as any cattle baron who ever walked." [128]

Lavicy's inhumane disregard for her horse also bothered her visitor, who had a soft spot for animals. When she complained to the wrangler, who also served as cook, about the girl's care of her horse, he acknowledged Caroline's gripe, saying sardonically: "They're pizen on horses all right. Them as has much dealin's with woolies gits so they don't know nothin' else." [129]

One evening while they were sitting on upturned starch boxes in the moonlight, Caroline got the Sheep Queen to tell her story: As a young widow in Utah with two small children, she had only a small band of sheep for support. She heard of the Copper Mountain country in Wyoming with its vast range and open grassland and decided that it sounded like a sheep's paradise. Subsequently, she greased the wheels of the rickety covered wagon, purchased a scanty supply of cornmeal, flour, and salt pork, and loaded her few belongings and children. Driving her small band of sheep ahead of the wagon, she traveled through bitter cold and snow and made camp with no fuel except buffalo chips or sagebrush. Despite frequent breakdowns, sick horses, and hungry children, she arrived in Wyoming with a larger band than when she started. During the drive she had not permitted a single sheep to be slaughtered for food. The children killed rabbits for the pot by stoning or running them down and digging them out of their burrows.

After she had selected her range, herding and control of the band posed the greatest problems. If the sheep were not watched every minute, wolves and coyotes quickly took their toll. "Her children were too young to be left alone," Caroline recalled, "so she solved the problem by placing the two kitchen chairs upside-down and lashing them to the side of a horse like a pack saddle." She placed the children inside the rungs, which left her hands free to lead the horse and carry them with her as she herded the sheep.

At first the cattlemen left her alone, thinking that the first hard winter would take care of her and the little band of sheep. Eventually, however, they came to respect her courage; and as Caroline discovered, "they quietly did many favors for her of which she knew nothing."

Lucy Morrison knew her business, and as the years passed her flocks and her fortune grew. Although it would have been financially possible for her to live in a mansion, she continued living in the sheepwagon. Her wealth, however, did leave an imprint on her attitude toward "poor" people. Caroline learned that the woman could be "utterly ruthless" in her treatment of homesteaders who came in later to file on the government land that was part of the Morrison domain.[130]

It is worth noting that this story as recorded by Caroline varies in considerable degree from the story of the Sheep Queen's origins as told by her granddaughter, Olga (Mrs. Hugh) Von Krosigk of Meeteetse. According to the granddaughter, the Sheep Queen's first husband, Luther Morrison, around 1880, helped bring in the band of sheep, the second ever to appear in Wyoming. The first severe winter killed all but 200 of the original 2,000, but they were able to build up their flock until they were shipping a full trainload out of Casper each year. The family, which included four small children, lived in tents on Copper Mountain, east of the Wind River Canyon.

In 1898 Luther Morrison died, leaving his wife and fourteen-year-old son, Lincoln, to take over the sheep ranch. At the age of sixteen, however, Lincoln Morrison was shot by hired gunmen while tending sheep on Kirby Creek. He survived, however, and eventually became a government trapper in the Greybull district. In 1906 Lucy Morrison married a "tall, gaunt Vermonter named Curtis Moore." According to the relatives, Lucy presented her new husband with two bands of sheep, "so people could say she married a sheepman instead of a sheepherder."[131]

Whether Caroline's version was the result of literary license or the Sheep Queen's desire to feature herself in a starring role is difficult to determine. It is obvious, however, that Caroline, for whatever reason, did not learn or record all the particulars of the Morrison history. Her firsthand observations of camplife, therefore, have more validity than her version of the family background and were most useful to her in writing the romanticized novel based on the Sheep Queen's life.

Caroline's recollections of her last evening at the sheep camp, for example, were memorable. Mitchell, the cook, had baked a big stack of doughnuts in her honor, and the sheepherders and guest were sitting around the table enjoying the feast when the Sheep Queen made a grand entrance. Caroline described the scene:

> She was in her bare-feet as usual and wearing a bungalow apron as was her wont but skewered in her fuzzy iron-gray hair was a dazzling, bejeweled ornament. Diamonds and jewels of every description blazed in a big breast-pin on her chest, in bracelets on her arms, and on practically every finger of each hand! [132]

Looking pleased at the sensation she created, the Sheep Queen explained that she had purchased the jewels in Paris, adding, "They cost several bands of sheep. . . . Looks like you'd read about me in the papers. They took my picture an' all." "Whether this fantastic tale was one she had dreamed to impress me or had some basis of truth," Caroline wrote, "I was never able to find out." [133] The next morning she left the camp. The writer never saw the Sheep Queen again but contributed to the legends that had grown up about her by writing a novel using Lucy Morrison Moore as the heroine.

After some initial marketing problems, the book, titled *The Fighting Shepherdess*, was published by Small, Maynard and Company in January 1919 and later was made into a movie starring Anita Stewart. The New York *Times Tribune* advertised the novel as "Better than Zane Grey at his best!" but Caroline was not pleased. "That tooth-pulling ass," she raged. "My *worst* is better than Zane Grey at his *Best*." Destined to be as popular and lucrative as her first novel, *Me-Smith*, the book went into its fifth printing by May of that same year. [134]

In *The Fighting Shepherdess*, acclaimed for its adherence to reality, the author departed from her usual tactic of using at least one female figure to represent eastern cultural values and placed the literary spotlight on a true woman of the West. Heroine Katie Prentice, daughter of Jezebel of the Sand Coulee Road House, is depicted as a distinctive and powerful character who carries on a remorseless struggle to make her mark. As one reviewer put it: "The Fighting Shepherdess . . . in our judgment, is her best novel and Katie Prentice her finest character. The story holds one's attention from the moment Katie, a mere child, leaves her disreputable mother and becomes a shepherdess, until her day of triumph in Prouty, which had scorned her." [135]

As the plot develops, the young girl is befriended by sheepman Uncle Joe (or Mormon Joe) after she is attacked by trapper Pete Mullendore. Uncle Joe teaches her the sheep business and takes her into partnership.

At this point in the novel, Caroline starts to lean heavily on her firsthand acquaintance with Lucy Moore for story line and atmosphere as the heroine overcomes numerous obstacles to become a wealthy sheep rancher.

In this book, as in most others, Caroline's appreciation of social position is apparent. Katie Prentice, for example, is found to be of good social background when her wealthy and highly connected father returns. Her position is further enhanced by her marriage to "Hughie," the dude rancher, who recognizes her as "a diamond in the rough" from the night she is first "snubbed" by Prouty "society." In the end, Katie who has long been suspected of murdering her benefactor, is vindicated by "Teeters," the cowman.[136]

Described by critics of the era as "tense, gripping, with drama and humor . . . that holds one breathless to the end," this book—like her others—when judged by today's standards appears melodramatic and overly romanticized.[137] But to the student of western culture and to the biographer, the novel has a distinct value in what it reveals about the author's attitudes toward small-town rivalries and society. The Prouty of the book is simply Cody revisited.

Borrowing a page from Cody's history, Caroline used her analytical talents, heightened by her personal experience in the Lady Doc controversy, to depict the maneuverings of those she considered to be petty, mean-minded, unscrupulous citizens. Even the town's founding father, despite personal friendship, became the subject of sociological analysis. Although she later assisted in establishing a memorial in his honor, Caroline used what she considered to be William F. Cody's personal foibles to delineate a similar colorful character in her novel.[138]

With the vision of a born entrepreneur, Major Stephen Douglas Prouty (alias Colonel Cody) casts a speculative eye about the countryside as he imagines the town-to-be:

> I'll get the post office, and name it Prouty! . . ." It seemed incredible that he had not thought of this before, for deep within him was a longing to have his name figure in the pages of history of the big new state. Tombstones blew over, dust storms obliterated graves, photographs faded, but with a town named after him and safely on the map, nobody could forget him if he wanted to.[139]

Thus Caroline illustrated her perception of the Major's motives for the establishment of Prouty and what she perceived as the self-aggrandizing aspects of his activities. In this respect, the author is not alone in her protest against what the towns and villages bred—or, by the same token, what bred the towns and villages. As western writing approached the present, a revolt against the negative aspects of urbanization was not atypical. Willa Cather took a similar stance in *My Antonia*, published in 1918. Much later, Mari Sandoz in similar manner would reject her hometown and native state of Nebraska. Bernard DeVoto also spoke disparagingly of his hometown of Ogden, Utah; although he, like Cather, Sandoz, and Lockhart, appreciated the West in its unpolluted, primitive state.[140]

For Lockhart, *The Fighting Shepherdess* represented the culmination of nearly fifteen years as a student of western culture. Although her novels were permeated with personal prejudices, her aptitude for capturing with relentless candor and acuity the internal makeup of both the people and the place resulted in outsiders lauding her work for "reality" and "texture"— that accurate portrayal of dialect, folkways, and local lore. And as she came to realize, there were many facets to her West, not only the cowboys, miners, and sheepherders but also a new breed that brought with them a special appreciation for the West in its natural state—the "Dudes."

Denver Days

I've a kind of pride in winning out big in the West. I've made my boast
that I would be the best known woman not only in Wyoming but in
the West.

Caroline Lockhart, 8 July 1918

FRIENDS AND RELATIONS

In 1918 American journalism still enjoyed a brawling youth. It was a robust,
action-oriented era when power rested in the hands of the press. It was a
time when a publisher could spark a war with Spain, ignite a cattle war,
or extinguish a miner's strike. Critics emphasized their views with horse-
whips and editors toted pistols. News stories were rawboned and emotional,
headlines filled with gusto.[1]

The Denver *Post* under the leadership of Fred Bonfils and Harry Tammen
was a prime example. Amid articles relating to atrocities of the Huns and
an eye-catching advertisement urging mothers to use California Syrup of
Figs as a laxative for bilious and constipated children, the *Post*'s front-page
feature, with great fanfare, introduced a new celebrity. "BOY, HOWDY!
MEET CAROLINE LOCKHART NEW STAR FOR THE POST," read the
three-inch headline, with subtitle: "Woman Famous for Her Stories of Adventure and Western Life Comes Back to Newspaper Field and Picks Post
as Best Paper in USA."[2]

The enthusiastic reporter invited Lockhart to "shake hands with the
Denver *Post* family," and presented her to readers as a novelist well known
in the field of literature and journalism for her "brilliance of . . . intellect"
and "the beauty of her vocabulary." She had been persuaded, he said, to
put aside her work as a novelist to write

> little stories of everyday happenings, here in Denver and throughout the
> West. A murder in Denver, a gold strike at Cripple Creek, a roundup at
> Durango, a horse race at Cheyenne . . . a social conclave at the Broadmoor,
> a starving mother and babies in the most humble home in the city—wher-
> ever there is news or heart action, Miss Lockhart will go. And she'll give her

impressions in the same inimitable way which has placed her books in the select circle of America's six best sellers.[3]

He assured his audience that "Lockhart is of the West and for the West," having "ridden the range with the cowpunchers, herded sheep over the vast expanse of Wyoming's grazing lands, [and] explored little known places." He noted that she could ride a bucking bronco, trail a grizzly, or swim a mile in close to thirty minutes, but hastened to add that the reader must not get the impression that Miss Lockhart was inclined to be masculine. "There isn't a masculine feature in this talented woman's makeup," he raved. "She is a thorogoing woman."[4]

Her books, he said, "have inked Caroline Lockhart's name indelibly on the roll of America's greatest novelists." In touting her forthcoming novel, "Jezebel's Daughter" (*The Fighting Shepherdess*), he pointed out that Lockhart had sought authentic "atmosphere" for the book by taking a job near Thermopolis as a sheepherder for Mrs. L. (Lucy Morrison) Moore, "Sheepqueen of Wyoming." This sort of experience caused Robert H. Davis, head of Munsey Publications, to claim: "Lockhart knows the West better than any living writer."[5] And why had she selected the Denver *Post* over an eastern paper? According to the reporter, Lockhart had been impressed by the paper's broad appeal—from cowpunchers to millionaires. "The *Post* is distinctly Western," she had explained. "I like it above all other papers."[6]

Acceptance of the position with the Denver *Post* marked still another stage in Lockhart's life and career. By the end of 1918, at age forty-seven she had largely accomplished her goal of becoming "well known in the West." But success had come at a price; real happiness continued to elude her. Her celebrity status and reputation as a writer of some renown did little to compensate for continual worries about finances, quarrels with family members, and unsatisfactory relationships with the men in her life. Now, in late December 1918 as the new year approached, she sat alone in her room at the Brown Palace Hotel and looked back on the circumstances that had brought her to Denver.

She had boarded the train out of Cody in May of that year on the first leg of a journey that took her to Denver to see about a job with the *Post*, on to Oklahoma to visit relatives, and then east to Boston and New York to market her book. Nellie De Maris saw her off at the Cody station.

Since publication of *The Lady Doc* six years earlier, personal relations with residents of the town had been strained, although time helped smooth ruffled feathers. As she admitted to her Diary, she seemed to be "coming into my own . . . and getting . . . the hold back that I had when I first came." Nevertheless, Caroline was glad to be leaving—at least for a while. She was experiencing one of her periods of restlessness and boredom. By this time, Cody had become for her "a living death . . . fruitless . . . inane."[7] A change of scenery would help her mood and, hopefully, her pocketbook.

In general, the first visit to Denver went well. She met with *Post* editor Fred Bonfils, who offered her a job, and with a reporter for the paper, Frances Wayne, who interviewed her for a complimentary biographical piece. Caroline also visited an uncle, Seward Woodruff, but that encounter ended on an unpleasant note. She came away shocked by his vulgar speech and upset because he criticized her smoking and made unfavorable comments about her appearance.

After finishing her business in Denver, she boarded the train for a two-and-one-half-day trip to Oklahoma. Her itinerary took her through Topeka, Kansas, where she stayed at the Shroop Hotel. The heat and discomfort of the marginal accommodations contributed to her general depression and gave her time to dwell on her affair with O.B. Mann, a gentleman rancher from Meeteetse. Mann, a dapper bachelor who always dressed neatly in dark trousers, white shirt, and tie, even when supervising work in the field, had a reputation as a philanderer—and a hold on Caroline's heartstrings. Realizing that O.B., or "Ornery" as she called him, had difficulty being loyal to any one woman, just as she had difficulty settling for any one man, did not make his casual behavior any easier for her to accept.

At the time, Caroline herself had several men on the string. She was seeing cowboy William M. "Jesse" Mitchell; banker Andrew Ross, who was married; Bill Miller de Colonna; and John R. Painter—men friends she referred to as the "bright spots" in her life.[8]

Two days later her train pulled into Hominy, Oklahoma, where she planned to visit her sister Grace and her younger brother Robert (Bob), who managed the family holdings. She stepped off the train in a drizzling rain, exhausted from riding in a chair car until 2:00 a.m. Fortunately, Grace and her daughter Sylvia were at the station waiting for her in their "machine."

Grace, younger by several years, did not resemble Caroline either in looks or personality. Her features were more refined and so were her attitudes and demeanor. Caroline was enchanted by her niece, whom she described as "dear, lovable, and quaint."[9] Sylvia, in turn, found Aunt Caroline "exciting and glamorous." She loved her aunt's visits because "things were very lively while she was there." Furthermore, Aunt Caroline always came with gifts, and "once with a handsome boyfriend!" The memory of Caroline's first visit to their home in the little cow town of Hominy remained with her always.

Sylvia's bedroom had been given to her aunt as a guest room; and when she went away, the youngster was shocked to find an ashtray with butts in it. "It was not the idea that it was 'naughty' to smoke cigarettes," Sylvia recalled, "but the impossibility of a *woman* doing so." "Sophistication had not yet come into our lives," she added; "Aunt Caroline was, indeed, a pioneer among liberated women!"[10]

On this occasion, however, the visit would be marred by a quarrel between the sisters over a love letter that Grace felt contained language that "no gentleman would write to a lady." The letter came from Bill Miller de Colonna, a soldier friend overseas, who referred to Nellie De Maris's hired man as a "pimp" and in speaking of the "Prussians" used the word "bitch." Grace also made derogatory comments about her sister's table manners, to which Caroline responded by charging her with "provincialism." According to Caroline's somewhat prejudiced viewpoint: "She [Grace] sits up there like a ramrod, the old maid school teacher at the head of the boarding school table and not knowing the day is past when people sit waiting to fall upon their food at a signal."[11] Caroline was never one to take criticism mutely, and by the end of the last day of her week-long visit, the two sisters were not speaking.

The only positive aspect of her stay was that she had been successful in getting a ninety-day loan for $500 from Grace's husband, Roy, a banker by profession. On 22 May, in a state of mental anxiety, Caroline left Hominy, where "the earth steamed like a vapor bath," for the cooler climate of the East. She fretted that she might be going through "the change" or worse yet, PREGNANT! "Wouldn't that give Grace something to get excited about," she thought ruefully. "Work is the panacea," she wrote in her Diary, "if I can work when I am hungry for love and affection."[12]

THE MARKETING OF JEZEBEL:
THE FIGHTING SHEPHERDESS

By June 1918, Caroline was in Springfield, Massachusetts, trying to regain her health and market her manuscript on the Sheep Queen of Wyoming. She visited a local physician, who gave her a prescription and assured her that her problems were related to the onset of menopause rather than pregnancy. The news brought mixed feelings of relief and despondency. "The change" meant that she was getting older, and in her depression, she regarded the prospect as "the beginning of the end."[13]

She found quiet, comfortable accommodations and gradually began to feel better. She saw producer Norman Jeffries about making her first novel, *Me-Smith*, into a movie and arranged for literary agent J. Berg Essenwein to read and edit the Sheep Queen manuscript, which she titled "Jezebel of the Sand Coulee" (published as *The Fighting Shepherdess*). Essenwein, she said, "chortles over the humor" in her story and told her that it would appeal to "a higher class of reader." [14]

His final verdict a week later, that it was simply "a very good story," did not meet her expectations; but her spirits were lifted by news that the noted critic H. L. Mencken, who at that time edited *The Smart Set*, had offered to read the manuscript. By mid-June, she still had two to three days of work remaining to have her manuscript in polished form. "Wish I could attain something like Joseph Conrad's style," she fretted. Conrad's *Victory* represented to her "the acme of elegance." [15]

June 26, 1918, found her in Boston at the Winthrop Beach, a plain, homelike hotel that rented for $14 per week. Bright and early Monday morning, she met with a publisher at Little, Brown. Described by Caroline as a pleasant, curly-headed chap, "Mr. Jenkins," showed his interest by the sudden, quick sparkle in his blue eyes. He promised to give her his decision within a week.

His decision when it came was not what she wanted to hear. Jenkins's comments to the effect that the story was "humorless," "too long," and that the love interest was not "sufficiently developed" threw Caroline into a fit of depression. Even worse, he touted the works of novelist Bertha M. Bower as a shining example of "really good" western writing. Jenkins's admission that Caroline's story provided an "excellent picture of the life of a sheep raiser" did little to help her faltering ego and state of mind. [16]

That night she went to bed crying, while outside her hotel a cold wind wailed and low gray clouds added a somber cast that matched her mood. She agreed with Jenkins that the manuscript was too long but rationalized that the story wasn't of the type to appeal to him in the first place. "He is of the East," she wrote in her Diary, "and wouldn't understand either the humor or the atmosphere." [17] While in New York she planned to see Mencken personally to enlist his aid, but she decided to try another publishing firm in Boston before leaving.

With time and the money from her brother-in-law Roy running out, she approached her father for an advance on her annual stipend. It became increasingly clear that she must think seriously of taking a job with a newspaper to ensure a stable income. Money problems caused her to consider marriage as a way out. "God," she fretted uncharacteristically, "if only O.B. would ask me to marry him and end all this worry and unhappiness." [18]

Her visit to "a Mr. Hale" of Small, Maynard and Company publishers offered hope. Hale told her that they had turned down her first novel, *Me-Smith,* and regretted it afterward. He looked forward to reviewing this newest manuscript. A letter from Cody friend Maude Altberger arrived, saying that Mencken had spoken to Moffitt-Yard about the novel and that they also showed interest.[19]

Although she was recognized as an established novelist at this time, the financial pressures and rejections caused Caroline serious self-doubt and feelings of inadequacy. Characteristically, she would never be satisfied with her accomplishments. Her make-up demanded continual recognition and reinforcement. She needed to prove her worth to herself as much as to others, but she carefully kept these feelings concealed beneath a facade of charm and good humor. Her Diary was her only confidant. "It's lucky," she wrote, "I have this diary in which to complain and whine and spare my friends."[20] In these private pages she revealed with embarrassing honesty her dark side and the depths of her emotional despair. To her dinner partners, however, she made it a point to be "lively and entertaining company." Her ability to charm people with her personality and intelligence was apparently a matter of personal pride. To her credit, she had the rare ability to laugh at herself, even in embarrassing situations.

One such occasion occurred while she was staying at the beachside hotel. To relax, she went for a swim in the ocean, but found the undertow so strong that it soon pounded her back against the beach, rolling her over and over. Spectators hanging over the porch railing at the hotel got quite a show when her trunks and the rest of her suit parted company. Undaunted, Caroline carried off the situation with good-natured aplomb. Later, the landlady told her that she hoped she would stay, that she "was the kind they missed." To Caroline, the words were a compliment. "Glad I've got some little charm and magnetism left," she wrote.[21]

The journal in which she confided these innermost thoughts served not only as her confidant but also as her silent analyst during stressful times. In a soul-searching and self-deprecating mood, she observed: "It is strange that when I can so easily attract and hold people, I've never yet met *the Man,* outside of O.B., a perfectly eligible man that was in love with me."[22]

In moods such as this, she chose to forget the handsome one-armed cowboy Jesse Mitchell, who loved her loyally, mining man J.R. Painter, and ranch foreman Dave Good. Both J.R. and Dave had asked for her "hand," yet she failed to recognize that, where marriage was concerned, she herself was the major obstacle. As she admitted in her Diary regarding Dave: "He wants me to marry him so he can be open and aboveboard . . . but what he doesn't see is the courage it would take for me to do this. With the difference in our positions and our ages, I and *WE* would be the talk and probably the laughing stock of the country."[23] Caroline fought marriage and its constraints to the end, perhaps because of a basic distrust of the men in her life, her concern for appearances, and also because she felt that marriage entailed fetters that would restrict her lifestyle and professional growth.

In addition to worries about placing her book with a publisher, Painter's financial problems concerned her, as did her own. "I worry about Jack," she wrote, "wondering if I should send him money even at the risk of going broke myself."[24] She considered sending him funds on deposit in the Cody bank, but knew that she should keep that money in reserve to pay for taxes and home repairs. She decided that she "should" be able to help him as soon as she placed the serial rights to her book.

By 7 July 1918, Caroline's fortunes took a turn for the better; the publishing company of Small and Maynard informed her that they had decided to publish the Jezebel (Sheep Queen) manuscript. In addition, her father wrote saying that he would forward the $500 that he intended to send next fall, "but nothing else."

The admonishment from Joseph Lockhart piled rejection upon perceived rejection. Her deep-rooted dislike for her father, going back to the circumstances of his remarriage and what she had always considered as his abandonment of her for her stepmother, was an emotional scar that would never heal. The fact that he subsidized her financially over the years made little difference. On this particular occasion, she vented her anger on the pages of her journal. "I hate him," she raged. "Damn his mean little soul, with his $10,000 a year income refusing to help me to hang on until I can make advantageous terms. . . . I can't curse him enough when I think how he has always failed me when I needed his help."[25]

Even for a successful writer, making a living solely from one's income as a novelist had never been easy. And in 1918, Caroline Lockhart was not among the fortunate few who did. Periodically, she was forced to turn to journalism as a source of steady income. Once again she had to think of alternatives. "Somehow," she wrote, "I can't make up my mind to tackle New York newspaper work. But if I can get a job, I am wondering if I wouldn't find the Denver *Post* more congenial."[26]

When the contract from Small, Maynard and Company arrived, she was disappointed to find that it did not appear to be as liberal as Lippincott's, her previous publisher. A telegram from H. L. Mencken in New York advised her to go ahead and sign, if the offer seemed fair. "These parlor publishers," he warned, "that are all eagerness today are scared to death tomorrow."[27]

In New York by mid-July, Caroline rented a room at the Hotel Calumet and began making the rounds of her publishing acquaintances, including agents Mabel Lee, Laura Wilch, and Andrew MacLean, editor of the *Popular*. MacLean, a friend from her days as a short story writer, had some bad news. Her contract with the Small, Maynard and Company, he felt, was a bad one. The publishers offered 10 percent royalties but retained the serial and movie rights. In desperation, Caroline had accepted their terms, but now thought better of the decision. MacLean advised her to join the Author's League, which he thought should offer some leverage in dealings with the publishing company. After some negotiating, Small, Maynard and Company agreed to return the rights in question. Caroline was then able to take the manuscript to agents Brandt and Fitzpatrick, who helped her in placing serialization of the book. Brandt and Fitzpatrick, she found to her surprise, were women.

During the frustrating process of placing her manuscript, she came to terms with herself about taking a job with the Denver *Post*. The *Post*, she decided, would provide her the "congenial atmosphere" necessary for her to succeed. "It'll be good groundwork for my forthcoming book," she wrote in her Diary, "and make those who may squirm when they see themselves in it afraid to squeak." [28]

OBSERVATIONS ON THE EAST, SUFFRAGE, AND SELF

With the business of marketing her manuscript completed, Caroline looked forward to a return to Cody. After only three weeks in the East she had regained her appreciation for the West. She found the eastern attitudes of "narrow precision and perfect propriety" too constraining, and admitted frankly that "the atmosphere of decay and emptyness [sic]" was driving her "nutty." [29]

These impressions stand in startling contrast to attitudes expressed in an essay on Philadelphia written approximately fifteen years earlier, before she had adopted the West as her home. The article, although published in 1905, apparently was written just after her return from a trip abroad. Arriving at night in Philadelphia, she had taken a room at a hotel where her open windows admitted the shrill, piercing noises of city life: "the incessant striking of signal bells and weird, prolonged cries, such as might be produced in fairyland by the giant ogre playing—very badly indeed—on a giant fiddle with one string." [30]

At the time, the city noises failed to bother her; and in the residential areas, the old Quaker buildings set among luxuriant trees and high hedges appealed to her sensibilities. More than a decade later, however, after having enjoyed the West's wide open spaces, the East—and New

York City in particular—grated on her nerves. She found the city to be "over-powering, crushing" with a "noise and pandemonium" that was bewildering. The incomparable West, by contrast, she described poetically as a country where "the smoke goes up in a cloudless sky, where snow-tipped mountains and endless stretches of sagebrush fill the eye." [31]

From her vantage point as a staunch westerner, Caroline expressed her observations on the East in various perceptive and humorous articles. Sketches such as "From Billings to Broadway" and "When I Came Back to Philadelphia" show her to be an astute, if biased, observer.

In the Billings essay she lampoons the East, where individuality is lost as one is submerged in the "teeming masses of humanity." "Out in the sagebrush," says the westerner, "I know all the dogs to speak to for miles around and can tell who is in town by reading the brands on the horses tied to the hitching posts. I am an individual, an entity." On the other hand, when this same observer walks down Fifth Avenue dressed in the latest fashion from Billings, Montana, she feels like "a Worm with a capital W, and not even a wooly one at that. They did not know I was there!" she declares in amazement. "Even the hat that I would warrant a Crow Injun in killing me for the feathers never got a look. It is the sublime indifference of New York that makes one feel like a worm," she concludes. [32]

Humorously chiding New Yorkers for their rudeness and fast-paced lifestyle, Caroline told how she was nearly run over by a beer wagon. En route to visit the Museum of Natural History, the driver suddenly bore down upon her but was foiled in his "murderous purpose" by a "policeman's regal gesture and the sound of his whistle." She noted somewhat ironically, "I should dislike to come from the land of adventure to be killed by a beer wagon." [33]

After her timely escape, she proceeded down the road to "Bohemia," described as "a smelly one" where "the babel of tongues, the filthy street, . . the swarming of children . . . would put a Belgian Hare farm to blush." Eventually, all trails led to the Waldorf, which she characterized as "more than a hotel, it is an institution." There she saw the "Who's Who of America," as well as lesser beings, and was fascinated by the cosmopolitan world housed beneath its roof. She chuckled in sympathetic enjoyment over a conversation with an old lady sitting in the lobby.

With hands folded comfortably on her abdomen, the old lady declared: " 'Well, Pa has made all the money we need, so now I'm going out and spend it.' Ma rambled on: 'When my boy took us to the depot he said: 'Look here, Mother, you just cut loose now and rip up the sod.' "

Later, Caroline heard "Pa" giving directions regarding "Ma." " 'She's

down the hall there buying herself a $40 kimono. Get her out if you can—
I gave up an hour ago.' "[34]

At lunch, Caroline also overheard the conversation of three women
sitting at a table next to her. She noticed that the chief topics of discussion concerned how to dispose of that superfluous forty pounds and "Votes
for Women." Considering Caroline's liberal views on various subjects, her
comments on the tête-à-tête reveal a surprising position on the suffrage
issue: "The subject of that forty pounds is of absorbing interest," she admitted, "but forgive me if I yawn over 'Votes for Women.' Although there
is nothing quite so terrifying as a suffragist who is contradicted or who finds
a lukewarm member of her sex, yet I dare be neutral. Figuratively speaking,
I sit on the fence and say 'Sic 'em.' "

Caroline explained that since women in Wyoming had been given the
vote, she had not seen "the direful disasters" predicted to come to pass as a
result of suffrage. On the other hand, neither had she seen "the iridescent
dream of purity in politics . . . come true." "Going to the polls," she added,
"has not 'hardened' or 'demoralized' any woman of whom I know; nor has
her presence there noticeably 'elevated' any man of my acquaintance."

The major advantage to suffrage, from Caroline's perspective, was that
it provided women with something to discuss other than each other: "Instead of spending all their waking hours working over the neighbors, they
now devote a share of them to the candidates and the issues. The result
is undoubtedly broadening and beneficial." "God knows," she concluded,
"that's a powerful argument in favor of suffrage."

Despite its faults, she admitted that city life in the East did offer certain
advantages: "The City of Big Things lays hold of one powerfully. The fascination of its restless life gets into one's blood. Its spirit of enterprise and
of achievement is contagious. It inspires, stimulates, and educates, for the
best in every line of human endeavor gets eventually to New York."

In a self-revealing comment she added: "It has to offer what isolation
most lacks, congenial companionship, the sympathy of kindred spirits, the
understanding of similar minds and tastes." Yet, when weighed in the balance, the advantages of city life in the East, according to Caroline's scales,
did not measure up to the benefits of life in the West. Despite the lure of
the East, she maintained that "the smell of sagebrush after a rain" and "the
purple peaks . . . prove more potent than the brilliance of Broadway."[35]

July found Caroline back in Cody, having her house cleaned and making
plans for the move to Denver. She also renewed her relationship with O.B.
Mann, much to the despair of her devoted cowboy friend Jesse Mitchell.

The townspeople—with some exceptions—were pleased to have her back. "Everyone waves their hands at the exuberant Caroline," she wrote in her Diary. "Ye, Gods! If they could see my heavy heart. Well, s'help me, if my hand hasn't lost its cunning, I'll make good on the Denver *Post* and achieve the ambitious goal I've set for myself—to be the best known woman west of the Mississippi."[36]

As if in response to her aspirations, a telegram from T. C. Bonfils arrived, welcoming her to Denver. "My dear Caroline Lockhart," the message read, "you had better come on back West where you belong. We can certainly use you on the Denver *Post*. . . . The sooner you come, the better we will like it. You belong out here."[37]

By the end of December she was in Denver, alone, but looking ahead.

REPORTING FOR THE *POST*

On 6 November 1918, not long before her departure for Denver, Caroline Lockhart made a revealing entry in her journal: "So like Kate [the Fighting Shepherdess] in my story, I am thrown back on myself and life resolves . . . into my taking my medicine with the best face possible."[38]

Caroline excelled at putting on the best face possible—a facade that concealed a growing despair. Arriving in Denver around the first of December, she was—to outward appearances—the vivacious woman novelist who had just landed an important job on the Denver *Post.* But the vital, energetic image presented to the public contrasted sharply with the middle-aged woman who sat alone in her hotel room at night with a bottle of scotch and poured out her worries and heartache on the pages of her journal. More and more frequently, she drank herself to sleep, awakening in the morning to put on her hat and smile. Admissions in her Diary such as "Finished a bottle of scotch during the night," and "My forty-year-old scotch is going fast" revealed the seriousness of her emotional state.[39]

During the day, however, her busy professional life revolved around interviews, public functions, and the hurried production of stories to meet deadlines. At first she found the new job stimulating and enjoyed the visibility that it afforded her. News of her "celebrity" status filtered back to Cody, where her friend Dwight Hollister made a speech at the Irma Hotel saying that the town should be proud of her.[40]

In Denver, she became increasingly involved in the affairs of the mile-high city and in the lives of its better-known residents. Relying on talent and charm, she wangled interviews with people ranging from Governor Oliver Shoup—"a nice, friendly chap"—to a local judge, a bigamist, and a woman bandit. She liked the latter "immensely" and resolved to help, if possible. In addition to the busy round of interviews, she played Santa Claus to a needy family of three children deserted by their father and served on the Home Welfare Committee, greeting soldiers returning to the States after the armistice.

With the exception of the story on the judge, felt by her editors to be too controversial, she transformed each experience into good news copy. Her stories ran the gamut from the human-interest genre to those of a more serious vein, such as an article on the need for regulation of the meat-packing industry. For this particular story, she interviewed L. G. Phelps, owner of a 127,000-acre cattle ranch in Wyoming and a member of the National Livestock Association. Phelps, who was staying at the Brown Palace Hotel, had come to town to lobby for passage of the Kendrick Bill, which would impose a system of licensing for meat-packing houses and prevent them from establishing monopolistic control of the stockyards and refrigeration cars. Judging from her favorable coverage, Caroline shared the cattleman's views.[41]

Another article, also in a serious vein but presented in the inimitable Lockhart style, had as its moral the old axiom of "practice what you preach." In the post–World War I atmosphere, Herbert Hoover had just sent out a letter to the schoolchildren of America urging conservation of food and resources. "Many millions of people have been made free by our victory, but they are in the greatest danger of starvation," she quoted Hoover as saying. "Consequently, we must go on saving and sharing with them as faithfully as ever."

Simultaneous with this plea to the youngsters and their elders "to tighten their belts" came the announcement that President Woodrow Wilson and his wife were sailing to the peace conference at Versailles accompanied by an entourage of fifty chefs, pastry cooks, and confectioners from the best hotels in New York. The timing of the two events was too much for Caroline to resist. "Ahem!" she wrote: "We politely cover our mouths with our fingertips and cough gingerly. We cannot help wondering if food conservation, like the game laws, is always made for the other fellow?"[42]

Ironically, the worse her emotional state, the more humorous her stories became—a fact she herself acknowledged. "I have felt rotten for two weeks, yet never wrote funnier stories," she confided.[43] In an article about the Kaiser, for example, as punishment for his war crimes, Caroline suggested that he be shipped to Cody, Wyoming. "My home town would take care of him, all right," she claimed, and proposed that a select panel of Codyites be chosen to give the Kaiser his just rewards. Peter Nordquist "every morning before breakfast . . . could take two turns around the saddle horn with his throw rope and drag him awhile." Or, "he could go for a joy-ride thru

Shoshone canyon in 'Jedge' Wall's machine with the 'Jedge' at the wheel."
Then—if he returns—"with his hair snow white," they could "tie him in
a chair while the late Democratic candidate for governor, Frank L. Houx,
delivered one of his famous lectures on the evils of drink." And, "if he did
not laugh himself to death," as a last resort she suggested, "they could call
in the lady doctor to operate. The sound of her surgical knife being whetted on the stove-pipe would bring him to himself long enough to gasp—
'Oh, why did I do it?'"[44]

In addition to capitalizing on her hometown, Caroline used her personal
notoriety as a novelist for a source of material. A tongue-in-cheek feature
on story writing offered advice to aspiring authors and claimed that writing
fiction was "a cinch" if one learned the appropriate bromides: One must
simply remember that any woman who wears black velvet is always "regal";
all debutantes are "popular"; and "any musician able to claw the ivories
in public has a brilliant future." Pauses in conversation are always "awk-
ward"; kisses are "chaste," to distinguish them from the other kind; and
gazes should be "riveting." Snowfields are "great, white wastes," and no
character should be able to gaze at mountain scenery "without feeling that
he is an atom . . . in the presence of his maker." "Nuances" is a great word
to use, Caroline advised, because "it lends class" and because the average
reader has to look it up in the dictionary—"so use it when possible."[45]

In addition to showing her awareness of shopworn literary clichés, Lockhart subtly interjected her opinion on stereotypic images of women. "All
women," she wrote, "pout prettily" in fiction. "In real life, they look
like thunder," she added, "but don't let that deter you." Furthermore, "at
twenty-eight or thirty a woman must retain 'only a trace of youthful beauty,'
for 'time,' undoubtedly must be graying her hair at her temples." Neither
could she resist adding facetiously that members of her sex should also be
portrayed as "pure as driven snow," and "if unmarried, she must be bitterly
conscious that she is 'a failure as a woman.'" Finally, she concluded: "If
searching for a good ending, have your hero 'go silently into the night.'"
And as for the heroine, "start her off somewhere, to a desert or an isolated
cabin, 'to find herself,' so that she can return later to 'take up the broken
threads of her life.'"[46]

In the meantime, Caroline herself was trying to tie up the broken threads
of her own life. Not long after her lover O.B. Mann visited her in Denver,
she received a letter from him saying that he had met a "lady friend of the
South" and planned to marry her. Strangely enough, the woman's name
was Nan Lockhart. Heartsick, and angered by O.B.'s betrayal, Caroline
filled the pages of her Diary with despair: "God *damn* him, I hope he'll never

know a day's happiness from now on. How could he . . . accept my love and mean to do this all the time? What a snake!"[47]

When scotch and sleeping powders failed, Caroline visited a seer who told her that she should go to California where she would meet a good, successful man and be married within a period of months. More important, she would find happiness. The fortune teller surprised her by being able to identify O.B. Mann by his nickname "Ornery" and Caroline's profession as that of a newspaper woman.

Considering the publicity she had received in Denver, the latter should not have been difficult to do; but more interesting was the fact that the seer told Caroline that she was assisted in her work by "a woman of fine figure" who, she said, "is always with you helping you in difficulties of your work. Her name is Kate." When Caroline told her that she knew no such person, the seer offered another name: "Fields." Caroline recorded that she "nearly fell off her chair," for she realized that the seer meant Kate Fields, the famous journalist long since dead. The woman also told her that her Uncle Luther was watching her business interests and that her Aunt Caroline (both deceased) loved her very much.

"It was her giving the names that knocked me off my pins," she wrote: "I don't know what to think." Prophetically, the seer also told her that it was not her fate "to be loved right, like other women, in the conventional way."[48] Of this sad fact, Caroline was already becoming very much aware. On 20 March, Mann himself wrote to her verifying that he had indeed married his southern lady. Fortunately, Caroline's good friends, Maude and John P. ("Willie") Altberger, who had moved to Cody from the East, arrived in Denver for a visit and provided her with much needed support and friendship during this time.[49]

The arrival of her cowboy lover Jesse Mitchell also boosted her morale. A handsome man, despite the loss of an arm, Jesse came courting dressed in a new black suit, shirt, and necktie, looking "almost like a gentleman," in Caroline's estimation.[50]

After only three months working as a journalist for the *Post*, she tired of the daily regimen of producing copy. Other factors, however, contributed to her state of mind. She was irritated because a perfectly good story on Honduras was "killed by someone in typesetting," who tagged the article with what she considered "an utterly stupid headline." She admitted her discontent: "No fun, no exercise, no recognition of my stuff in the jumble of trash—it is wasted, lost."[51]

Unhappiness with the paper, her former lover, and life in general, indicated that it was time for a change of pace and scenery. Consequently, she decided to follow the advice of an eastern publisher and write a story on the oil-rich Osage Indians in Oklahoma. She saw this as an opportunity to get away from Denver, enjoy the outdoors, and be with Jesse, who would act as her guide and general assistant. She proposed the field assignment to the managing editor of the *Post* who thought it a "novel idea," and she made her plans. Jesse was to precede her "to get the lay of the land." [52] Unfortunately, they were not too specific about dates and meeting places.

LOSING A "PARDNER"

As part of the preparations for her field assignment, Caroline made an unsuccessful attempt to borrow money from her father: "I am going to 'touch' Papa for $500 advance, which will put me on easy street until my royalties are due," she wrote in her journal for 31 March 1919. She hoped "Papa" would meet her in Topeka, Kansas, but illness, ostensibly, kept him from making the trip. Her alternative was to borrow money from a bank in Kansas. [53] Within a day or two, she had reserved a berth on the Union Pacific railroad. By 3 April 1919, she arrived in Tulsa, Oklahoma, tired and irritable, becoming even more so when she discovered that Jesse was nowhere to be found. After a few fretful days in Tulsa, she decided to go to Pawhuska where she rented a "dark and cheerless" room at the local hotel. She and Jesse had talked about Pawhuska in their plans, so she figured that he may have understood that he should meet her there. Regardless, by this time she was furious, wondering if Jesse would ever show and cursing him for his lack of intelligence. Still depressed over the "philanderer" O.B. Mann, she considered suicide, but concluded in her journal entry that she was "not so desperate as that YET." [54]

The 15th of April rolled around and still no Jesse. She decided she must get on with her assignment, with or without him. Her plan was to find work as a hired girl for one of the wealthy Osage Indian families in the village. The editor of the Osage *Journal* gave her the name of a Native American who worked in the local bank and she, in turn, referred her to a couple of prospects. The next day, after gathering her courage, she succeeded in being hired as a cook for Chief Baconrind's wife, described by Caroline as "a fat, good-natured squaw with such a stomach as I never did see." This firsthand approach to "getting atmosphere," she knew from experience, was a "sure-fire way" to get a good story. [55]

The next day, Caroline donned her working dress and apron and found the residence of Chief Baconrind. The royalties on Baconrind's numerous oil wells allowed the family to have not one but two hired women.

The other servant, Hattie, was a surly young white woman who quickly established her seniority.

In the kitchen, Caroline found Baconrind's wife sitting on the floor with a quarter of beef in front of her. Without acknowledging the new hired help, she methodically chopped off hunks of meat with a long butcher knife and tossed them into a big iron pot. The sound of a car driving up elicited a grunt: "Go out and git the stuff," she ordered.[56]

Outside, Chief Baconrind stood majestically by his large Lincoln, which was filled to the roof with boxes and sacks full of goods. On the roof of the car, the Chief had lashed rolls of quilts and blankets—all of which Caroline got to pack in, while Baconrind strode ahead looking like the chief that he was. After the evening meal, eaten in shifts, the chief and his extended family prepared for a stomp dance, while the new hired woman tackled the stacks of dirty dishes. Although snubbed as "poor white trash" by both the Indians and Hattie, Caroline was allowed to tag along.[57]

At the dance, Baconrind took center stage. His face was painted vermilion and ochre, and on his head he wore a magnificent headdress of white-tipped eagle feathers. On his ankles, bells tinkled as he rhythmically stamped to the drum beat. None of the other dancers could compare with the splendor of Caroline's boss, and she reported that she was "almost thrilled to be associated with the noble house of Baconrind." But the excitement of the ceremonial failed to make up for the drudgery of endless chores. After one more day, she decided that she had collected enough "atmosphere" to last "for quite a spell."[58]

Her timing was fortunate, as it turned out, for the next day she got "canned," as she put it, for her bad attitude and for burning the biscuits. Despite this initial experience sometime between mid-April and the first of May, Caroline actually took on one more servant job with a Native American family and fared little better. "The Walking Irons," she summarily dismissed as "sons-of-bitches all."[59]

While Caroline was getting firsthand research for her story on the Osage Indians, Jesse finally caught up with her—"just like the story where everything comes out right in the end," she wrote. By 1 May, they had decided to buy a car and "go rambling around." Their plans were to camp out. "Thank God for a pardner like Jesse," she added. "I couldn't do this at all if it wasn't for him."[60]

Caroline, a tomboy at heart, kept an eye out for good campsites as they traversed the countryside. Each day they pitched their tent, built a campfire, and set the typewriter on a stack of wooden crates. Jesse cooked while Caroline typed. The dirt and squalor didn't faze her, nor did the leaky tent, purchased from a freighter. She worked steadily despite cold, rainy weather, eyes blurred by tears from the smoke, and feet that were at times uncomfortably clammy from the damp. "No matter," she wrote in her journal. "It is an experience and I am more content than at the Brown Palace in my luxurious loneliness."[61]

Roughing it was no handicap to Caroline's creativity. The words flowed. The outdoor environment sparked her descriptive talents and made her writing that much easier. Still smarting from O.B. Mann's rejection, she basked in the light of Jesse's love and devotion: "He is patient and kindness itself to me . . . so that's all I can expect of him and I am learning his limitations, which may be useful to me," she added pragmatically.[62]

By mid-May, Jesse and Caroline were back in Pawhuska, where they set up camp on the banks of the Arkansas River near Fairfax. That first evening they enjoyed a particularly beautiful sunset. The simple homelike atmosphere of the campsite, with a makeshift table and boxes arranged for her work and the fire for cooking, struck a responsive chord.

Caroline was developing a real feeling and appreciation for her "pardner," as she referred to him. Under her tutelage, Jesse had become "almost civilized," which meant clean-shaven and as neat as camplife would allow. His devotion and terms of endearment touched her deeply. She loved being petted and shielded. It was a welcome respite not to have to rely totally on herself. Jesse and the outdoors were having a healing effect on her—both body and soul. She was happier than she had been in years.

Then one morning Jesse crawled out of bed early with plans to catch a fish for their dinner. Before leaving, he kissed Caroline goodbye and headed toward the deep hole at the bend of Salt Creek. Later in the day, Caroline took time out from her work to make new covers for their pillows. While doing so, she experienced a strange feeling—almost a premonition. The afternoon turned into evening, and Jesse still had not returned. Filled with an unidentified anxiety, Caroline walked up the road to the spot where she and Jesse stood the previous evening enjoying the sunset. From there, she caught a glimpse of the car on the bank near the stream, shiny from the polish that Jesse had so industriously applied. But there was no sign of Jesse.

As she neared the big hole half a mile away, a sickening fear washed over her. She knew—without knowing—what had happened and ran down the road crying. A man crossing a field saw her and offered to get help. Soon Indians from the village joined the search. In her Diary, she described the scene as "a Belasco setting with the blood and sun behind the trees and the Indians in their bright blankets running along the high, green bank shouting 'Jesse, Jesse!'" Sick with grief and shock, Caroline collapsed. "I laid down in the grass and cried," she wrote, "weak and perspiring with grief and horror of the future without my pardner who had grown so dear to me." [63] She knew there was little hope that he would be found alive.

Meanwhile, rescuers dragged the Salt Creek hole. Two hours after the search began, they recovered the body. Caroline then had to face the questions of law enforcement officers and newspaper reporters. Ostensibly to protect her sister Grace and husband from being associated with the accident, Caroline told investigators that she was Jesse's sister, then learned to her consternation that Jesse had told people in Fairfax that she was his wife. The contradictory information caused the local officials, Sheriff S. V. M. Lewis and County Attorney Corbett Cornett, to conduct a detailed investigation. [64]

Cornett and Lewis arrived on Thursday morning to hold the inquiry. At the place where the body was found, the creek made a big bend. On the side next to the road, the bank dropped some ten to fifteen feet into a deep hole of water. Clearly visible footprints leading down the steep embankment to the small foothold just above the water told the story. There, the ground had caved in, apparently throwing the victim into the water.

Whether Jesse could swim or not was unknown; however, his right arm was shorter than normal and bore an ugly scar above the elbow. His left arm had been amputated between the elbow and wrist. A handicap such as this would have severely impeded his ability to pull himself up the steep embankment, even if he could swim. The evidence was clear: death by accidental drowning. [65]

With Jesse gone, Caroline returned to Pawhuska to take care of shipment of the coffin to relatives and to make arrangements to sell her car and return to Denver. In the two-week interim, while grieving for Jesse, she met a traveling photographer who immediately fell in love with her and asked her to marry him. Her Diary account of this brief episode—testimony to her personal magnetism—revealed the importance she placed on career: "Had a curious day with the picture man. He asked me to marry him. Too funny for words, the brilliant future he painted for us. Me giving up my literary career to write letters for him, sew on his buttons, and collect his laundry. God! How it started the tears and my heart ached to go to the camp at Fairfax where I cooked on the grate Jesse had fixed for me." [66] By 6 June she was back at the Brown Palace feeling lost and depressed. The trip of two-months' duration had cost her $1,000 and the life of the one man who loved her unconditionally, the one man she felt she could depend on. She now faced a dilemma.

Although she enjoyed the notoriety afforded her through her affiliation with the *Post*, she was tired of the regimen of meeting deadlines and working as a full-time journalist. Moreover, the past year had not been one of her best. O.B. Mann had jilted her, and when she found someone who really cared for her, he was taken away. Furthermore, the pieces of another novel were beginning to form a cohesive pattern in her imagination; she needed the creative environment of her Cody workshop. After a few days rest in Denver, she boarded the train for Cody.

Willie and Maudie Altberger met her at the station. Caroline found that they had had her house cleaned for her return. Her good friend "Altie" (Alta Booth Dunn) also paid her respects, as well as Bill Miller (Sergeant Valentine) de Colonna, who had just returned a hero from the war in Europe. "It was good to be home," she wrote.[67]

THE PRODIGAL RETURNS A CELEBRITY

Cody offered Caroline Lockhart a sense of place. Despite the controversy that her writing generated—and which she secretly enjoyed—the little town was "home." And although she was still unaccepted by the "better element," she had her own circle of friends. The support of these friends and the recognition accorded her for her writing abilities boosted her spirits and made the loss of Jesse easier to bear. At last she held center stage. Despite being well-known throughout the region and in the East, she had heretofore shared the limelight in Cody with Buffalo Bill, but his passing the previous year (10 January 1917) meant that she was now the town's celebrity-in-residence.[68]

Not long after her return from Denver, she went to Thermopolis on assignment for the *Post*. The town newspaper, the *Independent*, covered her visit in a front-page article, and at the local "cabaret," one of the townsmen stood on a table to introduce her to a cheering crowd. The sheepmen, in particular, raved about her book, *The Fighting Shepherdess*, while the band played a waltz in her honor.[69]

Her fortunes also took a turn for the better. Not long after her triumphant reception in Thermopolis, she heard that Small, Maynard and Company had sold the film rights for the Shepherdess book to well-known movie star Anita Stewart, for $2,700. Furthermore, Douglas Fairbanks, actor and producer, offered her $10,000 for a western scenario from which his staff planned to develop a suitable film script. A local reporter quoted Fairbanks as saying: "Miss Lockhart is the one western writer that can give . . . something original." The reporter added his own plaudits: "Our local authoress is to be congratulated on her sudden rise to fame, which is a fitting reward for her continued and honest efforts to place before the public a true depiction of the real westerner."[70]

When the movie premiered in Cody, the film broke the record for at-tendance. The line of people waiting to get in blocked the street. Caroline enjoyed the notoriety, but the film's portrayal of pioneers of the sagebrush country made her angry. She found particularly offensive the scene where women were shown wearing "dowdyish, ill-hanging clothes with loud fig-ures." The reporter covering the story for the *Enterprise* noted that the authoress "suffered in silence"—but not for long.[71]

Characteristically, Caroline made her opinions known. The casting, she said, was "derogatory and unrealistic." Except for the hero and heroine, she didn't see "an intelligent face in the crowd." In reality, the authoress claimed, "nearly half of the cowpunchers of the early eighties were Harvard or Yale men, or young men from good eastern families."[72]

Despite her irritation, she made the best of the affair by hosting an "after-movie" party and dance for friends and out-of-town guests. Harry O'Donnell and Terry E. Barefield came over from Elk Basin, and Ralph Smith from Meeteetse. Others attending were Frances Phelps Belden and her husband Charles, Mr. and Mrs. Blen Holman, Mr. and Mrs. Edwin E. Dunn, Helen Davis and her husband Eugene Phelps, Caroline's friends Maude and Willie Altberger, Dwight and Orilla Hollister, Charles Hensley of Burlington, and Canyon Smith of Frannie.[73]

Her reaction to the film depiction of her novel reflected strongly held views that were evolving into a new crusade—a crusade that would add controversy to an already contentious life. Having lived and traveled in the region for more than a decade, her insights had broadened. She was completing *The Dude Wrangler*, a book that revealed her recognition of a West in transition. The changes she wrote about were especially apparent in Cody, where she saw a rising tide of eastern influence being generated by a vocal contingent of easterners who equated urbanization with progress. In opposition stood an equally outspoken sector who felt that the old ways were best. It was a situation with potential for political volatility.

These years were to be significant for Lockhart in other respects. In the halls of Congress, legislation was enacted that would add another colorful chapter to her life and career. The Volstead Act, which provided the en-forcement apparatus for Prohibition via the Eighteenth Amendment, was ratified on 29 January 1919 and became the focal point of still another con-suming personal crusade. Lockhart regarded the act making illegal the sale of liquor as a "travesty," an abuse of individual freedom and the rights of the individual.

With Prohibition scheduled to go into effect by 16 January 1920, she planned to "mourn" the new era by attending a rousing Prohibition party. Until the repeal of the Volstead Act, the beautiful mahogany bar that graced her living room would be draped in black. On that illustrious eve, however, she was belle of the ball. Escorted by Bill Miller de Colonna and joined by friends, Caroline whooped it up "until America ran dry at midnight." Len Leander Newton, editor of the *Herald* and a member of the Methodist church, made pointed reference in print to the disgraceful "rowdyism" that took place at a local hotel on the eve of Prohibition.[74]

Thus, by the time Caroline celebrated her fiftieth birthday, she had become involved in two new campaigns. As an ardent opponent of Prohibition and as a spokesperson for those who sought to preserve the ways of the West, she would increase her notoriety throughout the region and the nation. The next period of her life, therefore, was to be characterized by a journalistic activism directed toward the demise of Prohibition and the preservation of what she felt to be the best of the Old West. In both cases she employed her writing and promotional talents to good advantage.

THE DUDE WRANGLER

By the second decade of the twentieth century, the West could boast of a booming new industry that began to play a significant role in the region's development—dude ranching. Wyoming, as one of the northern strongholds of the industry, along with Montana and Colorado, would profit from this particularly western adaptation of the nation's vacation business.

The impetus for the dude-ranching industry can be traced to the advent of World War I, which made European vacations impractical, if not impossible. The war and the temper of the times following those years encouraged people to look to the West for rest and recreation. By the 1920s, dude ranching had entered its greatest growth period.

Whereas the word "dude" generally carried a derogatory connotation meaning "tenderfoot" or "greenhorn," the term "dude ranch" simply meant a resort or residence where a visitor would be offered food, lodging, and entertainment for a fee. The introduction of this new industry to the West not only stimulated the economy, it also promoted conservation of the area's scenic beauty and brought more women to the area, both as guests and as owners.

Considered as an entity, the dude ranchers were pioneers; although, as Lawrence R. Bourne observes, they came "later than most recognized pioneer groups." Nevertheless, Bourne maintains: "[They] were true pioneers; they opened the West, although not in the same way as the mountain men, or miners, or soldiers. But they did see the land in a new way, with a clear vision."[75]

In 1911, one of the most famous of these pioneers came to Cody as a dude himself and later returned to become a well-known dude rancher and conservationist. Irving H. (Larry) Larom, like Caroline Lockhart, had his interest in the West whetted by a performance of "Buffalo Bill's Wild West and Congress of Rough Riders of the World." The show, featuring the great scout himself, added action and a human element to the beauty of the western scenes Larom had so admired in paintings by Albert Bierstadt and other artists.

After several visits to the West, Larom and his friend Winthrop Brooks in 1915 purchased Valley Ranch, a seventy-five-acre homestead of spectacular beauty near Yellowstone National Park on the South Fork of the Shoshone River. There they began by raising cattle and entertaining friends from the East. Eventually, the operation grew into a full-fledged dude ranch encompassing 8,000 acres of owned or leased land. In 1918, Larom left the ranch in the capable hands of his partner and joined the army. After the war, he returned and married Irma Elizabeth Dew of Cody.

Over the years, the Valley Ranch expanded to include special programs for teenagers and a college preparatory school for boys. In 1926, Larom bought out his partner's interest in the ranch and became increasingly active in the promotion and organization of the Dude Ranchers' Association and conservationist activities. Along with Caroline Lockhart and others, Larom in 1917 was also instrumental in founding the Buffalo Bill Memorial Association and, later, the Cody Stampede.[76] Lockhart, in fact, shared Larom's views on conservation and his appreciation for western artifacts and Indian culture. Like him, she saw the positive aspects of dude ranching for the West.

During the years 1915–18, when Larom and Brooks were first establishing their ranch, Cody and its residents were still a major source of material for Caroline's literary endeavors. It is not surprising, therefore, to find her using the easterner's success story as a prototype for a novel on the subject. With publication of The Dude Wrangler in 1921, Lockhart, who had written novels featuring outlaws, cattlemen, sheepherders, and miners, acknowledged the place of dude ranchers as latter-day pioneers.[77] This book, which speaks well of the author's highly developed sensitivity to cultural change, also reflects her insight into the factors contributing to the acceptance and popularity of dude ranching.

The novel features three major characters: Helene Spenceley, the girl from Wyoming; Pinkey Fripp, the ex-soldier and cowboy from the same state; and "Wallie" [Wallace] MacPherson, the foppish easterner who becomes a dude rancher in the West. The story starts out at the Colonial

Hotel in Florida, where all three meet for the first time. Analyzing the societal temper of the postwar era, Lockhart speaks through the hotel proprietor:

> Pacifying disgruntled guests was now as much a part of the daily routine as making out the menus. . . . Threats to leave were of common occurrence. . . . The only way in which we could explain the metamorphosis was that the guests were imbued with a spirit of discontent that prevailed throughout the world in the years following the war.[78]

She then explains how dude ranchers, capitalizing on this discontent, lured dudes to the West with advertisements that spoke of "air . . . so invigorating that languor was unheard of" and of scenery of "such a variety that the eye never wearied"; of "salt baths that made the old young again"; of "big game in the mountains for the adventurous"; of fishing opportunities; and—last but not least—of the beautiful Yellowstone Park.[79]

As the novel develops, Wallie MacPherson, motivated by the beauty of Helene Spenceley and the need to prove himself, decides to accompany his friend Pinkey to Wyoming. There he stakes a 160-acre homestead in the middle of a wealthy rancher's spread. He tries farming, but his crop is overrun by a herd of the rancher's cattle. Through numerous trials and tribulations, Wallie the tenderfoot grows into a tough, courageous westerner. The theme is familiar to the western regionalist. As Fred Erisman has explained in his study of writers and the uses of "place": "The West fuels ambition."[80]

Among the numerous episodes charting Wallie's metamorphosis is a rowdy escapade into town where he and Pinkey partake of Mr. Tucker's homemade cache of raisin-and-brown-sugar brew. But the most significant scene occurs when the easterner rescues the rancher from drowning and, in the process, wangles repayment for damages to his property. It is this grub-stake that provides Wallie and Pinkey the means to set up their dude ranch, which they figure is the only thing—other than sheep—that can flourish amid the aridity, salt-water wells, and generally harsh but picturesque environment.

The cast of characters becomes more colorful as Wallie's former friends from the Colonial Hotel travel West to be his first guests at the Lolabama Dude Ranch. Among them is Miss Mercy Lane. In this character, the reader once again meets Caroline's favorite real-life antagonist, the Lady Doc. The passage of ten years has in no way diminished Caroline's intense dislike for Frances Lane.

To make sure that there is no case of mistaken identity—and almost as if daring the Lady Doc to file a libel suit against her—Caroline not only uses the physician's real last name but facetiously gives the character the first name of "Mercy." Leaving no room for error, the novelist describes Mercy Lane as a trained nurse, who has a "booming contralto voice," and wears "a masculine hat with a quill in it and a woollen [sic] skirt that bagged at the knees like trousers."[81] In addition to bearing a physical resemblance to the real Frances Lane, "Shady Lane"—as Caroline calls her—shows disquieting personality traits, like the Lady Doc of her earlier novel. In one scene, for example, Caroline writes that Miss Mercy "caught a butterfly . . . and pulled off first one wing and then the other in spite of Aunt Lizzie's entreaties." Presently, the woman "dropped it on the bottom of the surrey and put her astonishingly large boot on it. . . . 'There,' she snickered, 'I squashed it.'"[82]

Another character integral to the plot is the highly prized cook, Mr. Hicks, who, after being insulted by the guests, resolves to avenge himself. Methodically, the sly Mr. Hicks manages to drive off all of Wallie's dudes with his malicious antics—such as enticing the fat Mrs. Budlong to go swimming in a pool filled with leeches, and baiting a bear to attack Mr. Stokes.[83]

Throughout this novel—unlike her others—Caroline's major female character, Helene Spenceley, plays a rather low-key heroine. Helene simply appears now and then from the sidelines to pass judgment on Wallie's metamorphosis into a tough westerner worthy of her love and respect.

Finally, the cook successfully completes his campaign of harassment. All the dudes desert the West for the more civilized environs of the Colonial Hotel in Florida, and Wallie (who by this time has earned the right to be called "Wallace") sells his land to the rancher for "a magnificent sum," marries Helene, and goes into the sheep business. Friend Pinkey becomes his foreman.[84]

In The Dude Wrangler, her sixth novel, Caroline Lockhart makes a literary statement that records her recognition of how the West was changing. When she had first arrived in Cody shortly after the turn of the century, she carried with her a mixed cultural baggage that enabled her to look at the small town and its residents from the cosmopolitan perspective of one who had been a world traveler and an eastern city dweller. Underneath the acquired veneer, however, was the Kansas ranch girl whose innate appreciation for the West continued to grow.

This background, combined with her extraordinary experiences as a reporter, provided her with the insight and expertise necessary to produce in one decade six novels featuring a panorama of pioneers illustrating the cultural evolution and settlement of the West. In retrospect, the Me-Smiths,

Mormon Joes, Sheep Queens, and mining men—if not displaced—were forced to move over for the newest pioneers, the dudes from the East. And in the transition, as her novels so pointedly show, not only the "places" (the small towns) but also the people were changing. By recognizing (as Erisman has proposed) that "place has a human component," Lockhart transcended the local-colorist approach to join the ranks of the true regionalists.[85]

Of all her novels, *The Dude Wrangler* is particularly effective in illustrating how "place" influenced and directed the lives of those who lived there. This view—like that of Willa Cather, Mari Sandoz, and more-contemporary regionalists John Graves and Paul Horgan—hints at a basic geographic determinism.

At the time Lockhart's books were published, their highly readable and humorous style made them best sellers, read for their entertainment value. Then, like many popular books of a specific era, they were largely forgotten. For the student of western culture, however, the novels as a series have a lasting value because of the author's ability to capture the evolutionary process taking place. Moreover, the careful reader will find, under the biting characterizations and sometimes wicked humor, traditional moral and intellectual statements of the times.

Published in 1921, *The Dude Wrangler* would be Caroline's last novel for more than a decade. A journalist at heart, she had turned once again to the newspaper world.

The Iconoclast

The policy of this paper is to uphold the standards and perpetuate the spirit of the Old West.

Caroline Lockhart, The Cody *Enterprise*

THE PARK COUNTY *ENTERPRISE:* 1920–21

For Caroline Lockhart, the turn-of-the-twenties decade was a busy time of new beginnings. She rallied after a bout of depression that always seemed to descend like a cloud around Christmas and darken as her birthday approached in February. In early spring she left on a marketing trip that took her to Portland, Oregon, then to California. By March she was in Los Angeles, where she met with actress Anita Stewart and her agent. Lockhart had her picture taken with the star and completed her business. Before leaving, however, she had to have five teeth extracted, which caused her to wonder "what if anything will come out of my six weeks of misery in Los Angeles."[1] Back in Cody by April, she learned from local businessman William S. "Doc" Bennett that the Park County *Enterprise* was for sale—news that started her thinking.

Founded by William Frederick Cody and "Colonel" Peake in 1899, the *Enterprise* epitomized the American frontier newspaper. Its pages featured a plethora of local events, whimsical advertisements, and a smattering of state affairs. In Lockhart's estimation, the paper was a "dreary sheet."[2] But for her purposes, it had possibilities.

She explained her motives: "I thought it might be an outlet for my superfluous energy," she wrote in her autobiography, adding that she felt she could "inject a little color and life into it." More significantly, the Eighteenth Amendment was then in effect. "I was opposed to the prohibition law on general principles," she said, "and hoped I might contribute my two-bits worth toward getting this preposterous statute off the books."[3]

Accompanied by Bennett, she investigated the plant facilities on 30 April 1920. From where she stood, in front of a long hitching rack at the edge of a gravel sidewalk, Caroline saw a nondescript two-story frame structure listing noticeably to starboard. A sign on the high false front identified the building as home of the Park County *Enterprise,* one of the town's two local papers.[4]

The fly-specked windows and unimpressive facade failed to dampen the interest of the prospective buyers, who arranged to meet again. This time Irving H. Larom of Valley Ranch, Sid A. Eldred, and Charles M. Conger joined them. Both Conger and Eldred had been affiliated with the paper previously. Negotiations moved rapidly. Together the group, which included Caroline, successfully outbid Louis G. Phelps of the Pitchfork Ranch near Meeteetse, and on 12 May 1920, the *Enterprise* carried the official announcement of a change in ownership. The paper's policy statement, signed by W. S. Bennett, sounded little like Caroline Lockhart:

> It is our aim to publish a live, accurate 'home' paper which shall be independent politically and sincere in its treatment of the public. Americanism shall be our watchword and keynote rather than an acknowledgement of any political affiliation.[5]

If Lockhart had a hand in composing the paper's *credo,* she must have done so with tongue in cheek. Although she would not be the paper's first major contributor, she would sprinkle the pages of the *Enterprise* liberally with salty humor and mark it indelibly with her irreverent journalistic style.

Under Lockhart's influence, the "Americanism" referred to in the paper's policy statement would take on a distinctly western flavor. She would successfully add "color" to the "dreary sheet" and also to the faces of those who did not share her views. She would be "independent politically"—blatantly anti-Prohibition, that is—and she would be "sincere" in her treatment of the public. In a time when libel and slander laws packed little wallop, Caroline wrote whatever she chose. As part owner, and eventually as ramrod and editor, she permitted no sacred cows, or even bulls, in the Cody corral.

During the next few years, she divided her attention between problems associated with establishment of a financially sound newspaper, promotion of an annual frontier celebration, and the building of a memorial honoring "Buffalo Bill" Cody. All activities were closely related; but the *Enterprise* would be her common denominator, the "voice" that allowed her to work toward her goals to do away with Prohibition and promote the Old West.

THE CODY STAMPEDE AND BALL

In the same month that Lockhart and partners purchased the Park County *Enterprise,* preparations began in earnest for the annual frontier festivities.

Volunteers constructed a dance pavilion, called "Wolfville," and set up exhibits and games of chance around the perimeter. West of town, cowboys wearing brightly colored bandanas practiced riding, roping, and bulldogging. On the sidelines, ladies in long, divided skirts and high-top shoes braved the dust and dirt to watch and cast admiring glances. A row of prestigious, if primitive, box seats ran across the front of the grandstands. Valley Ranch, with its large contingent of dudes, traditionally reserved a special box along the eastern end of the grounds. The box seats, which quickly became status symbols, were jealously guarded.[6]

In the past, Cody residents had held smaller frontier-type celebrations—county fairs, the Red Lodge Dances, and in 1919, the three-day Entrance Celebration. That year on 23–25 June, townspeople and visitors, using the slogan "Powder River: Let 'er Buck," celebrated the opening of the eastern entrance to Yellowstone National Park—an event that signaled the beginning of the year's travel and tourist trade.[7]

Lockhart and others of similar persuasion saw these events as a positive trend. Such festivities, they realized, would provide an opportunity to promote the area, preserve the region's culture, and serve as a fitting memorial to the town's founding father.

By 5 May 1920, the annual celebration boasted a new name, "The Cody Stampede," and a formally organized association to promote it.[8] The success of the affair was largely due to the hard work and promotional abilities of the association's charter members, and to Caroline Lockhart in particular. Former association officer, Ernest Goppert explained the situation: "The Cody Club did not support the Stampede that first year. For some reason, everyone was in favor of the Stampede, but no one wanted to do any work. Caroline Lockhart took the thing over."[9]

Planned for the Fourth of July, the celebration was officially announced in the Park County *Enterprise* and bore the Lockhart brand:

Cody Boosters Plan Annual Frontier Event, Spirit of Old West to be Preserved and the Yip of the Cowboy to Drown the Honk of the Tin Lizzie for Three Whole Days.[10]

The article also announced officers for the newly formed association: Caroline Lockhart, president; Sid A. Eldred, secretary; and Ernest J. Goppert, treasurer. Irving H. Larom, William Loewer, and Clarence Williams were to serve as directors. At the outset the new president's attitude was positive: "Larom is keen on the Stampede, and I think he and I and Goppert will work together like triplets," she wrote in her Diary.[11]

As spokesperson and president, Lockhart expressed the association's philosophy as simply to preserve "some of the Old West that we love." "And surely," she continued, "there is no more fitting place in America for exhibitions of cowboy skill and valor than right here in Buffalo Bill's town at the foot of the Rockies." The organization's objective was therefore twofold: "To . . . [keep] alive the spirit of the West and perpetuate the memory of our late honored townsman, Colonel W. F. Cody." Stock subscriptions for the Stampede Association, offered at $10 per share, came in rapidly, a response that Lockhart claimed "Shows Community Love for the Good Old Days." [12]

With Lockhart as the first president of the Cody Stampede Board—a position to which she would be re-elected for six years—the new association did not lack for publicity. Her abilities were put to good use and ranged from contributing ideas for acts and exhibits to writing articles and designing advertising posters. To encourage stockholders in the association, she humorously appealed to her reader's aesthetic sensibilities. Subscribers would not only be supporting a worthy cause, she claimed, but the certificates, framed, "will brighten the walls of your home and lend an air of wealth and culture; in sickness they may be applied as a plaster to the parts affected; in winter they can be worn as a chest protector." [13] In sum, the Cody Stampede stock certificates were indispensable.

Such tactics were highly successful. That first year, according to treasurer Goppert, "The Stampede paid a 10 percent dividend." Credit for the success of the Stampede as a business venture, Goppert said, "went to Lockhart, despite the fact that she insisted on paying out $500 for a feature act involving an automobile stunt that failed." "That was the biggest scrap [over the Stampede] I ever had with Caroline," he added. "It made me sore as hell; I had to pay that." [14] Nevertheless, a total of $2,215 in donations was collected by the time the Stampede opened on the Fourth of July. [15]

The dispute over finances would be merely one of several well-publicized disagreements between Caroline and the up-and-coming young lawyer. Goppert, who counted among his friends Dr. Frances Lane, hailed from Belleville, Kansas, where he had "attended court as much as high school." As a young man, he moved to Wyoming and passed the bar exam. When World War I was declared, he joined the service and afterward resumed the practice of law in Worland. At the invitation of Judge William Walls, Goppert came to Cody in January 1919 to take over the practice when Walls was appointed state attorney general. The *Enterprise* for 14 July 1920 carried Goppert's photograph in his World War I uniform with a caption announcing his candidacy for "Prosecuting Attorney, Republican Party." "Although young in the legal game," the reporter (possibly Caroline) wrote, "he enjoys a considerable practice and is not afraid to speak his mind when occasion demands." [16]

Goppert was elected to the post of county attorney, and as such, he would be responsible for enforcing the Prohibition law—a position that would place him in political conflict with Caroline Lockhart. In the interim, however, he and other members of the association worked to make the Stampede an annual and paying affair.

The drawing card for the first Cody Stampede was Pinkie Gist, champion bulldogger. Caroline, who counted Pinkie among her numerous men friends, persuaded the rodeo star to give up a previous billing out-of-state to come to Wyoming and help launch the Stampede. The purses that first year were respectable: $200 for the women's saddle horse race; $150 for the one mile free-for-all; $500 for the bucking horse competition; and $335 for bulldogging, among other awards. Other performers at the early Stampedes included champion Roman rider Ralph McCulloch, bronco-buster Earl Hayner, relay winner Roy Stambaugh, and the two Coleman brothers of Sheridan, Lloyd and George. In 1921, Tim McCoy, the famous cowboy actor and movie star, was the featured guest performer.[17]

To make sure that all the essential elements were present, Caroline issued a special invitation to Indians from the Crow Reservation. Crow Chief Joseph Plenty Coups (as well as his wife and friends) were invited to stay in Caroline's home as her personal guests. She didn't object to her Indian friends' cultural habits, but she did note that her good perfume dwindled rapidly during their stay. The visitors gave Caroline a special name "Its-Be-Che-Loti" (White Woman Chief), and she developed a special friendship with Other Buffalo, Plenty Coup's wife. The Crow Indians became regular performers at the Stampedes.[18]

The earliest celebrations featured such exciting and dangerous events as a wild-cow milking contest and a wild-horse race where cowboys, working in pairs, rode mustangs counterclockwise around a track. Josh Deane's barbecue was another drawing card. Funded by various stockmen who provided steers or donated money, the barbecue was held originally at the city park.

As Caroline noted in the *Enterprise*, Josh became famous for his barbecues and approached his job with meticulous ceremony, a process he generously shared with readers of the *Enterprise*. The entire procedure, Deane explained, "took just 30 hours if the wind don't blow." Caroline concluded the article with her own accolades: "Long after Josh is dust he will be remembered for the oxen he roasted, and the children's children of the present generation will listen with watering mouths to accounts of the barbecues over which he presided."[19]

Another memorable feature of the first Stampede was a stagecoach rescue. Pursued by Indians, the stagecoach rumbled down Main Street until the rescuers prevailed. According to the scenario, one of the passengers, a young widow, Mrs. Jack Stone, was grabbed from the Indians by John "Blocker" Dodge. Holding the girl under one arm on the left side of his horse, Dodge galloped up to Judge Howard Brundage, who married the couple on the spot.[20]

During the Lockhart years of leadership, the annual affair became a well-established local institution despite the lack of support from certain elements and power plays designed to change management of the association. Although supporters of the event included such civic-minded individuals as Ernest Goppert and Jake Schwoob (elected vice-president of the association in 1922), the Cody Club, as Goppert indicated, was not numbered among them.[21] Marjorie Ross, companion of Dr. Frances Lane, led the opposition.

Before the second Stampede could be held, Marjorie Ross attempted to have club members pass a resolution asking that management of the association be turned over to another organization. But the resolution was voted down. Caroline regarded such actions as the equivalent of a declaration of war and Ross as the enemy. As always, Lockhart attacked frontally and publicly. "The above incident," she wrote in the *Enterprise*, "moves us to ask what in particular is gnawing on Miss Marjory [sic] Ross? In the two years that we have been obliged to ask the public for money to pay the initial expenses for the Stampede, we have yet to see Miss Margie's handwriting upon the business end of a check."[22]

When Ross went a step further by publishing in the Northern Wyoming *Herald* a resolution asking that the next Stampede be conducted "in accordance with law and order," Caroline got tougher. "We cannot but wonder," she responded pointedly, "where Miss Ross was that she saw so much during former Stampedes that she felt such a request necessary. We are very sure that Miss Ross was not insulted by any visitor, drunk or sober, for we are confident that Miss Ross is one of those women who could go anywhere in the world without fear of molestation from the opposite sex." Finally, noting that it was not possible to conduct a Wild West show "along the lines of the Chautauqua Assembly," Lockhart added: "On the whole, the Cody Stampede is as orderly an affair as may be found anywhere in the country, and conducted in a fashion which is wholly satisfactory to everybody except the Meddlesome Marjories of both sexes."[23]

Lockhart numbered among those "Meddlesome Marjories" of the opposite sex Len Leander Newton, editor of the Northern Wyoming *Herald*. Noting that Newton had published an article titled "Humane Society May Stop Cody Stampede," she translated by saying: "What Mr. Newton really means is that *he* would like the humane society to stop the Cody Stampede." Caroline noted that he was joined in this complaint by

> a merchant who probably reaps as much or more direct benefit from the Stampede than any one person in Cody, but who, like Mr. Newton, and his dwindling coterie, would rather wreck somethin' . . . and sacrifice their own and the town's interests, than to see it succeed under the management of some person or persons for whom they have a feeling of personal enmity.[24]

Getting to the crux of the matter, she reminded readers that the mistreatment of animals simply was not tolerated. Moreover, a representative of the State Humane Society had attended the Stampede for the last two years, she reported, "at the express invitation of the Committee."[25]

Caroline's personal love for animals was well known. Touched by the magic of the horseman, she herself was a familiar figure clad in long divided skirt and Stetson hat as she rode her buckskin horse "Sonny" at the head of the Stampede Parade. On horseback she struck an impressive figure, exuding a certain power and grace.

The association's mascot, "Miss Cody Stampede," was another of Caroline's pets. Wampus or "Wampie," as her master affectionately called her, was a bobcat. Caroline discovered her starving on a chain in a taxidermist's backyard, bought her, and brought her home. "I gradually tamed her," she wrote, "and shortly she was sleeping on the bed . . . purring in my ear like a sewing machine."[26] For exercise, Caroline put Wampie on a chain attached to the clothesline which permitted the animal to run up and down. The bobcat also accompanied her on outings, as on the day they visited Thermopolis. This particular visit earned Wampus a reputation as a healer of rheumatism when he clawed the screen off a window at the Washake Hotel, where they were staying, and got into the room of an old gentleman. "When the varmint appeared in the room," noted the reporter for the *Enterprise*, "the patient concluded that his rheumatism wasn't so bad after all and got out of his wheelchair and walked."[27]

Caroline's novels and short stories also reflected her appreciation for animals. In *Me-Smith*, for example, she characterized the outlaw's dark side by describing the man's cruelty to his horse. And the theme of her short story, "Never a Redeeming Trait," first published in *Popular Magazine* in 1929, centered around humane treatment of the horse and the boy's love for the animal. But Lockhart's appreciation extended beyond horses and bobcats to more exotic creatures as well, such as a pet skunk called "Whiffy," an eagle named "Uncle Sam," and a boa constrictor who had the run of the house. When the pet boa constrictor crawled out of the sofa cushions and into the lap of a visiting friend, the woman moved her belongings to the local hotel.[28]

Caroline directed literary tirades against "poachers" from the East who killed only for recreation, and she protested strongly a campaign by the Montana Fish and Game Department to exterminate bobcats. "I like varmints—four-legged," she began:

> Every man's hand is against them and his one thought is to kill them. Consequently, he never knows them, much less comes to like or even love them. Now I wince when I read that the Fish and Game Dept. is out to exterminate them for it reminds me of my lynx cat "Ampie" [sic] who once ate and slept with me.[29]

Considering her penchant for animals of various types, Lockhart's reaction to Newton's criticism is not surprising. With Caroline as spokesperson, the Stampede was in little danger of being closed down—by the Humane Society, Len Leander Newton, or Marjorie Ross.

While the frontier aspects of the Cody Stampede were generally held around the Fourth of July, the Stampede Ball was held on 28 October, despite blizzard conditions. Chief Plenty Coups and the Crow Indians graciously accepted Caroline's invitation to attend—"the weather and his rheumatism permitting."[30]

Entertainment that year featured the Red Lodge Orchestra with Mary Quilico on the "accordeen." Echoing Owen Wister's scene in *The Virginian* in which the cowboys switch babies, Lockhart promoted the event in the *Enterprise*, announcing that a "baby wrangler" and a room for herding the tots would be provided so mothers could dance. "Everyone can bring their papoose and be sure of getting the same one back," Caroline assured them. The event took place in the Irma Hotel barroom, where the cosmopolitan array of guests "lent a League of Nations flavor to the affair." Crow tribesmen in paint and war bonnets danced with Anglo women in evening gowns, while cowboys squired Indian women in blankets around the dance floor.[31]

Support from the townspeople for the annual frontier festivities began to increase in correlation to economic benefit, but the basic sociological dichotomy remained. Tom Ames of Valley Ranch, speaking before the Cody Club, expressed his view of the situation. "The name of the town itself, 'Cody,'" he maintained, "is a great and natural advertisement, and one that should be lived up to." He proposed an all-out effort to maintain the town in its rustic state, "with more riders, indians [sic], big hats, etc., and a general wild and wolly [sic] atmosphere." He acknowledged that such an environment might sound like fiction to transplanted middle westerners who arrived in Cody and tried to convert it to a replica of a small town in Iowa; but, he added pragmatically: "The western regalia induces tourists to linger while here, and spend their money." [32]

During its lengthy history, the Stampede survived the Great Depression—a time when financial strain severely limited donations—and a suspension during the war years. In the thirties, to escape a 20 percent amusement tax levied by the federal government, Stampede officials had turned the affair over to the American Legion. In actuality, however, management of the Stampede still rested with the community. When more prosperous times returned, the show was again acknowledged officially as a community project and it reverted to its previous status. Restrictions on materials and a shortage of contestants, many of whom were fighting in the war, resulted in a decision not to hold the Stampede during the years 1943–45. By 1946, however, the Cody Stampede Association was back in business. [33]

The Cody Stampede and Ball still thrive today, attesting to the longlasting success of the idea, first promoted by Lockhart and her associates. While present-day visitors to Cody see a country club and a collection of modern homes atop the bluffs above the city, along Main Street below, the Irma Hotel and many of the stores appear as if caught in a time warp. Reallife cowboys work and reside on nearby ranches. In well-worn boots and sweat-stained hats, they frequent the stores and small cafes, have a beer in the bars, or dance at night at the local cabarets. In Cody, it is perhaps easier than elsewhere to provide tourists a glimpse into the past.

Over the Fourth of July, the town is spruced up and its westernness exaggerated. The Stampede festivities lend a temporary Hollywood-like luster to the town and its people, but a rich patina of western reality lies just beneath the surface. The "scissorbills," as Lockhart labeled the "encroachers from the East," have made slow inroads in Cody.

AT THE HELM OF THE CODY *ENTERPRISE:* 1921–25

With her novel *The Dude Wrangler* completed and the Cody Stampede well established, Lockhart began to pay more attention to the *Enterprise*. What she observed did not please her. It was becoming more and more apparent that Sid Eldred knew little about the business. The quality of the publication, she felt, reflected his lack of experience. "The purpose of our purchase is to improve the paper and he has demonstrated he is only an amateur," she fretted. Eldred's numerous literary faux pas, such as placing an obituary in the middle of the front page, encouraged the owners to appoint a new editor. Lockhart seemed to be the logical choice.[34]

In reality, however, she knew less about the actual running of a publishing business than did the man she wanted removed. Although she had been associated with the newspaper world since an early age, her function in the field until 1920 was confined largely to handing in copy to managing editors. "Of the back office with all the grief attached, and of the advertising and business end, I was as ignorant as if I never smelled printer's ink," she admitted in later years. She described her own naiveté accordingly:

> All that was necessary, as I saw it in my innocence, was to advertise for an experienced small town editor in the *Publishers Weekly*. To him I would outline the paper's policy which would preserve the oldtime atmosphere of this lively and distinctive western town. . . . I would keep the old staff and the paper would be theirs and the editor's responsibility. It was as simple as that.[35]

Well, not quite—as Lockhart soon discovered. She did advertise in *Publishers Weekly* and received a response from a small town in New Mexico. The applicant, who claimed to have "worked with Dana on the New York *Sun*," arrived on Caroline's doorstep dirty and unshaven. The new editor exuded confidence, however, and assured her that he would soon convert the *Enterprise* into one of the outstanding small-town newspapers in the state. With some trepidation, Lockhart gave him a "free hand"—but only until the first paper came off the hand press.

To her consternation, the front page displayed an ancient woodcut entitled "The Greatest Mother in the World—The Red Cross," previously used only when there was an empty space to fill. The new editor enlivened news articles with what Caroline considered to be "pointless slang" and misspelled names. Children were referred to as "kiddies" and all social affairs ended with "an elegant repast." The next week, Lockhart sent "the Man Who Had Worked With Dana On The *Sun*" down the road with "all the cash he was able to pilfer from the office desk."[36]

"One editor followed another," Caroline recalled, "each a little worse than the last." Always one to laugh at herself as well as others, she joked with her readers about the situation. "Introducing new editors to its readers has become one of the *Enterprise's* favorite pastimes," she wrote, adding optimistically:

> There is no reason to believe, however, that with the coming of Mr. S. A. Nock of New York City, we are to be deprived of our weekly recreation of

hiring editors. Having proven to our satisfaction that he can write an obituary without referring to the 'Grim Messenger,' 'Silent Reaper' or 'Angel of Death' and about an accident without 'Snuffing Out' the victim's life, we have taken him to our heart.[37]

Regardless of the ongoing stream of editors, the *Enterprise* from 1920 to 1925 reflected Lockhart's inimitable style. Never an active suffragist, she nevertheless publicized the activities and accomplishments of women she deemed worthy. Just one week after the *Enterprise* officially changed hands, the lead article on the front page reported the victory in Jackson Hole, Wyoming, of a slate of officers consisting solely of women. "Jackson, Wy. claims to have the distinction of being the first city in the world which will be governed entirely by women," the report read. "The women won two to one after a campaign in which the only issue was a question of sex."[38]

To win the Lockhart stamp of approval, neither women nor men had to be pillars of the community. On the contrary, those who seemed to earn her public endorsement were more often than not characters she considered to be representative of the true West—characters such as the Fighting Shepherdess, Arizona Bill, and Poker Nell.

An article on Arizona Bill, subtitled "Hurt by Ridicule, Frontiersman of Another Generation Draws Rifle in Meeteetse," told how an old man with long hair, dressed in the fashion of the early West, drifted into Meeteetse leading two burros. Harassed by local toughs, Arizona Bill had been forced to draw his rifle to defend himself. Lockhart reported the incident in empathic if melodramatic terms, telling how Arizona Bill endured the ridicule in silence, then finally turned on them, "his eyes blazing."[39]

Another of Caroline's favorite "old-timers," J. D. Woodruff of Shoshoni, was active in Wyoming politics. Woodruff and Caroline became friends and correspondents. One letter in particular she treasured for its insightful commentary on a West in transition: "Where there was a trail, now there is a graded highway," Woodruff wrote, "and we have traded the sorenosed white-eyed cayouse for an automobile." With regret, he told of the people and places that he had personally witnessed taking their place in the pages of the past—the trapper, the prospector, the scout, and the old-time cattleman; the stage-coach and ranch stop with its bar, its flies, its bedbugs, and its greasy cook; the sheepherder with his dog who spent days and months of solitude and then took "the criticisms of those who did not understand why he blew his earnings on wine, women, and song." Woodruff also commented on "the derrick and drill, which . . . brought untold wealth to Wyoming," and the plight of the dry farmer, "whose only visible means of support seemed to be an oversupply of faith."[40]

The women Lockhart chose to write about also exhibited the individualism of the Old West, strength of character, or talent. One of her favorite
subjects was Poker Nell Hendrickson, who in the eighties and nineties was
well known among professional gamblers "from the Mississippi to the sun-
down slope." Described by Lockhart as a woman of good looks, quick wit
and sparkling personality, Nell survived abuse as a child and marriage at
the age of thirteen to become a successful detective, and later a professional gambler. Eventually, Nell retired in Cody, where she ran a saloon
and later a millinery shop. Her life ended as it began, on a tragic note, with
her husband Bruce hanged for murder and Nell herself dying in a mental
institution. A full-page illustrated article by Lockhart in the Rocky Mountain *Empire Magazine* told Poker Nell's life story. Published when Lockhart
was seventy-six years old, the story (possibly her last) glorified the hard and
independent lifestyle of a woman of the West.[41]

Although she did not bestow compliments lightly and, in fact, ruthlessly
attacked those individuals who did not share her views, Lockhart could
be generous, even to those whom she considered competitors. Margaret
Hayden, for example, received accolades for her "well-written and accurate stories of local happenings published in the Billings *Gazette.*" Friend
and aspiring poet Alta Booth Dunn also received encouragement from
Lockhart.[42]

Despite the fact that the *Enterprise* reflected the Lockhart style from the
time of initial purchase, her imprint became more apparent when she became both editor and owner. Lockhart never relished being "lashed to a
roll-top desk in a dingy office," as she termed it, but the conviction grew
that if she was to publish a paper even remotely resembling the one she had
in mind, she would have to exert more control. Neither did she want to
admit that she had failed and put the *Enterprise* up for sale. The alternative
was to take her place at the helm.[43]

To gain managerial control, she and C. M. Conger bought out their partner's interests, and on 22 June 1921, the Park County *Enterprise* officially
became the Cody *Enterprise.* [44] Throwing out the paper's alleged nonparti-
san philosophy along with the trash, she announced the *Enterprise* position
on the controversial issue of Prohibition not long thereafter. To her surprise, the issue hit the streets like a bombshell. Lockhart explained part of
the reason for the sensational reaction to her announcement: "It was the
only 'wet' paper in the state," she said, "for while other editors were with
me in spirit, they had families to support."[45]

Whether attacking the town's administrators or the Anti-Saloon League,
Lockhart's barbed wit became the journalistic trademark of the *Enterprise.*
Readers, as she said, "stood in line" (some with trepidation) to see if their

names would be in print. Blazoned across the masthead was the boast: "EVERYONE READS THE *ENTERPRISE*, EVEN IF THEY BORROW IT." One who "borrowed" it was Mayor Cox. Caroline told why:

Mayor Cox curtly canceled his subscription to our great moral uplift sheet sometime ago. Therefore, we were flattered to see him at Alto's cigar counter last Thursday, waiting like a cat at a mouse-hole for the *Enterprise* to come out, and to hear him remark, 'He didn't want to miss anything.' All of which leads us to reiterate: If you hit a balky hourse [sic] on the nose he may not love you, but he will be interested in your movements.[46]

Still another who did not care for the *Enterprise* was "Jedge" Webster. "We kinda thought that after 'Jedge' Webster had fined Mrs. McGinnis $50 for turning the water into the street that he would come in and pay us that $4.15 he still owes us," she wrote. "But no such luck! A while back the 'Jedge' stomped in and demanded his bill because he did not like our paper. For a time we contemplated suspending publication, but concluded to go on, although the withdrawal of the 'Jedges' moral and financial support has put an awful crimp in us," she added facetiously.[47]

Lockhart also panned Clarence Baldwin, the city constable. Dubbed "Hairbreadth Harry" after a humorous escapade with a porcupine he tried to evict from the pool hall, the constable skipped town with a large advance in pay provided by the "administration." In a series of articles, Caroline expressed concern over the "dauntless" constable's continued absence. "Where is 'Hairbreadth Harry' Baldwin, the Curly Headed Boy of the Mayor's Office?" she wrote. "We miss his tender smile, his artless ways, also his bludgeon. Tain't right for him to leave us here at the mercy of porcupines and bootleggers and go off to another state for ten days or more when we are paying him $150 a month to protect us." Some thirty years later, Lockhart confided to interviewer David Dominick: "Hairbreadth Harry kinda liked me in his heart."[48]

As the self-appointed conscience of the community, Lockhart enjoyed taking potshots at aspiring politicians as well as administrators already in office. Although it is difficult to measure her effectiveness in influencing the town's politics, her colorful style undoubtedly attracted attention. "Last week we had Lumbago or something equally terrible," she wrote with tongue-in-cheek. "At any rate, it hurt us to move, to laugh or even to smile, and then someone drifted in and told us that T. P. Cullen was coming out sheriff and nearly killed us."[49]

Friends fared little better. "Pinky Gist, who was formerly a champion bulldogger, writes from Omaha that he is married and is now a clown," she reported. "We take it from his letter that there is some connection between the two." [50]

Not all was lighthearted humor, however. Under Lockhart's leadership, the *Enterprise* also featured a respectable number of serious articles dealing with national and state affairs as well as local issues. Such items, presented in a relatively objective manner, ranged from a black-bordered headline announcing the death of President Woodrow Wilson and an article on the election of Nellie Ross (not to be confused with Cody's Marjorie Ross) as governor of the state, to coverage of the activities of Wyoming lawmakers. Articles with headlines such as "Big Gas Well Blows In Here" and "Train Drops into River Near Casper When Bridge Breaks" kept readers well-informed of newsworthy events in the region. [51]

Where local events were concerned, however, Lockhart rarely made an attempt at objective reporting. A case in point was the *State* v. *A. Strand*. Tried in Judge Percy J. Metz's court, the case involved a ten-year-old child who reportedly had been sexually abused by her father. Later, when the child's mother, who had shielded her husband, was charged with intimidating a witness and subsequently was released by the local justice of the peace, Lockhart publicly chastised the official. Referring to what she termed "one of the most revolting cases in the history of Park County," she reported that "the action of the justice of the peace has been severely condemned by many people." [52]

For impact, however, Lockhart's attempts at serious reporting did not compare to articles written in her characteristic humorous style. It was this tool—barbed humor—that she used so effectively to conduct her campaign against Prohibition.

In her unpublished autobiography, Lockhart explained how not long after assuming control of the paper, she launched her attack. "Since my views on the Eighteenth Amendment had not changed," she wrote, "it seemed to me as well as to state where the *Enterprise* stood on this contraversial [sic] question. This I did, putting it in a small 'box' on the front page." She told how the newsboy then left with an armful of copies for the newsstand in the post office store. Ordinarily, a dishearteningly small number of papers was sold, and many copies were returned. On that particular day, however, in less than thirty minutes a breathless messenger came to the *Enterprise* office asking for more. "Then the storm broke," Caroline recalled. "The town hadn't been rocked by such excitement since one of Buffalo Bill's employees took a bath in champagne at the new Northern Hotel in Billings and put it on his expense account. The news was out—the Lady Editor was wet!" [53]

The battle lines formed, with the "Roughnecks" on one side and the "Better Element" on the other. "The Methodist preacher," according to Lockhart, "denounced the paper from the pulpit, declaring that it should not have the support of law-abiding citizens and demanded that all subscriptions be stopped and business advertising be withdrawn at once." The preacher's campaign made an impact: "The only advertising space in the next issue was occupied by Lydia Pinkham's remedies for female trouble; the manufacturer of Pink Pills for Pale People, Smith Brothers Cough Drops, and a Sure Cure for Corns," Lockhart remembered.

There *were* advantages, however. The list of *Enterprise* subscribers lengthened despite threats of a boycott, and the newspaper and its editor/owner attracted national attention. H. L. Mencken, then editor of *Smart Set*, praised the outspoken editor, and Christopher Morley borrowed her witticisms verbatim for his column in the New York *Post*. Neither was Lockhart above tooting her own horn. She reveled in the popularity of her salty western style: "As the circles widen when one throws a pebble into the pond," she reported,

> so each week the fame of the Cody *Enterprise* grows until at last we can truthfully say we are known and quoted from coast to coast.
>
> Some little time ago the sober New York *Evening Post* gave nearly a column to clippings from our great moral uplift weekly, and now along comes a copy of the Oakland (California) *Inquirer*, reprinting one of our paragraphs.[54]

As the vehicle for her editorial voice, she created a biting, humorous column titled "As Seen From the Water Wagon," which became her trademark. Soon the column was moved from the back of the paper to center stage on the front—the better to be heard.

AS SEEN FROM THE WATER WAGON

Although doomed to failure, the attempt at Prohibition would span a thirteen-year period in the history of the United States. But a nation of individualists such as Caroline Lockhart could not and would not stay "on the water wagon." A Lockhart article in the *Enterprise* helps to explain part of the reason for Prohibition's failure and sheds light on the title of her column. "The United States is Falling off the Water Wagon," she quoted an investigator as saying. The official had surveyed the country for information, hobnobbing with bootleggers and talking with enforcement agents. After following the well-traveled rum routes that laced the country in organized traffic, he decided that this state of affairs existed because "Prohibition had become the chief butt of ridicule."[55] Lockhart apparently agreed.

Deriding Prohibition was a popular pastime, and one in which Lockhart participated with enthusiasm. "Baiting Prohibition officers and law enforcement departments promises to become one of the national sports," she wrote, "as entertaining and full of thrills as baseball."[56] Certainly Caroline enjoyed the sport, and she played it according to the emotion of the moment, occasionally with levity, but at all times with serious underlying intent. In the *Enterprise*—irreverently referred to by her enemies as "the booze sheet of Wyoming"—she staunchly supported the cause of moonshiners and bootleggers and took delight in exposing informers and flouting federal and local enforcement officers.[57]

One such article denounced a big drive then underway to enforce Prohibition locally which had begun by importing some 50,000 federal officials to carry out the law; however, local Prohibitionists were also subject to Caroline's opprobrium. She derided in print the actions of a Cody merchant who, after making a large sale of sugar and cornmeal, immediately informed the authorities, thinking that the foodstuffs were intended for the manufacture of moonshine. "It is so thoroughly characteristic of this individual, that to mention his name would be superfluous," she added.[58]

Lockhart also took pleasure in refuting some of the more outrageous Prohibitionist theories. She told of a lecturer who claimed that in families where one parent was an alcoholic, "degeneracy will pursue the family until the progeny become sterile in the fourth generation." Therefore, the lecturer theorized, since "a nation must renew its life through its families; a nation in which drink prevails must perish." To counter such theories, Caroline pointed out that the hard-drinking Scots people had produced renowned intellectuals, poets, and philosophers. She called attention to still another hard-drinking race—the Germans. "For a race of degenerates, the Germans put up a pretty stiff front a few years ago," she reminded her audience. "Whatever theories may be developed about inefficiency resulting from alcohol, they cannot refute history."[59]

In comparison with news articles on Prohibition, the vignettes in her personal column, "As Seen From the Water Wagon," were more succinct and humorous, but they relayed clearly the anti-Prohibitionist party line. Realizing that a humorous barb was often more effective than an angry accusation, she seemed to favor this tack: "We are informed that the sheriff's office has made the boast that within 30 days there will not be a bootlegger left," she wrote. "We are sorry to hear that there is trouble ahead for so many of our intimate friends." State officials were also fair game. In response to State Prohibition Director Carol Jackson's report that "the state is gradually drying up," Caroline quipped: "If the same thing would happen to the reformers, it would be a great relief." Lockhart also told how Prohibition officers dropped in for an evening call on the Reverend John Trout at his home in Mount Vernon, Illinois, and found thirty-two pints of liquor concealed on the premises. "The Reverend Trout must have drunk like a fish," she punned.[60] A similar one-liner read: "The news that beer may now be prescribed for medicine has made half the people in the country sick."[61]

Although Lockhart professed that she did not desire "to propogate [sic] Blasphemy" in her column, she had no qualms about publishing a parody of the Doxology. Ostensibly used by "the worthy and righteous advocates of the Volstead Act," the verse read:

Praise God from whom all blessings flow,
Praise Him who heals the drunkards' woe,
Praise Him who leads the Temperance Host,
Praise Father, Son, and Holy Ghost.[62]

A column in the *Enterprise* called "Sage Ticks" bore the Lockhart imprint as well. An entry under this column called attention to what she considered the irrational standards being promoted by the Women's Christian Temperance Union (WCTU). Established in 1874, the WCTU spurred the founding of the Anti-Saloon League and advocated women's rights. Despite their positive contributions, Caroline went on the attack: "The nice ladies of the WCTU have decided that men may smoke and women rouge, skirts may be short and stockings rolled, but hooch must go."[63]

Working closely with the WCTU were others who renounced the "demon drink" on religious grounds. Generally referred to by Lockhart as "the Methodist bunch," this group included members of the WCTU and Cody's "better element." Spokesperson for the faction was rival editor Len Leander Newton. As Caroline admitted to interviewer David Dominick: "Oh! L. L. Newton—he was head of the Methodist bunch. I just doted on fighting Newton. He was the breath of life to me. They frisked his place and found moonshine in the barn."[64]

Lockhart's battles with Newton ranged from politics and Prohibition to religion. When Newton announced that he would run for re-election as state committeeman, Caroline charged him with being responsible for the split in the Republican party. "L. L. Newton must have much in common with the rhinoceros unicornus," she wrote irreverently, "if it has not penetrated that outside of a few standpatters and Methodist reformers, the Republicans will not work with him."

Elaborating, she added: "While we are upon the interesting and prolific subject of the ubiquitous Len Leander, we are moved to call attention to the glowing tribute paid to S. A. Watkins in the last edition of the *Herald.*" She reminded readers that it was through County Commissioner Sanford Watkins that L. L. Newton was awarded a two-year contract for the county printing concession over the lower bids of the Powell *Tribune* and the *Enterprise*. As a result, taxpayers lost $1,300 in savings. To add insult to injury, in the lower right-hand corner of the *Enterprise* front page, she printed an unflattering out-of-date photograph of the county commissioner with hair parted slightly off center. Much to Watkins's irritation, Lockhart would reprint the picture repeatedly.[65]

A year later, she was still dealing Newton misery on the subject of the county printing concession. "Before the last election," she reminded readers, "we prophesied that if anybody ever got L. L. Newton by the hind leg and pulled his front feet out of the trough where he has fed so long and bounteously, his squeals would be long and earsplitting. This was just what Messrs. Powers and Markham did to him when they took away his monopoly of the county printing and perquisites."[66]

Newton and the "Methodist bunch," however, held their own quite capably. Attacks in the *Herald* on Lockhart's personal friends, or those she considered the "underdogs of society," seemed to be particularly effective in hitting a nerve. On occasion she lashed out in honest anger. "The brazen bigotry of the average so-called reformer is proverbial," she raged, "but it is rarely more unblushingly displayed as in the editorial published in the *Herald* last week entitled 'Not Over Yet.'" Newton's reference to "Enemies of the Home," she charged, was clearly "a scathing characterization of Mr. Russell Crane and those with whom he has associated himself in opposition to the 18th Amendment."[67]

Relations between Lockhart and Newton reached a new low when Caroline reported how the *Herald* editor had been kicked in the seat of the pants by A. S. McClain after a wrangle over the "electric light question." On the front page of the *Enterprise* she told in picturesque terms how Newton followed McClain into the Electric Light Company's office on Third Street with the intent of continuing the argument that had started outside. McClain, however, lost patience. The discussion ended quickly when he grabbed Newton by the collar and firmly planted his foot on the seat of the unfortunate editor's trousers. Newton limped to the courthouse and swore out a warrant for McClain's arrest, whereupon the "Police Judge" held court in his barber shop and fined McClain the sum of $1.00. Newton felt this was too little to pay for the privilege of kicking an editor and subsequently swore out another warrant, with the result that Justice of the Peace Marston fined McClain $10.00. Lockhart gleefully reported the incident in full detail under the headline "Costs $1.00 to Kick an Editor."[68]

This story and others of similar kind inspired Newton to descriptive heights as he retaliated by expressing his opinion of the lady editor on the front page of the *Herald*. But Newton's personal attacks on Lockhart appeared to be less effective in raising her ire than his attacks on her political friends. Her response in "As Seen from the Water Wagon" capitalized on Newton's literary tirade:

> We learned that we have a 'maggott mind,'—whatever that may be—something lively, we take it—'exude venom,' are a coward and a liar, malign Methodists, ridicule all . . . and behave like a daughter of Satan generally.[69]

The game of verbal darts went on for months, but Lockhart had the last word: "As between a 'maggott' and the characteristics of a buzzard we see small choice."[70]

When Lockhart tired of battling Newton, she took potshots at another enemy of long standing, "Lady Doc" Frances Lane. Under the subtitle "Following the Ponies," Lockhart reported seeing Dr. Lane "in appropriate costume" out in the middle of the street with a shovel collecting manure to place at the roots of "the vigorous young Balm of Gilead trees" growing about her residence. Lockhart noted wryly that although Lane's motives were commendable, considering that residents were anxious to have Cody recognized as 'The City Beautiful,' the editor questioned Lane's rights in removing the fertilizer without permission from the town council. "However," Lockhart concluded, "we do not anticipate that any legal steps will be taken in the matter, as it can readily be seen that a serious obstacle to the successful persecution [sic] of such a case would be the difficulty of proving property."[71]

Lockhart's acidic sense of humor and frontier style of journalism earned her notoriety far and wide. Editors from nearby towns read the *Enterprise* as avidly as did the local townspeople. Ralph Smith, editor of the Meeteetse *News*, was one of the first to call attention to Lockhart's liberal style and the differences between the *Enterprise* and the *Herald*. Caroline liked what he had to say and quoted his observations for the benefit of her readers:

> In one plant the halo is seen encircling every press and type case. The propaganda spread here is so drastic in reform as to become nauseating. This sheet concludes that it is the saint and the other fellow the devil.

The attitude of the other is altogether different. Here you can go with your chewing tobacco, cigarette, and jug—if you have any—and be perfectly at home. This paper believes that people yet have a few rights, that they are not created to consult their fellowman when they wish to partake of a glass of sparkling burgundy.[72]

The descriptive comparison left little doubt as to the identities of the respective papers. Caroline expressed her appreciation by inviting Smith to bring his jug and visit her office anytime. "He can put his feet on our desk and we will wash a place on our fly-specked window large enough for him to watch the chickens passing," she offered hospitably.[73]

The editor of the Inland *Oil Index,* also a Lockhart fan, complimented her in the provincial style of the times: "No wonder it is the popular journal it is with a woman at its head and one who is so efficient and who wields so ready a pen. We salute you sister, in the blossoming field of journalism."[74]

Others, however, were not so impressed. Ed Mills of the Greybull *Standard* regarded the editor of the *Enterprise* with a jaundiced eye. "To read the Cody *Enterprise,*" he observed, "one gets the impression that Cody is made up of a class of temperance people who never take a drink until some contemptible stool pigeon comes along and persuades them to fall or takes 'em out and pours it down them by force." To which Lockhart responded: "We may as well confess that we have long held the opinion that what Ed Mills really needed himself was about three fingers in the bottom of a washtub."[75]

In such a manner, Caroline turned criticism into colorful news copy. Judiciously, she printed both the comments of her detractors as well as the compliments of those who supported her. With her talent for making the most of negative comments, Lockhart was a tough opponent whose talents soon became widely known. Her journalistic antics attracted the attention of such luminaries as Christopher Morley, essayist and editor of "The Bowling Green" column of the New York *Post.* Morley praised Lockhart highly, both as a newspaper woman and as a novelist: "Whenever we feel low in our mind about the general state of human morals, manners and intellects, we turn for cheer to that admirable newspaper The Cody *Enterprise . . .* run by Miss Carole [sic] Lockhart, the seemliest editor west of the Appalachians."[76]

By this time, Lockhart's book *The Dude Wrangler* was out and arrangements were being made for its production as a movie starring Tim McCoy. LaDura Fein, art director of Mountain-Plains Enterprises, planned to film the picture in nearby Thermopolis.[77] The book's favorable reception and Lockhart's assessment of the impact of dude wrangling as an increasingly important western industry also attracted Morley's attention. In his column in the *Post*, he quoted the inimitable Caroline extensively:

> The ranch house swarmed with folk in weird costumes and strange ways while the erstwhile proud and independent rancher has a hunted look—the look that comes sooner or later from wrangling dudes and is due chiefly to answering questions, changing stirrups and teaching novices to ride.[78]

Morley concluded with a comment on her talents as a humorist. Lockhart, he said, was one of those who had the ability to "make the human lung crow like chanticleer."[79]

Although her novels were well known for their western humor, her news column "As Seen from the Water Wagon" remains the best repository for a synthesis of the Lockhart brand of wit. Through the vignette and the one-liner, she punctured the egos of the town Puritans and Prohibitionists while promoting her own views—rarely impartially, but certainly effectively and with humor—as Mencken, Morley, and other members of the trade readily acknowledged.

When she was not acting as militant spokesperson for the anti-Prohibitionist faction or keeping the local politicians in line, Lockhart during the years 1921–25 worked to establish a memorial honoring the town's founding father, William F. Cody.

THE WILLIAM F. CODY MEMORIAL

William Frederick Cody, last of the great scouts, rode into the sunset on 10 January 1917. Better known as Buffalo Bill of the Wild West extravaganzas, he left behind a significant and long-lasting legacy—one that Caroline Lockhart had the foresight to appreciate. As owner and star of Buffalo Bill's Wild West, Cody would arrive via private show-train in cities and towns across the nation, set up his Wild West circus, and treat cheering audiences to a vicarious glimpse of a colorful era in the nation's past. While the shows did little to enhance the image of the Native American, the roping, trick shooting, and Indian attacks helped to establish in the mind's eye of the audiences an image of the cowboy as the archetypal American.

For years Lockhart and Cody shared the limelight in the small Wyoming community. At times, as her novels and Diary entries reveal, this went against Caroline's competitive grain. She was not above using Cody as inspiration for subtle social criticism, nor did she spare him in the pages of her Diary. Yet in terms of posterity, she realized that the dashing frontiersman personified some of the better aspects of the Old West. Consequently, to perpetuate the myth and to promote the town, she worked diligently to establish a memorial honoring Cody as the town's founding father.

The Wyoming state legislature in 1917 took the first step by appropriating $5,000 for the project, but for several years the money lay unused. In the interim, the Cody family's primary interest lay in carrying out what they understood to be the Colonel's personal vision. Mary Jester Allen, Colonel Cody's niece, was the first member of the family to learn of her uncle's desires.[80]

Allen, a political writer, speaker, and promotional director for the National Republican Committee, started her professional career at the age of eighteen when she became publicity agent for her "Uncle Will's" Wild West show. The two remained close, and during his later years Cody visited his niece annually in Seattle, Washington.

It was on his last visit, 15 May 1915, that he told Allen and a gathering of old friends of his wish to establish "a great American Pioneer Center built about the heart and hearth of a ranch homestead." Such a center, he felt, would enable coming generations to see how the pioneer lived and worked. He wanted the focus of his last pioneering efforts, his TE Ranch home at Cody, Wyoming, to be the central scene in an expansive diorama of the West. Those present at the gathering pledged themselves to carry out the Colonel's wishes. Thus it happened that the Buffalo Bill Museum, the Cody pioneer center at the gateway to Yellowstone National Park, as Allen so aptly phrase it, "was selected by Colonel Cody himself as his gift to the world of today and tomorrow."[81]

World War I interrupted the efforts of Mary Jester Allen to carry out the pledge to her uncle, but after the Armistice, she founded the Cody Family, Inc., with the intent of building the ranch-home museum envisioned by Buffalo Bill. Then word came that the appropriation set aside by the Wyoming legislature must be used or lost.

Meanwhile, in the Colonel's hometown, Caroline Lockhart and members of the Cody Club appointed a committee to look into the matter of a suitable memorial. They kept in mind that the Wyoming legislature had indicated that they felt that a statue of the Colonel would be appropriate. Caroline contacted Cody's niece, who was then living in New York City, and urged her to take on the project at that end. Mary Allen later admitted: "I was so desperately busy with my own work and affairs that I paid little attention. Miss Lockhart pounded away with telegrams and letters and I finally said that I would do the pioneering here in the East."[82]

Committee members in Cody—Jake Schwoob, Samuel C. Parks, and Colonel Arthur W. Little—suggested that the famous American sculptor Gertrude Vanderbilt Whitney, also of New York, be commissioned to do the statue. Lockhart announced the proposal in the *Enterprise* and conducted a personal survey to determine if the citizens of Cody would be receptive to the idea.

Mayor Cox expressed concern about the large sum of money required—$50,000—but nonetheless offered his support. The Honorable L. R. Ewart encouraged the committee to take action: "Something ought to be done and done soon! The next session of the legislature will probably throw the five thousand dollars already appropriated . . . back into the general fund if it is not used," he warned. J. M. Schwoob advised everyone "to put on their thinking caps and work out some plan to raise the money." Clay Tyler already had an idea—why not raise the money for the statue through an organization such as the Boy Scouts? But he opposed the idea of placing the statue in front of the Irma Hotel. Tyler thought it would be more appropriate and more accessible to tourists if it were situated in a park setting. Dave Jones also liked the idea of a park and suggested acquisition of land west of the courthouse. Others, such as Paul Greever, favored the Irma location. Lockhart's survey showed that the community largely supported the statue as proposed.[83] She also wrote to the Colonel's niece suggesting that she make arrangements to meet personally with the famous sculptor and persuade her to accept the commission.

Mary Allen did just that. "I told of Uncle Will and his dream," she recalled, "and before I was finished, Mrs. Whitney had caught the fire of far-flung vision and was walking about the room selling me the West."[84] While Allen worked in the East, the "Sammy Girls" of Cody, Wyoming, launched the campaign for funds in Buffalo Bill's hometown.

The *Enterprise* carried front-page coverage of their efforts. "Take off your hats to the Sammy Girls of Cody," Lockhart wrote. "It is fitting that the fund for the memorial to the country's best-known American should be started by the Sammy Girls of Cody since the society itself was organized by the Colonel's daughter, Irma Cody Garlow." To raise funds, the Sammy Girls planned a ball to be held at the Temple Theatre with music furnished by the Melody Boys of Billings. Lockhart concluded her article on the affair by calling attention to the benefits that the town would derive from such a memorial. She pointed out that the statue would become a tourist attraction and a "mecca for thousands of hero worshippers throughout the world to whom the Colonel was the typical American."[85]

In October 1922, the chairman of the Buffalo Bill Memorial Committee, Clay Tyler, received word that Gertrude Whitney's first designs for the statue were soon to be submitted.[86] By 1923 the project had progressed to the stage where the sculptor made arrangements for New York architect Albert Ross to visit Cody to plan the setting for the statue. To give the architect a true feel for the West, Whitney insisted that Ross arrive on the Fourth of July in time for the annual Stampede celebration. Apparently, his visit was a memorable one, if a news article reprinted from the *Evening World* is any indication.

The article, written in a bantering style with an East versus West theme, gave Ross's observations on his visit. He was particularly impressed with Caroline's house, with the trophy animals she had shot, and with her pet bobcat. Ross concluded his article, inviting Lockhart and "her Wild West crowd" to visit New York. "Coney Island," he claimed, "is wilder than Cody!" On a more serious note, Ross reported that the Whitney statue was to have a lofty setting on a granite bluff, with the figure of the Colonel and his horse rising about twenty feet in height.[87]

In its style, the story reprinted from the *World* bears a strong resemblance to the prose of Caroline Lockhart. One suspects that the enterprising editor may have conjured up the story with Ross's consent to obtain national publicity for the project. Or the whole writeup may have been fabricated initially especially for the *Enterprise*, since no dateline for the *World* article is given.

By May 1924, Robert D. Dripps, executive secretary of the Buffalo Bill American Association, arrived from New York to confer with the local committee. By this time, the cost of the statue had increased from $50,000 to $250,000; but Dripps, who had the task of raising the money, assured local supporters that he did not anticipate much difficulty. The executive secretary completed arrangements for the unveiling and reported favorably on the granite plinth, or base, for the statue, which was being constructed by Russell Kimball.[88]

On Tuesday, 27 May 1924, the bronze equestrian statue of Buffalo Bill, one of the largest ever commissioned from a woman sculptor, was taken from its casting and started on its journey westward to Cody. The previous week, artisans assembled the statue at the bronze foundry in Brooklyn where it had been cast, and a private exhibition of the monumental piece was held for newspaper photographers, motion picture personnel, and news reporters.[89]

In final form, the bronze stood twelve feet high, measured thirteen feet long, and weighed almost two tons. Jane Garlow, granddaughter of the Colonel, presided at the formal unveiling held suitably on the Fourth of July in Cody, Wyoming. More than 10,000 people witnessed the ceremony. Lauded as "the triumph of Mrs. Harry Payne Whitney's career," the statue also represented the successful efforts of Caroline Lockhart and others who joined together to preserve and pay tribute to "the West that was."[90]

CAROLINE IN COURT

During the years 1921–25, Lockhart succeeded in establishing the *Enterprise* as an effective organ of anti-Prohibition and as a vehicle for promotion of the Stampede, the Buffalo Bill memorial, and other special interests— but not without personal cost. The irrepressible image that she projected as the frontier editor of the *Enterprise* stands in contrast to the self-portrait of the middle-aged, unhappy woman who emerges from the pages of her Diary. Tough and independent to all outward appearances, Lockhart in reality continued to suffer from periods of depression. Despite her accomplishments, she was plagued by feelings of failure and inadequacy. On 24 January 1921, she wrote in her Diary: "A month from today Caddie Lockhart will be fifty. It is at once incredible and horrible." She had received a love letter from O.B. Mann and admitted his "lasting hold" on her.[91]

As she approached her fiftieth birthday, the prospect of living out her life without the respectability of marriage also weighed more heavily upon her. When Mann had appeared on her doorstep, contrite and unhappy in his new marriage, she succumbed to his charm at the expense of her self-esteem. Her inability to put an end to this self-destructive affair, combined with financial worries related to the *Enterprise*, led to many a sleepless night. Alcohol remained her homespun cure for insomnia, although the companionship of any one of several lovers, in addition to O.B. Mann, seemed to help. She continued to hear from former soldier Bill Miller de Colonna, the banker Andrew Ross, and John R. Painter; but the newest man in her life was Lou Erickson, cowboy and horse wrangler. "Why, God knows," she conceded in her Diary, "but he attracts me and I do not fight it for it helps take my mind from O.B. He [Lou] reciprocates with equal warmth and he is not a skirt-hound."[92]

When able, she provided financial support to Erickson's horse-trading ventures by acting as a silent partner. She eventually entered into a short-lived partnership in a dude-ranching business as well, but the focus of her financial interests, of necessity, was the *Enterprise*.[93]

The paper monopolized her time and her money, which was a concern. Nevertheless, she felt that she had made the right decision in buying out the interest of W. S. Bennett and proceeded systematically to gain control. In March 1921, in order to settle personal debts, Larry Larom offered to sell his interest; and a few days later, Lockhart responded. She recorded the transaction in her Diary: "Am the more or less proud possessor of another interest in the paper. I gave Larry my check yesterday for $450"; adding as an afterthought, "I wish I could close up with that damned Eldred."

In April she was able to write jubilantly: "Sid's share is cinched and he is *out!*"[94]

These acquisitions made Lockhart the majority shareholder in the *Enterprise* with four-fifths interest and Conger controlling one-fifth interest. Soon, however, disagreement over editorial policy created a break between Lockhart and her remaining partner. "I'll have to buy him, too, ultimately," she confided.[95]

Lockhart's expanded interest in the *Enterprise* meant that she had to shoulder a larger portion of the paper's expenses. Financing became a major worry. "I'm sick of the dreary sheet and worried over payroll," she admitted, "but I'll hang on grimly and win if I can." She was forced to sell her car for $250, but this loss did not seem to bother her. "Thank God to be rid of the incubus," she wrote. "I never want another until I can afford a Cadillac."[96]

By the end of September she had arranged to finance the *Enterprise* by borrowing another $250 from Andrew Ross and by giving her brother-in-law Roy a note for a $250 loan. The strain of trying to make the paper a paying proposition began to tell on her, but she refused to leave it in incompetent hands or sell it to her enemies. She especially resented the fact that it kept her from her other literary endeavors. "I'm wasting time and energy," she noted dejectedly in her Diary.[97]

In the interim, Conger was becoming increasingly disgruntled. As a cost-saving measure, Lockhart considered relieving him or limiting his work hours, a right granted her according to terms of their partnership. She found him "disagreeable and obstinate," but admitted that she "would miss him . . . if he means to get out, for he is competent and faithful though irritating." Conger sensed Caroline's ambivalent attitude and accused her of trying to "squeeze him out." Disregarding the fact that she was $212 in arrears on his salary, she blamed another individual for Conger's discontent and suspicions.[98]

The new year, 1922, brought with it a heavy snowfall and both good and bad news. Caroline learned that she would receive $500 for the film rights to *The Dude Wrangler,* which raised her spirits momentarily; but on 12 January, she received what she termed "the jolt of my life." "That crazy old fool of a Conger has brought suit against me, asking for dissolution of the partnership, charging me with habitual drunkenness and being incompetent to manage a newspaper!" she wrote in disbelief. The news was upsetting, but she rallied quickly, vowing to "fight like hell, now I'm in it."[99]

Conger's suit against Lockhart was the first of several in which she would be involved. Her tenure as editor and owner of the *Enterprise* would be fraught with contention and litigation. In addition to charges of drunkenness and incompetency, Conger accused her of misrepresentation and fraud. He claimed that her beliefs and policies as expressed in the *Enterprise* were "destructive, against law and order," and in effect damaging to his investment. Lockhart, he said, had rejected his offer to buy her out; therefore, he wanted the partnership dissolved, the property sold, and the proceeds divided according to their respective percentages of interest.[100]

Lockhart denied most of the allegations and in cross-petition charged Conger with breach of contract. She acknowledged his offer of sale, but produced as evidence a partnership agreement of November 1921, designating her clearly as "the managing partner with authority to control and dictate the policy of said newspaper . . . with full authority to employ and discharge such agents, operators, and assistants, as she deemed necessary."[101] It was in this agreement that Lockhart, according to Conger's charges, had misrepresented herself. Whatever her motives in having Conger sign the "Memorandum of Agreement," the document stands as testimony to Lockhart's shrewd business sense. Largely on the basis of this evidence, the case of *C. M. Conger v. Caroline Lockhart* was "selected and dismissed."[102]

In early 1923, in addition to Conger's lawsuit, Lockhart was busy moving the *Enterprise* into new quarters. Lou Erickson helped her with renovations on the building, and by mid-February, she was able to announce the relocation to her clientele:

> It may be that among those who saw the *Enterprise* going down the street in a wagon last week there were some who hoped it would keep on traveling. We are sorry to disappoint them. The fact is we are now established on a safe and firm cement foundation in the new *Enterprise* building on Second Street which we recently purchased from F. J. Hiscock.[103]

Simultaneous with the move, Lockhart installed a new Intertype machine, which she declared to be "nearly human." "Seven linotype operators," she said, had "lost their immortal souls" cursing its predecessor; therefore, she felt "pretty snuffy" over the new purchase.[104] By 23 March 1923, Caroline closed her legal affairs with Conger by purchasing his interest in the paper for $300.[105] The Conger suit, however, was only one of several in which she would be involved, either as plaintiff or defendant, during her tenure as editor and owner of the *Enterprise*.

Another minor but colorful altercation involved a cook in a local restaurant, Blanche Gokel. The woman, it seems, objected strongly to a statement in the *Enterprise* to the effect that she had served as a character witness in a local divorce case. When Gokel threatened to beat up the editor of the *Enterprise*, Lockhart attempted to have the fractious lady placed under peace bond. But Caroline lost. Moreover, she received a lecture from the judge, who advised her to refrain from using Gokel's name in the paper and "to temper her articles with some reasonable sense of justice and regard for the truth."[106] Lockhart did not appear to take the remonstration too seriously. She did, however, start carrying a blackjack to protect herself against the possibility of attack, and she published her own entertaining version of the affair in the *Enterprise*.

Under the title "Couldn't Convince Judge Blanche Gokel Is Dangerous" with subtitle "Pugilistic Cook Goes on Rampage—Out to Whip Editor of the *Enterprise*, City Attorney and W. L. Simpson," Lockhart told how Gokel had been ordered from both the *Enterprise* office and the office of William Lee Simpson for using vulgar language and making a general nuisance of herself. Nevertheless, Paul Greever, representing the defendant, convinced the judge that Gokel was merely a hard-working woman who was "relieving her feelings," whereas the plaintiff "slung a wicked pen and otherwise took advantage of her petticoats." In her usual lighthearted manner, Lockhart reported that, when Greever had concluded, "the Judge scratched his head with a troubled expression and expressed the opinion that Blanche Gokel's boasts were largely conversations and that the plaintiff, Caroline Lockhart, was not so much afraid of the defendant as she would have it believed." Case dismissed.[107]

The *Herald* attempted to present the case in a more serious light. "Caroline Lockhart Seeks Help From Law Which She Ridicules, Judge Refuses Her Protection from Enemy She Maligned in *Enterprise* on Grounds She Is the Instigator," read the headlines. To which Caroline responded: "The *Enterprise* has always contended that the Workman's Compensation Act should include editors in its list of those engaged in extra-hazardous occupations." In support of her contention, she recalled how the town marshal gave Ernest F. Shaw of the *Herald* a black eye in a fast round at the post office, and how two weeks earlier: "L. L. Newton finally got a kick out of life when A. S. McClain assisted him out of his office."[108] Such was a day in the life of the editor of a western newspaper.

Not long after dismissal of the Gokel case, an event of a much more serious nature occurred. It, too, would lead to litigation and Lockhart's involvement in what she characterized in an autobiographical draft as "the outstanding incident of my career as a small-town editor."[109]

Local newspaper reports and an account in Caroline's unpublished autobiography reveal that the scenario began one June afternoon in 1923. On this particular day, Harry Tipton, with an air of contained excitement, pulled his lanky frame out of the chair he customarily occupied in front of the Irma Hotel and went to join J. T. McGonagle. McGonagle, who worked as the courthouse janitor, and Tipton were about to embark on a special assignment for County Attorney Ernest J. Goppert and Sheriff William H. Loomis. A tip from an informant had led to the discovery of an illegal liquor cache in a dry gulch near Cottonwood Creek, and Tipton and McGonagle were to stake out the site. Loomis deputized the two men as Prohibition agents, gave them orders to shoot "if fired upon," and drove them out to Cottonwood Creek. There they waited for the owners of the cache to appear.

About dusk, a Nash automobile drove up and pulled quietly to a stop. The deputies heard some men enter the brush, then the sound of jugs knocking together followed by the gurgle of liquid being siphoned. When the deputies heard the car door slam, they quickly crawled up a dry gulch to get a better view of the road and make the arrest. As the car passed, the deputies jumped up. Tipton yelled, "Put em up, goddam you!" Seconds later, both men opened fire.

At a fifty-foot distance, the fusillade of bullets from the high-powered rifles peppered the car with holes. One bullet shattered the windshield, seriously wounding the driver, A. E. Carey, and killing his companion, George "Scotty" Sirrine. The car swerved to the side of the road, momentarily out of control, then gathered speed as the driver tried to escape the barrage of bullets. Beside him in the passenger seat, Scotty Sirrine slid to the floor of the car in a pool of his own blood. Carey, with his hip shattered and bleeding, managed to drive the car into Greybull.

Meanwhile, the deputies hitched a ride with a passing motorist and returned to Cody where they notified the county attorney of the success of their mission. Goppert drove out to the cache and brought in some eighty gallons of liquor, while Sheriff Loomis arrested Carey at his home in Greybull. The bullet-riddled Nash bore mute testimony to the truth of the janitor's boasts that he had shot sixteen bullets into it. Loomis and his deputy, Earl Pulley, found sacks saturated with moonshine in the vehicle— evidence that would later convict Carey of violating the liquor law over the protests of citizens who considered the action of the agents akin to cold-blooded murder.[110]

Caroline Lockhart was one of those who shared this opinion. In a detailed story in the *Enterprise*, she stated that "the business had been engineered by the prosecuting attorney, E. J. Goppert." As soon as the paper hit the streets, Goppert fired off a letter of protest, charging the editor with libel. He objected specifically to Lockhart's claim that he had "engineered" the affair.[111]

Within two weeks, the attorney had filed formal suit against Lockhart for $30,000 damages. The petition, drawn by Paul R. Greever, declared that Goppert's popularity had "suffered irreparable injury," that the article in question held him up to the "ridicule, opprobrium, criticism and hatred of the people of Park County and greatly injured him in his good will, patronage and standing." He demanded $30,000 to assuage his injured feelings, restore his popularity, and repair the damage to his business. And Caroline's response? "Go your best, Mr. Goppert!" [112]

Rather than motivating Lockhart to alter her reporting style, the prospect of a court battle seemed to goad her further. Over the next few years she would rag Goppert relentlessly. The attorney, in later years, summed up the situation: "She raised hell with me on that paper," he said. "I was a prohibitionist and she wasn't. She offered me drinks right in her house, but I turned them all down. I don't think I would now," he added retrospectively. [113]

Goppert, who came from a "dry" state, recalled that he had not seen a man drunk "until after I was twenty-one. After I got out of Kansas, that was about the first thing I did see. As county attorney I had to enforce the Prohibition law." On the other hand, the libel statute, as Goppert noted, "was in effect, but not enforced." And as for Caroline Lockhart: "If she had been tried and convicted, she would have gone ahead anyway. I was more interested in the principle of the thing. I felt if I could get a judgment on her, it would keep her shut, but it didn't. She printed good and bad—all about it." [114]

Over the course of the next few years, Lockhart would avail herself of every opportunity to harass Goppert relentlessly. The Stampede celebration for 1923 became the scene of still another embarrassment for the young attorney. Goppert, mingling with the crowd at the Wolfville pavilion one night, saw V. F. Rotter carrying a sack that looked as if it contained bottles. Anxious to do his job, Goppert rushed to Marshal Sam Forrest and asked him to investigate the suspicious package. According to Caroline's version of the encounter, the conversation went like this:

> "Wot-chu-got?" inquired the Marshal when he located the suspect at his automobile.
> "Moonshine," replied Mr. Rotter, gaily, not knowing he was being raided.
> "Let me see it!" demanded the Marshal.

Whereupon Mr. Rotter opened the sack and produced only a pop bottle, much to the embarrassment of the young attorney trying to do his job. Lockhart publicized the affair in a front-page story titled "Gop Gets Pop in Raid on Car." [115]

Rival editor Len Leander Newton read of such goings on with great interest. As Lockhart dutifully reported in the *Enterprise:* "Newton is much elated over the fact that we are being sued for defaming the character of E. J. Goppert." While she admitted that being sued was "annoying and a nuisance," between "being sued and being kicked, we really prefer the former. It cost a husky citizen only $10 to kick the editor of the *Herald,*" she reminded him, "whereas it will cost the prosecuting attorney many times that amount to sue the *Enterprise,* which is some solace as we reflect upon it." She concluded with a colorful postscript: "In his last issue Mr. Newton referred to us as an 'Amazon,' for the purpose, we take it, of leading strangers to believe that we chew Climax and spit against the wind." [116]

Although Lockhart continued to take journalistic jabs at Newton, she focussed on Goppert unmercifully. She printed an unflattering photograph of him in the *Enterprise,* captioning it with indecipherable letters and symbols. Caroline took every opportunity to make the man look foolish, calling him "Mr. Gumpertz," and comparing him to a penurious New York tailor of her former acquaintance (possibly an anti-Semitic allusion to Samuel Gompers). [117]

Editors of neighboring papers also got into the act. The editor of the Inland *Oil Index,* for example, claimed that although he really did not know about the "merits of the case," it appeared that Goppert was "playing the baby act." Caroline quoted the editor's comments verbatim under the headline: "Here's Chance for Goppert to Sue Casper *Oil Index,*" then elaborated on the attorney's penchant for litigation:

> What with rumors of a $100,000 damage suit against W. L. Simpson and $50,000 against the County Commissioners, a $30,000 suit against the *Enterprise* and another against a local rancher, it looks to us as if Mr. Goppert was figuring on retiring at the expiration of his term of office. [118]

But neither did Lockhart go unscathed. By this time a newspaper editor from the state of Montana was referring to her as the "hard-boiled editor over the line." But that was all right. According to Caroline, "He smiled when he said it." The controversy did have its positive aspects; her notoriety increased and so did circulation of the paper. The editor of the Inland *Oil Index* reported that *Enterprise* exchange papers were being quickly grabbed up by customers who wanted "to see what kind of wop we are handing Gop." In response, Caroline added: "We hear that Gop does the same thing." [119]

Meanwhile, in late February 1924, a jury found the driver of the car in the Prohibition raid, A. E. Carey, guilty on four counts of violating the liquor law. On the strength of incriminating circumstantial evidence, Judge Percy Metz fined the defendant $2,750 and sentenced him to eleven months in jail. According to Caroline, however, Carey was not the only guilty party. "We will give Mr. Goppert the opportunity of suing us for another $30,000 by stating that in our opinion he failed to do his plain duty when he did not arrest Harry R. Tipton and J. T. McGonagle and charge them with the murder of Scotty Sirrine," she wrote in the *Enterprise*. As she had explained earlier: "In the case of a misdemeanor, it is a general rule that an officer has no right, except in self-defense, to kill the offender to effect his arrest, and the killing of a person fleeing under such circumstances amounts to murder." [120]

Lockhart did not retreat from her public stance throughout the four years that it took the libel case to come to trial. The suit proceeded slowly for various reasons. Lockhart's attorney, William Lee Simpson, felt that a change of venue was warranted and that caused some delay. Editor of the *Herald* Len Leander Newton announced this newest development with an attempt at levity, saying: "Now that Caroline has secured a change of 'venom' to Washakie County, the heartening news comes that the county may not have occasion to have a jury term this spring." Not to be outdone, Caroline reprinted Newton's humorous tidbit in the *Enterprise*, noting speciously that: "The last issue of the *Herald* is a fair specimen of the wit with which little len leander [sic] brightens its chaste columns." [121]

The libel case, originally set for 13 April in Worland, was delayed again because of the illness of Judge Percy Metz. While Goppert fretted because he "could not get to the law" and made demands for a complete retraction of Lockhart's statements, the contentious editor continued to entertain her readers. "Whether the Judge's relapse was due to the prospect of listening to the evidence in this case for several days is a matter of conjecture," she wrote. Due to postponements, the case would not be heard until 1926. [122]

When the libel case finally came to trial in the little town of Basin, some seventy-five miles from Cody, the once-peaceful village, according to Caroline, "looked like a circus had moved in." Throngs of people, buggies, and lumber wagons crowded the streets, and saddle horses nudged each other at every hitching rack. The trial was held on the second floor of the largest building in town. Outside, in the row of tall cottonwoods surrounding it, spectators "perched like blackbirds." "Feeling ran high," she recalled, "and the situation between wets and drys was tense." [123]

The case attracted widespread interest throughout the state, and Lockhart dreaded it, despite her self-confident facade. In retrospect, however, she felt that the person who suffered the most was the plaintiff's attorney, a young man who was trying his first important case. "In his nervousness," according to Lockhart, "he waved his arms, and raised his voice while he laid great stress upon the mental anguish his client had endured because of my unwarranted attack." When the attorney finally wiped his brow and sat down, Caroline presented her case in as few words as possible. If Lockhart's recollections are correct, Goppert did not take the stand at all. In conclusion, she said, "Those who came long distances did not feel they had their money's worth." [124]

Ultimately, the judge rendered a verdict of not guilty and ordered the plaintiff to pay court costs. In this manner, Caroline concluded, Goppert "became, and still is, one of my favorite enemies." [125] Lawyers throughout the state were interested in the verdict, which was as widely publicized as the case itself. Denver newspapers were especially congratulatory. After all, the verdict had meaning for their modus operandi; for a while longer they would have free rein to print largely what they pleased. [126]

As if to render support to Lockhart's charges of litigiousness, Goppert filed still another suit against Lockhart while the libel case was pending. The irrepressible editor announced the new case with a front-page feature headlined "GOP HAS ANOTHER TANTRUM; DEMANDS $50 DAMAGE FROM THE CODY ENTERPRISE." According to the story, Goppert also demanded the return of the unflattering photographs of himself and County Commissioner Sanford Watkins that Lockhart persisted in printing. [127]

Justice of the Peace A. B. Campbell came in from Garland County to hear the case. But Lockhart, who professed to be too busy to appear at the hearing, was represented by her attorney. After all was said and done, the judge ordered her to give up Goppert's photograph and pay him a reduced fee of $20 in damages and court costs of $7.60. Caroline felt it a bargain price for having dealt such misery to one of her favorite foes, but even the victories began to wear on her. [128]

Part of the fun of battle went out of the business in 1924 when rival editor Len Leander Newton, sold the *Herald* to his partner. [129] The following year, even before the Goppert libel case came to trial, Lockhart also decided to sell. She planned to write another novel about the West; and following a familiar pattern, not only would she write about it, she would live it.

Lockhart announced her departure with a flourish and praised the new owner highly: "With this issue, our great moral uplift sheet, the Cody *Enterprise*, becomes the property of Victor H. Abrahamson," she wrote. "We have had our play out and feel we must get down to work if we are to accomplish anything in our own field before we are in our dotage."

As for "Vic" Abrahamson, she noted that he had worked for her and that she found him to be "honest, truthful, loyal, and efficient—a man

altogether worthwhile." Therefore, from her "vast experience with bur-
glars, blacksmiths, ignoramuses and imbeciles . . . hired under the mis-
apprehension that they were editors, printers or machine operators," she
felt eminently qualified to judge. "Taking the office cat in one hand and
S. A. Watkins' picture in the other," Lockhart handed over the keys to the
Enterprise, but not without a final, revealing benediction: "May God have
mercy on his soul!" [130]

Although the Better Element and the Prohibitionists heaved a deep sigh
of relief, friends and compatriots in the field of journalism hated to see her
go. "Tartly refreshing contributions of wit, wisdom and wilfulness to the literary potpourri weekly compounded by Wyoming newspaper workers have
ceased with the retirement of Caroline Lockhart from the editorship of
the Cody *Enterprise,*" read one wordy salutation written in the style of the
times. Her imagination and pungent style, according to this well-wisher,
made the *Enterprise* "a novelty among newspapers," and in some ways
"unique." "Even a prohibitionist," the journalist claimed, "could not avoid
the element of entertainment, rasping as the *Enterprise's* editorial viewpoint might be to his convictions." Her skilled use of irony and ridicule,
he said, "penetrated many a Achilles' heel" that appeared invulnerable to
formal argument. [131]

Those who knew her personally provided additional insight relating to
the impact of her journalism on both the western community in which
she resided and, through reprints of her work, on an even wider national
audience. Paul Eldridge, who worked on the *Enterprise* for a short time,
explained:

> She found this shopkeeper and dryfarmer class backing to the mountains and
> crowding off the range the more picturesque trappers, sheepmen, cowmen,
> Indians, and assorted outlaws. . . . For the straggling, outnumbered, and
> well-nigh routed forces of the invaded, she became a leader and a voice. She
> was Rob Roy putting horn to lip, rallying the clan. . . . She put on a Cody
> Stampede and brought to the town, in their colorful regalia, the cowboys,
> the bronc busters, and the Indians that the . . . tide of the town's civilization
> was driving down the sunset slope.
>
> I should say that, conservatively speaking, she stemmed the Middle West-
> ern tide for about 10 years. [132]

In addition to serving as the voice of the old-timers, Lockhart, as attorney David Dominick observed, became even better known as "the brilliant
spokesman for the anti-Prohibitionists of Cody and the nation." [133] And in
this campaign, she may have been more successful. Although Prohibition

would not be repealed until 1933, the law was practically non-enforceable in Cody and elsewhere by 1925. Sheriff Frank Blackburn, who came into office in Cody during the latter days of Prohibition, summarized the situation: "It finally got to the point where you could not get a conviction in a liquor case. People were not willing to sign an affidavit, so search warrants were only hear-say and no good."[134]

In February 1925, almost as if proclaiming a final ruling on the subject, Lockhart published an editorial that gave a fair assessment of the situation. "PROHIBITION, THY NAME IS FAILURE" read the headline, with a discourse following on how the case of the *State* v. *Williford* strikingly illustrated the inefficiency of the Prohibition law. Although nine out of every ten people in the courtroom believed that the defendant was guilty, the jury disagreed. "The American people, pledged to liberty, can be educated to temperance, but they cannot and will not have their rights taken abruptly from them," she concluded.[135]

As one editor noted, "People might deprecate the *Enterprise,* but it was hardly feasible to ignore it." Her distinctive, if contentious, style had a galvanic effect that made "folks sit up and take notice." In more recent times, she stated, "after a series of good editors have come and gone, Caroline Lockhart will still be remembered as the most colorful, without a doubt."[136]

The Cattle Queen

But if you are part an artist; . . . if you have any desire to understand, and thus help to steer, a civilization that seems to have got away from us, then you don't choose between the past and the present; you try to make one serve the other.

Wallace Stegner, "History, Myth and the Western Writer"

ACQUISITION OF THE L SLASH HEART

"Petticoats are no bar to progress in either writing or ranching," Caroline Lockhart told a news reporter in 1928.[1] She spoke with the voice of authority, for two years earlier she had become the owner of the L Slash Heart, a large cattle ranch in the rugged Dryhead country of Montana. The land lay to the west of the Big Horn River canyon, some sixty miles southeast of Billings, Montana, south of the Crow Indian Reservation and east of the Beartooth National Forest.[2]

Accompanied by cowboy Lou Erickson, Lockhart first visited the area in July and August 1924. Lou, who was part Indian, and his brother Bud ran horses on a family spread in the Dryhead canyon. Caroline loved the primitive beauty of the country and planned another trip into the Dryhead the following summer. With the *Enterprise* no longer an all-consuming responsibility, she was able to think seriously of bringing to reality her long-time ambition to own a ranch in the West.[3]

The journey into the rugged isolation of the Dryhead was a feat that discouraged even the most venturesome souls—but not Caroline. Fuller of figure and years older, she still retained the spirit of young "Suzette," the daredevil reporter who went down in Boston Harbor in a diving suit and jumped from a rooftop into a fireman's net to get her story. Her goals were now bigger: a new novel instead of a news article, and a cattle kingdom to call her own.

Traveling into the Dryhead country was a formidable undertaking. Inaccessible in winter, it was difficult to get to in summer. The few intrepid souls that had reason to visit usually took the train to Kane, Wyoming, the nearest railroad point south. From there an old-time stage made the journey into the Dryhead on a twice-a-week schedule. By automobile, one could get some ten to fifteen miles inland to the Strong Ranch on Crooked Creek, which wound tortuously through the canyons. Early visitors, like residents of the area, relied largely on wagon or horseback for transportation. By the 1930s, however, mail driver Charles "Tuff" Abbott braved the rub-board roads and inclement weather to deliver the mail twice a week in his Ford-V8 pickup.

Although the trip was treacherous at points, Caroline and other visitors found the area impressive. The Big Horn Mountains and the Little Pryors made silhouettes against the skyline and created rock walls that jutted up from shadowy canyons below. The deep canyons, like permanent wrinkles in the landscape, expanded the distance to be traversed. It was western terrain at its primal best, reminiscent of the Grand Canyon.[4]

Beyond the ditch-fed alfalfa fields of the Strong Ranch, a red desert spread out before them, then merged into a stretch of badlands strewn with lava rock and dotted with an occasional juniper. The Dryhead, rough as it was, gouged by coulees and unfit for cultivation, kindled Caroline's imagination. She saw that it had value as pasture and grazing land for cattle and horses, particularly if adjoining lands could be obtained.

Farther on, they came to a log house at the bottom of a large clearing. Some three miles beyond, they reached the Philip Wasson ranch, the object of their journey. The headquarters site lay in a cottonwood canyon. Nearby, a shallow creek, bordered by a stand of mint in the summertime, trickled toward the Big Horn. The land adjoining the ranch house was sparsely occupied with trails leading from a bachelor squatter's shack to outlying neighbors' cabins nearer the mountains. The closest village of sorts was Hillsboro, which included the Grosvenor W. Barry ranch, the area post office, and a blacksmith shop. Caroline and Lou stopped at the Barry ranch on their first visit to the Dryhead, and for a while she carried on a correspondence with Grosvenor's wife, Edith Barry, who kept her informed of Dryhead news. But the friendship would not last.[5]

Back in Cody, Lockhart reflected on her trip. The scouting expedition had shown her the strategy she must take if she wished to realize her goals. "It is what I have wanted all my life and there's damned few years left in which to enjoy the realization of my dream," she wrote pragmatically. At age fifty-four, she envisioned the ranch not only as the realization of a personal dream, but also "as a headquarters for Lou who has been so unselfish." For herself, the ranch represented a final bid for happiness: "I believe I shall be comparatively happy, once I get my ranch in the Dryhead country; work, and life in the open—the life I have longed for always."[6]

Fortuitously, her financial situation had improved. By mid-October

1925, she finalized sale of the *Enterprise* and received a windfall of $10,000 in Liberty Bonds. Her father, Joseph Lockhart, was dying of cancer. His passing would mean the inheritance of ranch lands in Kansas and Oklahoma and funds that would enable her to operate the ranch on the Dryhead.

Lockhart and Lou Erickson agreed that he should negotiate the purchase of the ranch with Wasson; she would provide the funds. Always the shrewd businesswoman, she had also persuaded Erickson, her housekeeper Lou Tiffany Ketcham, and hired hand Clay Jolly to go to Billings with her, where each would file homestead entries on adjoining grazing land. By prearrangement, she would purchase their entries after they had "proved up." She learned from Edith Barry that the Caldwell place was also available and added that to her list of lands to acquire.

On 29 October 1925, Erickson blew into Cody at the height of a blizzard to discuss terms of the sale of the Wasson place and then out again to drive his horses to Lovell and to complete the negotiations for Lockhart. By 12 November he called from Kane, Wyoming, to report his success. "The ranch is mine for $2,250!" she wrote jubilantly.[7] She was to pay $500 in cash and the remainder when Wasson proved up on a homestead parcel.

Within two weeks, however, complications had developed. Lockhart learned that Wasson would not be able to prove up on the adjoining land if he sold the homestead site. Caroline therefore agreed to pay the necessary $500 "and let Erickson take it (the ranch site) as a lease." She was determined to have the place at this point. "Want it even if I pay $2,250 for the homestead alone," she wrote.[8]

The deed for the homestead in question would be in Erickson's name until she purchased it back from him some months later. In the interim, Caroline, accompanied by Lou Ketcham, drove to Billings where Erickson and Clay Jolly met them to file their individual entries on adjoining land and carry out the remainder of Lockhart's plans for the acquisition of what would become the L Slash Heart.[9]

According to homestead law, to prove upon their claims, Lockhart and her associates had to be in residence on their land seven months of the year. Improvements had to be made on the property within five years from the allowance date of filing. Although they filed their claims in late November, the allowance date was listed as 24 April 1926, which meant that final proof had to be made in July of 1931.[10]

During the latter part of 1925 and over the next few years, Lockhart made good use of her time, systematically carrying out the steps necessary to realize her goal. On 18 December she wrote: "Yesterday I took the plunge. Had Mr. McGee write Mrs. Caldwell to send on the abstract and deed, and I would give her my note for $1,400."[11] She also arranged to purchase three carloads of longhorns in the spring.

Her ability to pull together the different facets of her grand land scheme, including the carefully orchestrated acquisition of adjoining territory and water rights, gave her great personal satisfaction. "It gives me more a thrill than I have experienced for a long while," she confided.[12] In addition to publication of her last novel, *Old West and New*, the acquisition and successful operation of the L Slash Heart would be the major accomplishment of the autumn years of her life.

Meanwhile in Cody, despite numerous irritating interruptions from her talkative housekeeper Lou Ketcham, she worked on the novel, waited for a warming trend to melt the winter snows, and dreamed of becoming the "Cattle Queen of Montana." She had even come to terms, at least temporarily, with her solitude and respite from business and civic duties:

> It is such a grand and glorious feeling to get back into my old routine before the paper and constant companionship. Guess I was meant to live alone, though I do long for a congenial spirit now my work is done. Thoughts of the ranch make me happy in a way; it is something I look forward to.[13]

Throughout 1925 and for the first few months in 1926, Lou Erickson worked the ranch and reported to Caroline in Cody. She delighted in his glowing reports and found his enthusiasm about the ranch to be contagious. Her Diary reflected her own excitement:

> The Caldwell and Wasson place for headquarters will be a valuable ranch that can be sold if ever we want to dispose of it—which I hope will never come about. It is what I have wanted all my life and I am going to stick with it.[14]

RANCHING ON THE DRYHEAD

By early summer of 1926, the warm winds known as "chinooks" melted the snow to the extent that Caroline was able to join Lou Erickson on the Dryhead. In April she had won the Goppert libel trial, and in June she consented reluctantly to consolidation of the *Enterprise* with the *Herald*. "The name of the *Enterprise* is retained," she recorded in her Diary with some consolation; yet, she admitted "it made me cry—like handing my gun over to the enemy, though Shaw declares he will treat me right."[15] The transaction brought her some $5,600 in cash, which she needed for the operation of the ranch, and permitted her to pay off money still owed on the paper by Vic Abrahamson. More important, it closed that chapter of her life completely. She could now devote her energies to writing and to development of the ranch.

Lockhart approached ranching much as she approached all of her business dealings—with vigor and with objectives clearly in mind. "If only I can bring the same excitable ability into action in putting the L/ ♥ (L Slash Heart) ranch on the map that made the *Enterprise* and Stampede a success, I shall be happy," she wrote, adding as an honest afterthought, "not happy but satisfied." [16]

There were improvements to be made, fences to be erected, cattle to be purchased, and additional sections of land to be added at the opportune time. The main cabin had to be enlarged, a fireplace built, and outbuildings and barns constructed. Hired-hand "Harry" Miller helped Lou chink the cabin logs, and Lou Ketcham came to the Dryhead to serve as cook. Caroline also had a pen built for the newest addition to the barnyard—a pig named "Gop." Clay Jolly, who took one of the adjoining homestead entries, also helped out as a ranch hand. Despite the fact that he was "getting up in years," Caroline found him to be loyal and hardworking. In September when he had to leave, she rewarded him with $100 rather than the $70 owed, "because he has been faithful and done his best." [17]

At first, hard labor and tasks associated with getting the ranch operational interrupted the time she hoped to spend on her novel. In addition to work on the main spread, she was required to spend time on the adjoining homestead entry. To carry out the residency requirements, Lockhart moved a chicken shack from the main ranch up the hill to her homestead. The shelter, a small one-room building, was just large enough to house a built-in bunk, a table and chair set on a plank platform, and an iron stove used for heating and cooking. At times she used the cabin as her writing hideaway. The plank table served as a desk for her papers and typewriter.

Whether working there or not, on days that the mailman came she made sure that smoke billowed out of the stove pipe extending from the roof to give the illusion, if not the reality, of her presence in the cabin. Early on, she knew that the subterfuge was necessary to stifle the curiosity of neighbors, who quickly became suspicious of her control over more and more of the surrounding land. Their fears seem to have been justified. By 18 June 1927, she was able to write in her Diary: "I now have six sections of 640 acres each, my principality." [18]

Lockhart irritated her neighbors at the outset by fencing the access road. This meant that gates had to be opened and closed even to deliver the mail. She did allow the neighbors' cattle to get to water, but only because they knew that she was required to do so by law. Later, much to her disgust, she would be forced to remove the gates and fence both sides of the roads to allow free passage. Relations with Edith Barry—referred to on the Dryhead (according to Caroline) as "Old Satan"—and her son, Claude St. John, the postmaster at Hillsboro, deteriorated rapidly. These neighbors and others soon showed their displeasure with Lockhart's territoriality by cutting fences, killing her burros and dogs, and poisoning her cattle.[19]

It was a hard life on the Dryhead in other respects. There were few amenities, although she like to claim that her bunkhouse was as warm and comfortable as any around and that the shelves in the springhouse by the creek were always filled with eggs, butter, and milk. Nevertheless, ranch hands seemed to come and go. Although they were a continual source of frustration to Caroline, she wrote of them with characteristic humor.

Among those who held a prominent place in her gallery of singular characters was "John the Baptist." This particular hand arrived in the middle of a fearful winter when the snow was belly-deep to a horse and icy blasts from the north found every crack in the old-fashioned log house. One of the hands discovered him trying to survive the winter in a deep canyon some two or three miles away. Caroline gave instructions for the man to be invited to stay at the ranch until the chinooks arrived, bringing warmer weather.

A few hours later, the ranch hand returned with a strange-looking human who, to Caroline, resembled "a cinnamon bear rampant." Above average height, with wide, thick shoulders and a barrel chest, the visitor appeared to be a man of prodigious strength. Speaking in a strong German accent, the newcomer expressed surprise that anyone should be concerned about his welfare. He indicated that he had been living quite comfortably in a cave in the side of the canyon.

For the time being, that was all she learned about his background. The man agreed to stay at the ranch until the weather warmed and chose an old log cabin as his private quarters, making it clear to the bunkhouse crew that he preferred his solitude. Because of his air of aloofness and the mane of long hair that gave him an apostolic look, the ranch hands dubbed him "John the Baptist." John paid them little mind, however, and went about his business. As it turned out, he proved to be a diamond in the rough, a man of strength and talent.

The chinooks blew in, but John stayed on. He cleaned out the creek, dragging out soggy logs and fallen trees that would otherwise have required a team and horses. And as a blacksmith, John proved to be a genius. His ringing anvil produced from iron scraps a variety of ornamental hinges and latches that were works of art, and practical as well. He made a wash bench for the cook and grafted every tree, bush, and shrub in sight. But basically,

John remained a man of mystery. One day Caroline saw him stand flat-footed and vault onto the back of a tall horse with the ease and grace of a panther. Astonished, she asked where he learned such a feat and discovered that he had been an officer in the Prussian cavalry.[20]

Being the ramrod of a cattle ranch was not an easy task, even for a liberated woman accustomed to running things. Controlling a motley assortment of ranch hands who ranged from hoboes to former members of the Prussian military proved to be a real challenge. She found that her managerial problems were compounded by the availability of bootleg whisky, which made the men quarrel and neglect their work. A second complicating factor was rivalry among the cowboys over her own affections.

By March 1928 Caroline's affair with cowboy Lou Erickson had cooled, and a new man by the name of Bill Poole, alias "Miller," had joined the bunkhouse crew. In addition, a friend of long-standing from the East, referred to by Lockhart only as "Marie Louise," also arrived for an extended visit. "Marie," Caroline noted in her Diary, "is the only woman outside of Maudie for whom I ever cared." It was Poole, however, who suggested to Caroline that the way to solve her bootleg whiskey problem was to build her own still (which he offered to do) and promise the men a drink after work each night—if they agreed to stop buying it from a local source. Lockhart decided to give it a try. "After considerable expense, I acquired a small still with a copper coil and boiler," she recalled.[21]

Bill set up the still in a secret place along the creek and prepared the corn mash for fermentation. Sometime before it was ready for distilling, however, Caroline noted that the crew and Bill showed signs of having sampled the batch. She and her guest, Marie Louise, decided to investigate. Taking a circuitous route to the creek so as not to alert the ranch hands, they found their suspicions confirmed. The liquid, which had all the alcoholic content of the finished product, had been siphoned off the mash. The result was a drunken and raucous crew.

Furiously, Caroline called to Marie Louise to get a bucket and help her throw the stuff out. But Marie Louise had another suggestion: "Give it to the chickens; don't waste it." Each of the women filled a bucket and treated the chickens to a corn mash feast. Not long after, Caroline and her guest heard a series of shrill squeals and much cackling from the barnyard. "There I saw a sight that made my jaw drop," Caroline wrote. "The pig was jumping and squealing; the roosters were fighting and the hens lurching, while laughter, shouts, and the sound of scuffling came from the bunkhouse. In other words, everything and everybody on the place were tight."[22]

In retrospect, Caroline was able to appreciate the humor of the situation, but the problems relating to rivalry over her own affections took a much more serious turn.

LOVERS AND LAWSUITS

The arrival of new ranch hand Bill Poole, alias Miller, soon complicated matters. "Bill and I do great teamwork together and we like each other a lot," she wrote. Caroline admitted also that she had "taken quite a shine to him," a fact that was apparent to Lou Erickson as well. Although reveling in her continuing ability to arouse such feelings in her suitors, Caroline realized that the situation was a potentially dangerous one. "I fear that sooner or later Bill and Lou will lock horns," she predicted.[23]

True to Caroline's prophecy, the ranch romance soon became a real-life melodrama. Tensions erupted into a full-fledged gunfight when Bill appropriated Lou's saddle blanket. With the help of another hand, Caroline broke up the fight, bandaged her new lover's badly wounded arm, and transported him in the back of a jitney to the hospital in Billings.

Coverage of the affair in the Lovell *Chronicle* provided a slightly different version of the incident. According to the news report, Poole initiated the fight by attacking and knocking Erickson to the ground with a hammer. Erickson, trying to escape, retreated into the house where he grabbed a 30-30 gauge shotgun and fired at Poole in self-defense. The authorities apparently accepted this version because charges were never filed.[24]

Lou's departure put an end to the volatile situation, and by 16 October, Bill had recovered enough to return to the ranch. Caroline rented an airplane to get back into the Dryhead in maximum comfort. It was her first flight, and, much to her relief, the plane landed safely. While adventuresome by nature, she admitted that flying "was a great experience . . . but a nervous strain for me who fears heights."[25]

Rather than return to Cody for the entire winter as she usually did, Caroline decided to stay on the Dryhead with Bill for a while longer. Although half her age (which was fifty-eight), Bill was extremely jealous. "I have never seen such a jealous person in my life," she wrote, "worse than Lou and like a savage, yet tender and lovable . . . when we are by ourselves."[26]

Caroline and her lover spent the winter trying to keep the cattle from starving in the snowdrifts and the ranch hands from killing one another when drunk on homemade whisky. The still continued to be a problem. After a particularly violent fight between Bill and another of the ranch hands, she decreed that "there will be no more booze making on this place unless I am on deck every minute to see that they don't take too many samples of the mash." "Bill," she observed, "acted like a wild man."[27]

Toward the end of January, Caroline decided that she must go into Cody to take care of business and on to Kansas to check her cattle on the ranchlands inherited from her father. The trip out of the Dryhead proved more dangerous than anticipated when she and her driver got caught in a blizzard. At twelve degrees below zero, the roads were icy and treacherous. Even at the thirty to forty miles per hour they were traveling, Caroline felt that Ed was driving too fast. A few miles outside of Cody, the car hit an ice slick and slid off the road down an embankment where it overturned. Fortunately, the three- to four-foot snowdrifts acted as a cushion and kept them from being injured. They were able to escape from the car by pulling out the broken side windows and climbing through. They ploughed their way through the snowdrifts, crawling back up the bank, where they then flagged down an old oil truck to get into town.[28]

In Cody Caroline took advantage of the amenities offered by the small town, such as the local beauty shop, and made arrangements for the painting and repair of her house and rental properties. She spent a nostalgic couple of days pouring over old love letters, some of which she decided to burn. In a rare moment of insight, she acknowledged how little she had valued friendships, how guilty she had been of being "headstrong and supersensitive." She amazed herself by counting up the number of men who had loved her, recalling how they all spoke in complimentary terms of her "figure," "strong individuality," and "independence." She reflected on:

> Andrew MacKenzie, brilliant mind, sensitive, refined; Bill Miller . . . toughest of the bunch and young enough to be my son but willing to go to hell for me; . . . Harry J. Scott, district attorney of Philadelphia; . . . Jesse Mitchell, cowpuncher; Pinkie Gist, champion bulldogger; Lou Erickson, jockey; of all them, 14 I count up, O.B. [Mann] was the only one I wanted to marry.[29]

Back at the Dryhead, however, she had to deal with the most recent addition to her long list of suitors. She managed to return by 30 March, although ice and snow still covered the ground. Not long after, true to form, Bill went into another drunken, jealous rage. He accused other hands of being in love with her and also made threats that promised a repeat of the shooting incident with Erickson. Finally, no longer able to tolerate such irrational behavior, Caroline insisted that Bill leave for good.[30]

With winter approaching, it was imperative that she find another foreman soon. She heard of David Franklin Good, a cowman with an excellent reputation, who at the time worked on a sheep ranch called the Two Dot.

Dave Good was a roughly handsome man with a leathery face and a shock of white hair. People said he resembled Will Rogers. Anxious to work "in cow country" once again, Dave accepted Caroline's offer and in October 1929 joined the L Slash Heart as ranch foreman. "Now that I have Dave Good, I plan to be Cattle Queen right," she wrote jubilantly.[31]

Despite the momentary optimism, Caroline's goal was far from being realized. Dave provided strong support, but relationships with neighbors in the outlying areas worsened. She suspected the Barrys of castrating one of her bulls and another neighbor, Hank Lane, of fence cutting. She became involved in a legal dispute over water rights, and an infestation of crickets and grasshoppers stripped her dry-land barley fields. The crickets were so bad they hung in the trees in bunches; Dave decided they would have to mow the fields immediately to salvage the crop. Expenses mounted, but financing became increasingly difficult to obtain. The fates seemed to be against her.[32]

By the early thirties, the depression was being felt even in the small towns and outlying ranches of Wyoming and Montana. The bank at Belfry tottered on the brink of foreclosure, and the Joliet bank had already gone under. "Sheepmen and cattlemen alike are suffering," she noted. "Rancher offered to sell me 2 of his $250 bulls for $50 each. Things are that bad outside." [33] With sources of financing drying up, she was forced to accept a loan from friend Marie Louise in the East.

It was Marie Louise, in fact, who came to help care for her when, in October 1931, she suffered a mild stroke that caused one side of her face to be paralyzed. After a brief stay in the hospital in Cody, where she underwent "electric" treatments, Caroline was able to return to the Dryhead. Marie Louise had remained with her while Caroline recuperated in Cody, and later accompanied her back to the ranch. Although Caroline had little patience with many of her friends, she thoroughly enjoyed Marie's company and appreciated her assistance. "Marie cheers me up," she wrote; and again, two weeks later, "Marie is a lot of help to me." After several months, the paralysis affecting Caroline's face disappeared completely.[34]

The 1930s were tough years, but all was not bleak. One bright spot was the development of a romantic relationship with her foreman Dave Good. Dave, who held women in high esteem, proved to be a rather difficult conquest. Nevertheless, Caroline in her early sixties was still a handsome, earthy woman who had an incredible ability to make men fall in love with her. The relationship developed slowly—too slowly for Caroline's taste. They spent their first New Year's Eve together, dancing in the cabin, but he refused to spend the night. Caroline, accustomed to a more direct approach, was unimpressed by Dave's "exceptionally high principles" and admitted to her Diary with some astonishment that this was "the first turn down of this kind I ever had!"[35] High standards didn't stand a chance, however, against Caroline's charm and determination. Although Dave claimed that he had not cared for a woman in twenty years, by summertime he had joined the long line of Lockhart conquests.[36]

In July 1931, Lockhart and her former housekeeper Lou Ketcham filed for final proof of residency on their respective homestead entries, but even this was not to be accomplished without attendant problems. "The long dreaded has happened and I am broken up," she wrote. "The land office turned down my homestead on the grounds of insufficient evidence filed by the inspector." She had thirty days from notification to submit affidavits in her defense and appear at a hearing. Accustomed to legal frays and knowing that the inclement weather and lack of time made it impossible to contact the necessary witnesses, Lockhart immediately hired an attorney in Billings to obtain an extension for her.[37]

Although her neighbors were in back of the move and testified against her at hearings held 3–4 October 1933 in Bridger, Montana, Caroline rallied her own supporters. In the local area, Merle Abarr expressed his willingness to help, indicating that he had seen her working at the homestead shack when he was hauling poles from the mountain. Abarr's moral support gave her "courage to fight harder than ever."[38] Joe LeFors, U.S. Deputy Marshal and cattle inspector, also sided with Lockhart and Ketcham. The well-known cattle inspector had conducted investigations in the area and was familiar with the habits of the Dryhead residents. LeFors, who claimed that he "had never in all his experience seen so many unprincipled, conscienceless scoundrels congregated in one small community," wrote a letter to the U.S. Land Commissioner on the women's behalf. "The element in the Dryhead basin," he said, "is very antagonistic to Miss Caroline Lockhart and will resort to nearly anything. They want an open range."[39]

Lockhart, as always, proved to be a fierce adversary. Knowing that she had little support in the local area, she called upon influential friends and acquaintances, including Governor Nellie Ross of Wyoming; Senator Joseph C. O'Mahoney of Montana; president of the First National Bank of Cody, Fred T. McGee; president of the Wyoming National Bank of Rock Springs, John W. Hay; and John F. Cook, Democratic state committeeman, Park County, Wyoming. Letters from these individuals certified to her "excellent character" and financial reputation, indicating that over twenty-some years of acquaintance they had found her to be "most honest in all of her dealings."[40] Cody banker F. T. McGee revealed that he had loaned her up to $5,000 on secured notes, as well as smaller loans,

all of which she had repaid satisfactorily. McGee also spoke highly of Lou
Ketcham, saying that he had never known of her honesty and integrity
being questioned in any way. Letters on Lockhart's behalf were forwarded
to Fred C. Johnson, the U.S. Land Commissioner in Washington, D. C.,
whose personal interest in the case proved to be of benefit.[41]

For her own part, Caroline never let facts stand in the way of winning.
Her rendition of the circumstances leading to acquisition of the L Slash
Heart and proof of homestad, as presented to the land commissioner and
at the hearing, stands in sharp contrast to the step-by-step strategy worked
out with Erickson's collaboration and revealed in her Diary entries.[42] Con-
solidated hearings for Lockhart, Lou Ketcham, and Clay Jolly were held in
Bridger, Montana, on 3 October 1933. The government attorney claimed
that the Lockhart homestead shack was in actuality a chicken house moved
from the headquarters property, and that Lockhart had not spent the required amount of time in residence. Caroline contradicted all charges,
claiming that she had lived on the place for more than seven months a year
for the required three years. Lou Ketcham also refuted the government's
accusations, contending that she went to her house on the homestead a
mile from the ranch and resided there each night from spring until late fall.
In the case of Clay Jolly, the attorney pointed out that the homestead was
Jolly's sole residence. Gilbert T. Marchand also testified on behalf of the
defendants.

Even more blatant, but harder for the government attorney to disprove,
was Lockhart's denial of charges that she came to the Dryhead solely for
the purpose of buying a cattle ranch and adding to her holdings by having
others file on land for her. Diary entries prove that this was indeed the
strategy employed, yet Lockhart testified that she had first entered the area
simply to visit friends living on the Bighorn not far from St. Xavier. Lou
Erickson, she claimed, was her driver on the trip; and it was he who later
asked her for a loan to buy the Wasson place, saying he would repay her
from his mother's estate. When the estate turned out to be a myth and
Erickson could not pay, according to Lockhart, he deeded the place to
her in payment. "My job is writing books," she wrote to the land commissioner, "and the last thing I had in mind when I came to the Dryhead
was filing on land and engaging in the cattle business, and certainly not
in locating in a country where a fresh wagon track in the main travelled
road is an event."[43] In reality, the Dryhead—however godforsaken—provided Lockhart an avenue toward realization of a compelling desire, and
one important enough that she did not mind stretching the truth in order
to retain it.

Support for her position from people in influential positions paid off;

the U.S. Land Commissioner reversed the decision rendered by the district office. A subsequent appeal by the federal government to the Secretary of the Interior was unsuccessful; and in June 1936, final certificates were issued to Lockhart and Ketcham. After three years of legal wrangling, Lockhart had the L Slash Heart securely under wraps and official title.[44]

From the personal perspective, the decision represented a sweet victory over her enemies on the Dryhead. In the broader view, however, it was only one of many hardships she had to overcome during that first decade as she fought to become a successful ranch woman. The fact that she did survive against all odds stands as testimonial to an exceptional character— tough-minded, determined, and capable—if at times somewhat unscrupulous. In 1935, when articles in the Lovell *Chronicle* and the Billings *Gazette* reported that three carloads of Lockhart steers had topped the market in Omaha, she must have felt that she had indeed earned the sobriquet of Cattle Queen.[45] More amazing, during the early years of getting the L Slash Heart established, despite seemingly never-ending struggles, she somehow found time and energy to tap that inner source of talent to produce what would be her final published novel.

CONNECTIONS: *OLD WEST AND NEW*

In Dryhead, Montana, the weather at times seemed to exhibit no season other than slight variations of winter. On 20 March 1932, when inhabitants of more civilized environs were enjoying warm spring breezes, snow was falling on the L Slash Heart. The winters of 1932 and 1933 would be remembered as long-lasting and fierce. At the Lockhart ranch house, beams of sunlight reflecting off the snow filtered through the barren branches of the tree outside the main cabin where Caroline sat writing to cast patchwork patterns of light and shadow on the pages of her manuscript. With fingers stiffened from the cold, she pecked at the Remington Rand situated center-front on the table that served as her desk. In the other room, she could hear Dave stomping snow from his boots and dumping an armload of logs by the fireplace as she put the finishing touches on the novel then called "18 Karats." Such details of her life and surroundings she continued to record religiously in her Diary.

Throughout the month of April, she took advantage of the inclement weather to concentrate on her writing, after which she was able to say: "The only thing that gives me any comfort these days is the thought that my book is typed and is by now at the publishers." She was hoping that proceeds from publication would improve her financial situation. "So much depends on the verdict that I am afraid to think of the consequences if they turn it down," she wrote. "Acceptance . . . would pull me out of the hole I am in." A month or so later, exciting news arrived: "We like '18 Karat' fine and want to publish it." The editor did want her to come up with a better title, however.[46]

By the time the novel was published in 1933 under the title *Old West and New,* civilization had made noticeable inroads on those states traditionally recognized as the last bastions of the frontier. Although the Dryhead remained a primitive stronghold, Lockhart, as an astute observer of human behavior and changing mores, saw the cow paths becoming paved highways, the automobile replacing the horse and buggy, and cowboys—like her characters "Hungry Jim" and "Pole-Cat Jack"—tending gas stations instead of cattle. And these were the observations she recorded. At least one critic would claim that the book made no intentional sociological analysis, saying that the author had "tailored" it to suit her publisher's literary whim, but entries in her Diary and Journals show that she was well aware of what was taking place around her.[47] As such, *Old West and New* was an appropriate finale to her literary career.

Lockhart divided her final novel, as the book's title suggests, into two parts. Part One, depicting the Old West, begins with a scene at Roadhouse Fanny's in which she introduces her main character, cowboy Vance Galloway. Vance, goodhearted but naive, finds himself with an unwanted wife (Fanny), whom he has acquired in exchange for a cook stove.

Through the voice of characters such as Vance, Lockhart reveals the impact of the changing West on its inhabitants. Vance, who has been driving a freight wagon, tells Fanny of his need to get back to ranch work he so enjoyed. He will have to move on, he explains, because South Dakota is becoming too populated with scissorbills and pilgrims "bringin' in pennies and lockin' their doors like they thought the country was full of petty-larceny thieves."[48]

Frank Spivey—the calculating cattleman of her earlier novel *The Dude Wrangler*—is reintroduced, this time as the father of Fanny's illegitimate child. As the story progresses, Fanny returns to her "roadhouse ways," whereupon Galloway sells his freight outfit and heads off. On his travels West, he meets up with Nellie Kent, another western heroine in the Lockhart mold—self-reliant, adventurous, and attractive.

During the course of the usual hard-luck episodes, Vance Galloway meets other representatives of the Old West, characters such as Turkey Track, who always falls on his head to save his feet, and Charles E. Summers, who hopes to keep step with the advance of civilization by becoming a politician. Typically, Lockhart patterns certain of her characters after real-life acquaintances. Charles Summers is a thinly disguised Buffalo Bill Cody.

Like Cody, Summers anticipates the effects of Progress. Quoting from a speech, Summers talks of "law and order, substantial citizens, . . . churches, better schools *and* good society." But cowboy Vance Galloway is unimpressed. "I hope I'll be under the daisies when it arrives," he replies shortly. "I've seen enough of the East to thank God there's a West." [49]

The same brand of western humor animates the pages of this novel as in *The Dude Wrangler.* One of the most amusing characters is Waldo Haller, who aspires to become a judge. Repressed by his overbearing wife, Doc Haller observes that he has not lived fifteen years with a woman of his wife's temperament without learning something of the art of diplomacy. In fact, he says, this has made him "well qualified to handle delicate situations in foreign parts—Poland or the Balkan States." [50] Haller's ego is revitalized when he is elected to the legislature through the political plotting of his cowboy friends.

The Press, as still another personification of Progress, comes to town and operates out of a wagon for lack of better accommodations. Nellie reappears as a self-sufficient newspaper woman and niece of the editor, Homer Frizelle. Galloway in the interim has become an anti-Prohibitionist candidate for the legislature. Unknown to Galloway, it is Nellie who champions his cause through the newspaper.

In addition to Prohibition, Lockhart in *Old West and New* throws verbal darts at other favorite targets—stepmothers and the pseudo-religious. To do so, she sets up a scene where heroine Nellie runs away, then encounters a "wolfer" (trapper) who empathizes with her plight. [51]

"Why did you run off?" he asks.

"I couldn't stand it—at home—any longer." Nellie replies.

"Stepmother?"

Nellie nodded.

"I had one—she was a cruel Christian," the wolfer offers. [52]

Part Two features a twenty-years-after sequel in which the same characters reappear in modern guise as dude wranglers, filling station operators, and Prohibition agents. Prohibition, not surprisingly, is the town's most controversial issue.

In this final novel, Caroline not only acknowledges that the West in its primitive state is passing but also that people pass on. The *Old West and New* reveals for the first time the author's cognizance of the transient nature of human existence and of her own mortality. In the fall of 1926, she had made a "whirlwind" trip to Kansas to visit her eighty-nine-year-old father, who was in ill health. His obvious pleasure at seeing "his Caddie" apparently assuaged some of the lifelong anger she held against him; and when he died a few months later, she admitted that she wished "it could have all been different," and that she could have continued "worshipping" him as she had when she was a little girl. In March 1931, she received a telegram informing her that her older brother George had died in Tucson, and by the time her novel was published in 1933, she had also lost her friends "Lizzie" Hollister and Maude Altberger, and former lover Andrew Ross. At sixty-two years of age, Caroline, too, was beginning to feel the effects of time; her eyes in particular were becoming an increasingly serious problem.

In *Old West and New,* a character named Fender observes that the hospital had impressed upon him "the surprising fact that he *could* be sick—that he *could* die like everyone else." "Supposing I don't make the grade, what's going to become of the ranch?" he frets, much as Caroline herself worried about the L Slash Heart—and her own mortality.[53]

The main character, Vance Galloway, also reflects on the prospect of death. In a half-waking state, Galloway experiences a symbolic dream:

Tum! Tum! Tum! A funeral march played on a million muffled instruments. . . . He looked without surprise at the procession. Skeletons—sexless, repellent, rigidly erect as they passed him, beating on deadened drums monotonously—Tum! Tum! Tum! The dead of a million worlds, of a million years, marching in a line that had no end, through all eternity.[54]

The novel concludes on another semi-autobiographical note. Vance learns that Nellie is not only a successful newspaper woman, but an heiress with oil lands in Oklahoma. "Why is it you've never married?" he asks. "The kind of men I might have liked—don't often marry girls who work," she replies. "By the time I was no longer in that class some other woman had gobbled them up."[55]

In this novel, as in others, Lockhart freely interjected portions of her own life experiences to create a book that was a fitting culmination to a long and interesting career as an expert observer of human behavior and the influence of changing times on the West. The novel did not meet Caroline's personal standards—on one occasion she referred to it as that "dog"—but reviewers were more generous. "Many who care for westerns," wrote one critic, "will find a robustness and a realism about this book with a masculine attitude toward life that a mere male would hesitate to express. It is different enough from most cowboy stories to be well worth the reading." The hiatus of twenty years, in the opinion of a reviewer for the New York *Times,* detracted from the "artistic unity" of the book. "It is a good story, nevertheless," he added, "and stands out from the average run of conventional westerns."[56]

In the local area, the book was anxiously awaited; by the end of May 1933, it was selling "like hotcakes" at the Cody Drug and the Broadway Pharmacy. Caroline enjoyed the town's reaction to her characterizations: "Old Blanche is about half-crazy on the warpath on account of being in my book," she chortled. "Everybody likes it—thought it my best!"[57]

THAT WICKED WOMAN

The following year, Caroline began another novel, alternately called "The Madam," "The Witch of Willow Creek," "Web of the Black Widow," and "That Wicked Woman," in which she tried to polish off Edith (Mrs. Grosvenor) Barry, the individual she considered her major enemy on the Dryhead. But the novel would remain unpublished despite the assistance of her most loyal and supportive critic, professor of English literature Paul Eldridge, and the efforts of various editors in the East.[58]

A longtime friend, Eldridge had once worked for Lockhart on the *Enterprise*. The professor, who made an annual pilgrimage to the Dryhead for twelve consecutive summers, considered her cottonwood canyon homesite as "an oasis worth the rough ride," especially with Caroline to enliven it. He spent at least one holiday on the Dryhead as well, which was made memorable by Caroline and Dave Good retiring to the living room after dinner to compile a list of people they would most like to kill.

Eldridge recalled that Caroline's bizarre sense of humor also surfaced when she discovered that Dave was enamored of the young hired girl. Secretly hurt by Dave's lack of fidelity, Lockhart handled the situation by placing a farcical announcement of their forthcoming marriage in the local paper.[59]

As time passed, there were fewer typed pages for Eldridge to peruse on his visits to the L Slash Heart, but greater numbers of sleek cattle, new corrals, and well-fed horses. He later wrote nostalgically of the pond below the spring that served as a swimming pool for visiting Indians as well as professors, of waking to walls brightened by full-page western illustrations from the Denver *Post*, and of Caroline's yellow buckboard with a black L Slash Heart stamped on the back of the seat.[60]

Between visits, Lockhart sent him chapters of "That Wicked Woman," which he returned with high praise and suggestions for improvement. "Congratulations," he wrote after receiving the first chapter of the manuscript, "You've done a grand piece of work. Any reader will like it. . . . You are writing a seller!" Despite the compliments, however, Lockhart's work did not go well. She finally hired a professional editor in New York,

Eleanor Shoemaker, to do a complete rewrite. Both Eldridge and Shoe-maker suggested that a new title might help market the book. Eldridge wanted something more western in connotation, such as "Mrs. Sinclair of Silver Creek." Shoemaker suggested "Web of the Black Widow." After reading Shoemaker's revised version, Eldrige concluded that the organiza-tion of the book was indeed improved, but "some of it doesn't sound as Caroline Lockhartish as I could wish."[61]

Shoemaker felt that the crux of the problem was not so much in Lock-hart's style, which had remained the same, but the change in "public demand and appeal." Other professionals in the eastern literary market seemed to agree. New York agent Ellan McIlvaine, who at Lockhart's re-quest critiqued some of her short stories, focused on the same aspect. "Current stories are virtually all action; little explanation is in order," she advised, adding: "Writing has changed completely, and it is not so good in my opinion."[62]

Agnes M. Reeve, a reader and critic for the Oldest Writer's Service, was not quite so subtle. "It is not often a writer is so capable of criticizing his own manuscript," she wrote Lockhart, "for you hit the nail on the head when you said that you may be 'outdated,' for I fear that is the case to some extent."[63] Indeed, the popular literature of the day—books such as Evelyn Waugh's *The Loved One,* parodying Hollywood's Forest Lawn Cemetery, and Norman Mailer's *The Naked and the Dead*—were a far cry from the old-fashioned Western. Lockhart did not care for the change, for under the earthy exterior, the facade of a gentlewoman was deeply ingrained. *"The Naked and the Dead,"* she wrote to a friend of her later years Dorothea Nebel, "is too nasty and obscene for words. . . . I may be old-fashioned, but I think this is carrying realism too far."[64] Eldridge summarized the situa-tion best. "Lockhart," he wrote, "was a victim of a change in climate in the American publishing scene." Unconventional as her life was, she was not prepared "to follow the frontier of free speech as far as Hemingway, Faulkner, and the tribe of younger writers."[65]

The death of Charles Agnew MacLean, well-respected editor of *Popular Magazine,* also contributed to Lockhart's lack of publishing success during the later years of her life. For decades, she had found a ready market for her literary wares in MacLean's prestigious magazine. One of her last stories published in 1929 in the *Popular,* "Not a Redeeming Trait," contained an almost prophetic observation. Speaking "as a representative of the 'True West,'" she noted that "times, conditions and people have changed so rapidly and so much that I cannot keep up. Nor can I adapt myself. I belong to the past."[66]

MacLean's death ended an era—for the magazine and for Lockhart. Although not a sentimental woman, she was devastated by the news. "I wept," she wrote Paul Eldridge.[67]

High of quality and characterized by good, clean literature, the *Popular* was followed in its demise by two of its closest competitors in the Western genre—*Adventure* and *Short Stories*. Contributors such as Bertha M. Bower and Caroline Lockhart lost a valuable outlet. For Western-style literature, only two markets remained—the Western pulps, which she scorned, and the "literary publishers," which she found unacceptable for their modern latitude in language and morals. "She was," as Eldridge termed it, "in limbo between two worlds"; and that western world, as she portrayed it, was changing.[68] But Lockhart could not adapt.

The *Old West and New*, therefore, would remain her final benediction on the region she had come to know so well. From her beginnings as an eastern newspaper reporter and a writer of short stories utilizing the local-colorist approach, she had developed into a popular western novelist, acclaimed at the time but today largely forgotten. From *Me-Smith*, the story of a cowboy antihero, she had progressed over the three-decade span of her productive literary career to the *Old West and New*, in which she dealt with the larger themes of social change—primitivism versus civilization, the evolving process of society and human life, and the manner in which the unique aspects of the West determined human experience. While the Lockhart novels are of value to the student of the West for what they reveal about a region in transition, from the current literary perspective, they have not endured. Modern biographical sources such as *Women Writers* and *Notable American Women, 1608–1950*, edited by Edward T. James, and *American Women Writers*, edited by Langdon Faust, contain no reference to Caroline Lockhart. Although she would work on an autobiography, "Nothin'll Ever Happen to Me," during her autumn years, this work—like "The Black Widow"—would also remain unpublished and eventually would pass to the safekeeping of attorney David Dominick and the American Heritage Center of the University of Wyoming.[69]

Failing eyesight also affected Lockhart's literary output after age sixty-five. In 1938, she underwent the first of two cataract operations, one at Johns Hopkins University Hospital in Baltimore and still another in Oklahoma City. By 1950 when her foreman and long-time lover, Dave Good, became a victim of ill health and old age, Lockhart was forced to consider selling the L Slash Heart and retiring to her home in Cody.[70]

Epilogue:

The Last Leaf on the Tree

What do these newcomers know of the old days? There are no old-timers left anymore. I feel like the last leaf on the tree.
Caroline Lockhart, quoted by Kathryn Wright,
Cody Enterprise, 1962

On 11 June 1950, Caroline wrote to Dorothea Nebel: "I forgot whether I told you or not that I am going to sell the place? With no help except Dave, and his health so poor, I have no choice." She admittedly "hated to do it," and did not relish the thought of going back to Cody, but there was no alternative. "I had a buyer from Meeteetse about two weeks ago," she added in a more lighthearted vein. "He liked it—except the *road.* Then he went home and the next day *dropped dead.* I suspect the strain of driving a big, new Buick round the curves had something to do with it."[1] Isaac Tippetts, however, was more successful. In 1952 Caroline Lockhart's reign as "Cattle Queen" came to an end some twenty-five years after it began.

The Nebels of Kane, Wyoming—Harvey and Dorothea—assisted with the move into Cody. Over the years, an association begun as a business relationship had deepened into a friendship that approached or even surpassed that of family. An initial arrangement with the Nebels to winter her stock had led to correspondence and visits that allowed Caroline to enjoy vicariously, and perhaps for the first time, the ups and downs of a successful young ranch family that included a son Rex, and a daughter Cameron, named after Caroline Cameron Lockhart.[2]

Throughout these last years, the Nebels would watch over her, checking on her welfare and supplying her with items from kitchen and garden. More important, when she had been largely forgotten by others, they provided her with companionship and a sense of family. Caroline reciprocated—with letters full of concern and generous gifts—a Shetland pony for Rex, a fur robe and words of encouragement for Dorothea, books and sundry gifts.[3]

Not long after the move into town, when Dave was thrown from his horse and suffered a severe back injury, Caroline insisted that he move from his quarters in a rental apartment nearby to her guest bedroom. She made light of her ministrations: "I have the gentle, soothing touch of a blacksmith, so he is improving under my care," she wrote Dorothea. When Dave's condition worsened, she admitted: "My steam gets pretty low by night, but I can stick to it a few days until we learn the outcome and what to expect." She signed herself "Florence Nightingale."[4] Dave, who spent twenty-three years as foreman of the L Slash Heart, would spend his final days in a rest home in Cody. Like Caroline, he lived to the age of ninety-one.[5]

Still another who brightened the later years of her life was the attractive and talented Eloise Jensen Stock. Eloise, a former schoolteacher and author of a book called *Stories of Western Ranch Life for Boys and Girls*, was the wife of oil man Paul Stock. Of Eloise, Caroline wrote to Dorothea: "She is a swell gal . . . the sort you will like!"[6]

Paul and Eloise joined the Nebels in taking a special interest in Caroline during these final years. Paul treated her like the lady she dreamed of being, on occasion presenting her with roses or a fat duck for her table. She enjoyed seeing Eloise dressed smartly in furs and elegant clothes, but had no compunction about calling on her for assistance in getting her house ready for an influx of relatives from Oklahoma. On one occasion, Eloise remembered whimsically: "Caroline followed me around with one of her cactus china teacups in her hand while I scrubbed her floors." "I was glad to do it," she added.[7]

Highlights of these autumn years included celebrity appearances, along with other old-timers, to lead the Stampede parades. With that indomitable sense of humor that she retained almost to the end, she wrote of one guest appearance: "I lost my damn hat, the high wind almost blew my shirt off, and the horse cut capers so I had to pull leather to keep my seat; but aside from that, a pleasant time was had by all."[8]

As of 1951, Hollywood still showed an interest in making *Me-Smith* and *Old West and New* into screen plays. And in 1952, she paid for a reprinting of *The Lady Doc*. Its distribution in Cody livened up her life and brought a renewal of the public attention she loved so much.[9]

Spunky and contentious to the end, Lockhart also maintained an uncanny ability to attract the opposite sex. The companion of her autumn years was long-time Cody resident Vernon Spencer, who became her caretaker and devoted friend. Although their affinity for each other is perhaps most accurately described as a mother-son relationship, acquaintances recalled that "Vern worshipped her and kept a vigil during her final illness."[10]

One day not long before her death, she called early in the morning: "Dorothea, will you come up at your convenience? I have something for you." Dorothea asked if something was wrong. "Not really, my dear," Caroline replied, "but I see the shadow of the Old Grim Reaper around the corner. I don't mind the dying, but I hate missing out on what will be happening in the next decade or so."[11]

By 1959, Caroline Lockhart was nearly blind and growing increasingly feeble. On 6 October she wrote poignantly to her sister Grace:

> This is a dark day, and I don't know that you can read this scribble, but while in the writing humor will let you know I am thinking of you. I am well but lonely since the death of [friend] Betty Rumsey. I have a good woman to help me, but . . . no company. Is your leg growing together and does it still hurt you?
>
> Love to You,
> Caroline[12]

After a two-month illness, Caroline met the Grim Reaper on 25 July 1962. Two years earlier she had written to Vern: "It is my wish that when my number comes up that there shall be no services but that I will be cremated and my ashes scattered by you over the landscape from the most convenient peak."[13]

Despite her instructions, the prospect of no memorial at all bothered Eloise Stock and Dorothea Nebel. They arranged for a simple ceremony and invited those who wished to attend. Dorothea recalled the scene:

> Reverend Buswell of the Presbyterian church spoke beautifully, giving the 121st Psalm. "I will lift up mine eyes unto the hills, from whence cometh my strength." Then a simple prayer and the service was over. A few old-timers attended—some with canes, others holding on to someone as they came to pay their last respects.[14]

Family members traveled to Denver to pick up the crematory urn, then rented a plane to scatter her ashes over the L Slash Heart. It is possible that Vernon Spencer accompanied them, because thereafter he kept some of Caroline's ashes in an urn on his "side-board."[15]

There are still those individuals in Cody who maintain that Caroline Lockhart's positive imprint on the community was never fully recognized, nor was the extent of her generosity. Well remembered, however, are the flamboyant aspects of her life and personality. As one Cody resident phrased it: "She was ahead of her time, and as such, was always a bit out of place."[16]

In addition to helping many people privately, she provided generously for friends and relatives in her will; established an annual award for a Cody High School senior showing talent in creative writing; and supported

Colonel Cody's niece, Mary Jester Allen, in her attempts to establish—according to the Colonel's wishes—a Pioneer Center. Professionally, she earned regional recognition for her lifelong accomplishments, with selection to the roster of Who's Who for the State of Wyoming.[17]

Colorful, contentious, and controversial as editor and owner of the *Enterprise*, Caroline Lockhart assumed the role of gadfly to a region. Through reprints of her news articles in the East, she became a national spokesperson for opponents to Prohibition; and as a novelist and writer of short stories, she interpreted the West to a nation. Today, largely forgotten, her books and stories, humorous editorials and news quips remain a little-known treasure trove for the student of the West.

Notes

1. Historiography of the American West and the frontier continues to grow, both in length and in controversy. Among the numerous sources available, see Frederick Jackson Turner, "The Significance of the Frontier in American History," *The American Historical Association Annual Report for the Year 1893*, pp. 199–227; Arthur R. Huseboe and William Geyer, "Herbert Krause and the Western Experience," in *Where the West Begins*, ed. by Huseboe and Geyer (Sioux Falls, South Dakota: Center for Western Studies Press, 1978), p. 9; and Walter Prescott Webb, *The Great Frontier* (Austin: University of Texas Press, 1951), 434 pp. See also Necah S. Furman, *Walter Prescott Webb: His Life and Impact* (Albuquerque: University of New Mexico Press, 1976), pp. 33, 46, which discusses expansion of Webb's thesis from the Great Plains to the Great Frontier; Jerome O. Steffen, *Comparative Frontiers* (Norman: University of Oklahoma Press, 1980), pp. 4–5; and Wallace Stegner, "History, Myth, and the Western Writer," in *The American West* (May 1967), p. 77. Patricia Nelson Limerick, in *The Legacy of Conquest: The Unbroken Past of the American West* (New York: W. W. Norton, 1987), reconsiders the Webb and Turner theses and suggests that the frontier closed, even became "museumized," when Indian war dances became tourist spectacles; yet the 1980s reappearance of major issues in the courts—legal disputes over Indian resources, depression of the oil industry, farm crises—signaled a reopening of the region, a watershed era (pp. 3–26). Revisionist interpretations of the West, such as those presented in the text for the Smithsonian's National Museum of Art exhibition, *The West of America: Reinterpreting Images of the Frontier, 1820–1920*, posit that western expansion was basically racist, capitalistic, and ecologically unsound. Opponents of this interpretation, such as former Librarian of Congress Daniel Boorstin, point out that the positive achievements of those pioneers who settled the West (e.g., the evolution of a legal system and the completion of the Transcontinental Railroad) are being denigrated. Quoted by Washington *Post* columnist Charles Krauthammer, Boorstin terms the exhibition "perverse, historically inaccurate, [and] destructive." In this case, Boorstin voices the opinion of scholars who see value in perpetuating the positive side of western expansionism in opposition to "political correctness." See Charles Krauthammer, "Smithsonian Exhibit Takes Revisionism Back to the Frontier," Albuquerque *Journal*, 4 June 1991, A-3.

2. Like Wister, Lockhart—both in her personal involvements and in the manner in which she portrayed the heroes and heroines in her novels—seemed to view a marriage of East and West as the ideal union.

3. Ray Allen Billington, "Cowboys, Indians, and the Land of Promise," in *America's Frontier Culture* (College Station: Texas A & M Press, 1977), pp. 74–97; John R. Milton, "The Western Novel: Whence and What?" in *Interpretive Approaches to Western American Literature,* ed. by Daniel Alkofer, Richard Etulain, William A. Gibson, and Cornelius Hoffman (Pocatello: Idaho State University Press, 1972), p. 14.

For discussion of stereotypes, see Joan M. Jensen and Darlis A. Miller, "The Gentle Tamers Revisited: New Approaches to the History of Women in the American West," *Pacific Historical Review* 49, no. 2 (May 1980):173–212; Sandra Myres's chapter on "The Madonna of the Prairies and Calamity Jane," in her *Westering Women and the Frontier Experience, 1800–1915* (Albuquerque: University of New Mexico Press, 1982), pp. 1–11; Grace Ernestine Ray, *Wily Women of the West* (San Antonio: Naylor Co., 1972); Burton Rascoe, *Belle Starr: The Bandit Queen* (New York, Random House, 1941); Peggy Robbins, "Calamity Jane! Hellcat in Leather Britches," *American History Illustrated* 10 (June 1975):12–21. Dee Brown's groundbreaking book, *The Gentle Tamers: Women of the Old Wild West* (Lincoln: University of Nebraska Press, 1958) is being reanalyzed. As Jensen and Miller point out in "The Gentle Tamers Revisited," the older male images of western women are in the process of change. See also Paula Petrick, "The Gentle Tamers in Transition: Women in the Trans-Mississippi West," *Feminist Studies* 11, no. 3 (1985):677–94; Joan M. Jensen and Darlis A. Miller, editors, *New Mexico Women: Intercultural Perspectives* (Albuquerque: University of New Mexico Press, 1986); and Susan Armitage and Elizabeth Jameson, editors, *The Women's West* (Norman: University of Oklahoma Press, 1987).

Robert L. Griswold discusses the complexity of western women in "Anglo Women and Domestic Ideology in the American West in the Nineteenth and Early Twentieth Centuries," in *Western Women: Their Land, Their Lives,* ed. by Lillian Schlissel, Vicki L. Ruiz, and Janice Monk (Albuquerque: University of New Mexico Press, 1988), p. 15. Griswold maintains that "domestic ideology in the West was less . . . a well defined 'cult of true womanhood' than a way common women made sense of everyday existence." Certainly this was true in the case of a survivor such as Lockhart. See also Barbara Welter, "The Cult of True Womanhood, 1820–1860," *American Quarterly* 18 (1966):151–74; Elizabeth Jameson, "We Always Knew We Were Here: Women as Workers and Civilizers in the American West," in Armitage and Jameson, editors, *The Women's West* (Norman: University of Oklahoma Press, 1987), pp. 2–3.

Frederick Jackson Turner in his essay on "The Significance of the Frontier" claimed that the West was fundamentally liberating. For some women—the Lockharts of the world—it became so, but even Lockhart was not freed totally from the mores and constraints of "acceptable female behavior." See Susan Armitage, "19th-Century Western Women Beginning to Come into Focus," *Montana: The Magazine of Western History* (Summer 1982):2–7. Nevertheless, Lockhart's free-spirited morality and her liberated lifestyle reflected then what some analysts refer to as "a particularly western view of morals," a precursor or "vanguard for the rest of the nation." See D'Ann Campbell, "Was the West Different? Values and Attitudes of Young Women in 1943," *Pacific Historical Review* 47, no. 3 (1978):453–63.

4. Lockhart's political activism was not unique when considered in light of the 1920s era—for example, women were then holding high offices in California, Texas, and Wyoming, and were filling lesser-known offices in other states. Such notables included Miriam Ferguson, governor of Texas; Nellie Ross, governor of Wyoming; and Annette Adams and Katherine Edson of California. As an outspoken anti-Prohibitionist, Lockhart found herself pitted against the doyennes of small-town society. Women had marched in the forefront of the temperance movement since 1884. Traditionally, men built the saloons; women built the churches. Lockhart built neither, but she undoubtedly would have felt more at home in the former. For good analyses of women's reactions to the West, see Julie Roy Jeffrey, *Frontier Women: The Trans-Mississippi West, 1840–1880* (New York: Hill and Wang, 1979); and Vera Norward, "Women's Place: Continuity and Change in Response to Western Landscapes," in *Western Women: Their Land, Their Lives*, edited by Schlissel et al. (Albuquerque: University of New Mexico Press, 1988), pp. 155–81. As Mari J. Matsuda notes in "The West and the Legal State of Women: Explanations of Frontier Feminism," *Journal of the West* 24 (January 1985):45–55, the West did provide a refuge for feminists who found in the region a receptive and fertile landscape. And, because Lockhart chose to deviate from accepted norms of female morality, she suffered criticism and rejection. In so doing she resisted what Glenda Riley has termed the "female frontier," meaning the shared experiences and responses of frontierswomen which transcended geographic section. See Glenda Riley, *The Female Frontier: A Comparative View of Women on the Prairie and the Plains* (Lawrence: University of Kansas Press, 1988), pp. 2–4.

5. Lucille Patrick Hicks, *Caroline Lockhart: Liberated Lady, 1870–1962* (Cheyenne: Pioneer Printing and Stationery Co., 1984), 678 pp.

INTRODUCTION

1. Caroline Lockhart, "Cody Boosters Plan Annual Frontier Event; Spirit of Old West to Be Preserved and the Yip of the Cowboy to Drown the Honk of the Tin Lizzie for Three Whole Days," Park County *Enterprise*, 5 May 1920, pp. 1–3.

2. Wallace Stegner, *The American West as Living Space* (Ann Arbor: University of Michigan Press, 1987), p. 82.

3. Ibid., pp. 82–83.

4. Theodore Roosevelt, *Ranch Life and the Hunting Trail,* 1888 (rpt., New York: McGraw, 1969), p. 24.

5. Frederick Jackson Turner, "The Significance of the Frontier in American History," *The Annual Report of the American Historical Association for the Year 1893,* pp. 199–207.

6. See Judy Nolte Lensink, "Expanding the Boundaries of Criticism: The Diary as Female Autobiography," *Women's Studies* 14 (1987):39–53.

EARLY ADVENTURES

1. "Local Notes," newspaper clipping [Cody *Enterprise?*], 19 October 1904, in a scrapbook belonging to the late Agnes Chamberlin, Cody, Wyoming. My appreciation to Lucille Patrick Hicks for locating this clipping. See also interviews by Nell B. Kelley, "Cody Life Appeals to Writer—Caroline Lockhart Deserted Career in East for Western Atmosphere," Billings *Gazette,* 7 February 1960, and "Caroline Lockhart, Writer and Rodeo Sponsor," Northern Wyoming *Daily News,* 28 August 1958, in scrapbook at Spring Creek Antiques. In several of these interviews, Lockhart explained how she came to make Cody her home.

At the time of my research, Spring Creek Antiques was located in Lockhart's white house at 1126 Rumsey Avenue in Cody. Subsequently, the house was sold to the Lloyd Londerville family, who moved it to the West Cody Strip. The Londervilles converted the house into a bed-and-breakfast inn. I appreciate the geographic information provided by Paul Fees, senior curator, Buffalo Bill Historical Center, Cody, Wyoming. Letter, Fees to author, 8 May 1984.

2. William A. Connelly, *A Standard History of Kansas and Kansans,* vol. 3 (Chicago: Lewis Publishing, 1918), pp. 1593–94. "Miscellaneous Autobiographical Material," Box 5, and "Autobiographical Draft," Box 10, Folder 5, Caroline Lockhart Collection (henceforward CLC), American Heritage Center, University of Wyoming, Laramie. Obituary notice, "Joseph C. Lockhart is Dead," n.p., n.d. Copy provided by Caroline Lockhart's niece, Elizabeth Sutton, daughter of Grace Lockhart, from personal family papers. The obituary also notes that one child (unnamed) had died in infancy.

See also two unpublished biographical accounts of Lockhart's life: Paul R. Eldridge, "Woman on Horseback," 35 pp., Box 7, CLC; and David Dominick, "An Introduction to Caroline Lockhart," 58 pp., Box 9, CLC. The Dominick manuscript is particularly valuable as Lockhart entrusted drafts of her autobiography to him. Excerpts from the autobiographical notes are interspersed throughout the manuscript. David Dominick, an attorney, is the son of the late Dr. Dewey Dominick, Lockhart's personal physician. Paul Eldridge worked for Lockhart on the Cody *Enterprise* before his graduation from Harvard. In addition, Mary Shivers

Culpin generously provided a portion of her own manuscript draft focusing on the Dryhead Ranch, along with copies of a manuscript by Lockhart, "From Billings to Montana," and a copy of the Eldridge manuscript, "Woman on Horseback." The Culpin manuscript is especially useful because a part of it is taken from an interview with Vern Spencer, now deceased.

3. "Autobiographical Draft," Box 9, CLC. Interview, Dorothea Nebel, Cody, Wyoming, 8 July 1982.

4. Caroline Lockhart, "Incident of Childhood Makes Lincoln Birthday Memorable to Writer," clipping, n.d., Box 9, CLC.

5. "Autobiographical Draft," Box 9, CLC.

6. Ibid.

7. Ibid. Sylvia Crowder (daughter of Grace), in her letter to the author, 25 October 1982, records that "there was 8 or 9 years between my mother and Caroline, but Caroline and George [he was the older] were close in age and also in feeling for each other [which stands in interesting contrast to comments in the Lockhart Diaries]. My mother was Caroline's 'little sister,' and she had in the early years a protective attitude toward her. Their mother, Sarah Woodruff Lockhart, died of a fever when Caroline was 16 or 17 and my mother was 9, so you can understand the protectiveness Caroline felt. My grandfather remarried about a year afterwards, and his new wife was bitterly resented by George and Caroline, and they struck out into the world to make lives of their own."

8. Ibid.; photocopied page (436) from *Who Was Who*, n.d., Box 5, CLC.

9. "Autobiographical Draft," Box 9, CLC.

10. Ibid.

11. See Truman J. Backus, *Shaw's New History of English and American Literature* (New York: Thelden, 1884), 480 pp. Lockhart's notations are on pp. 239, 390 in copy of book in Box 13, Booklets and Pamphlets, CLC.

12. "Autobiographical Draft," Box 9, CLC.

13. Ibid.

14. Ibid.

15. Ibid.; William A. Connelly, *A Standard History of Kansas and Kansans*, vol. 3 (Chicago: Lewis Publishing, 1918), p. 1593, gives names of wives. Obituary notice, "Joseph Lockhart is Dead," n.p., n.d., records that Caroline's father married her stepmother at Cedar Rapids, Iowa, in the year 1890.

16. "Autobiographical Draft," Box 9, CLC.

17. Ibid.; "Miscellaneous Autobiographical Material," Box 5, CLC. See also Dominick, "An Introduction to Caroline Lockhart," pp. 6–8, Box 9, CLC, quoting a more extensive autobiographical version of the episode.

18. Dominick, "An Introduction to Caroline Lockhart," p. 8, Box 9, CLC.

19. "Autobiographical Draft," Box 9, CLC. Caroline's philosophy of "doing it before you wrote it" was to be reinforced by her newspaper experience when, as a

reporter, she was encouraged to get firsthand knowledge for her assignments. See also Eldridge, "Woman on Horseback," p. 7, Box 7, CLC.

20. "Autobiographical Draft," Box 9, CLC; Dominick, "An Introduction to Caroline Lockhart," pp. 5–6, Box 9, CLC.

21. "Miscellaneous Autobiographical Material," Box 5, CLC.

22. Ibid., Lockhart recalled that she was not yet seventeen, but because the interview followed her school days at the seminary in 1889 and her father's remarriage in 1890, she would actually have been about nineteen years old.

23. Ibid.

24. Ibid.; Dominick, "An Introduction to Caroline Lockhart," pp. 9–10, Box 9, CLC, quotes excerpts from a slightly different draft. As a writer, Lockhart typically revised what she wrote, even her autobiography. At one time, she became so disillusioned with her efforts that she tried to burn the manuscript, but it was saved by Ann Harper, a friend and neighbor in Cody.

25. "Miscellaneous Autobiographical Material," Box 5, CLC.

26. Ibid.; Dominick, "An Introduction to Caroline Lockhart," pp. 9–10, Box 9, CLC.

27. "Miscellaneous Autobiographical Material," Box 5, CLC; "Autobiographical Draft," Box 10, CLC.

28. "Autobiographical Draft," Box 10, CLC. See also "Caroline Lockhart, Dryhead Rancher and Author, Has Had Life as Colorful as Any of Her Books," Billings Gazette, 25 April 1943; "Miscellaneous Autobiographical Material," Box 5, CLC.

29. Nearly all the biographical and autobiographical sources cited give coverage in one form or another to unique events in Lockhart's career. See Eldridge, "Woman on Horseback," pp. 6–8, Box 7, CLC; and Dominick, "An Introduction," p. 13, Box 9, CLC, for synopses of some of these incidents.

30. "Autobiographical Draft," Box 10, CLC.

31. Eldridge, "Woman on Horseback," p. 8, Box 7, CLC; "Young Wyoming Girl Is Creator of Me-Smith," Denver Times, 18 May 1912; Culpin, Lockhart Manuscript, p. 7.

32. "Autobiographical Draft," Box 10, CLC.

33. "Miscellaneous Autobiographical Material," Box 5, CLC; "Autobiographical Draft," Box 10, CLC. See also "Caroline Lockhart, Dryhead Rancher and Author, Has Had Life as Colorful as Any of Her Books," Billings Gazette, 25 April 1943.

34. "Caroline Lockhart," Billings Gazette, 25 April 1943. See also Caroline Lockhart, "Cody Writer Recalls Meeting with Former Heavyweight Champion," Billings Gazette, 20 October 1955, clipped to "Autobiographical Draft," Box 10, CLC. If Lockhart's memory is accurate and the upcoming bout was against Jim Corbett for the heavyweight championship of the world, the fight took place on 17 March 1897 in Carson City, Nevada, where Fitzsimmons knocked out Corbett in fourteen rounds. Lockhart, however, may have confused this match with the

one between Fitzsimmons and James J. Jeffries at Coney Island on 9 June 1899. Fitzsimmons lost on an eleven-round knockout. Lockhart's disregard for dates challenges the biographer. In this instance, considering that Fitzsimmons was training at Coney Island, this may well have been the Jeffries bout.

35. Miscellaneous autobiographical materials, found out of folder and unlisted in Box 5, CLC. The three different drafts of autobiographical materials, located in different sections of the Lockhart Collection at the American Heritage Center of the University of Wyoming, are written in conversational format, thereby enabling one to quote Lockhart's rendition directly. Written on the backs of pieces of correspondence or advertising leaflets, these pages are filled with typographical errors and are seldom paginated. Autobiographical materials can be found in Boxes 5, 9, and 10. All of these materials are restricted and can be used only with permission of David Dominick.

36. For another version of the Cody interview, see also "Caroline Lockhart" by Dewey Dominick in the *Dude Rancher Magazine* (Spring/Summer 1982):8–9. The article, provided courtesy of Elizabeth P. (Mrs. Dewey) Dominick, contains the story of Lockhart's interview with Colonel Cody, with some variation in detail. Dr. Dominick, for example, reveals that Lockhart was invited to sit in the Colonel's box at the Wild West show the night following the interview; letter, Elizabeth P. Dominick to author, 11 November 1982.

37. "Miscellaneous Autobiographical Material," Box 5, CLC. Caroline Lockhart's printed version of the interview, "Cody Writer Tells of Meeting Buffalo Bill," Cody *Enterprise,* can be found in Box 9, CLC.

38. "Miscellaneous Autobiographical Material," Box 5, CLC. In her unpublished autobiography, Lockhart claims that her trip coincided with Peary's second attempt to reach the North Pole, but the chronology is suspect. It appears more probable that it coincided with his second trip to Greenland in 1891. On this trip, Peary was accompanied by F. A. Cook and seven companions, including his wife. Although Peary announced his intention of reaching the North Pole in 1898, he did not achieve his goal until 1909.

39. "Miscellaneous Autobiographical Material," Box 5, CLC. See also A. K. Stone, "Boy Howdy! Meet Caroline Lockhart! Famous Woman Novelist of West Joins *Post* Staff: Writer of Range Stories Has Known Adventure in Many Parts of World, but West Is Her First and Last Love and *Post* Her Choice of Newspapers," Denver *Post,* 3 December 1918, Denver *Post* Archives, Denver, Colorado.

40. Ibid. See also "Autobiographical Draft," Box 10, CLC.

41. "Autobiographical Draft," Box 10, CLC.

42. Ibid.; Lockhart Diary, 21 May [1918], Box 3, CLC. Interestingly, an analysis of Lockhart's handwriting by Professional Handwriting Analysts, Inc., a group used by large corporations for personnel selection services, supports the personality analysis and conclusions drawn from a study of her life by her various unofficial biog-

raphers as well by this author. See Betty Link, "Personality Evaluation of Caroline Lockhart," 6 pp., including letter to author, 5 April 1984, Buffalo Bill Historical Center, Cody, Wyoming.

43. U.S. Department of Commerce, Bureau of the Census, Twelfth Census of the United States, 1900: vol. 179, e.d. 671, sheet 22, line 10. I am indebted to Mary Shivers Culpin, historian for the National Park Service, Denver, Colorado, for the lead to this information.

44. "Miscellaneous Autobiographical Material," Box 5, CLC.

45. Ibid.

46. Ibid.

47. Ibid.

48. [Caroline Lockhart], "Suzette Sees Machine That Can Level Cities, End Wars," Philadelphia, n.d., n.p., Denver *Post* Archives, Denver, Colorado.

49. Caroline Lockhart, "Cody Author Recalls Pleasant Interview with Famed Financier," Billings *Gazette*, 7 August 1955, Box 7, CLC.

50. "Autobiographical Draft," Box 10, CLC.

51. Ibid.

52. Letter, Lockhart to "Betty," 2 January 1951; John La Cerda, "Mother of Mother's Day." Both items in Box 1: B-J298a, CLC. Dorothea Nebel, Lockhart's friend and benefactor in old age, recalls that Anna Jarvis and Caroline Lockhart first became acquainted as schoolmates at the seminary.

53. Caroline Lockhart, "The Greengrocery Man," *The Orphan's Bouquet* (1 June 1893):337, 340, 338–52, Box 20: Oversize, CLC. This story is annotated as "my first printed story."

54. Caroline Lockhart, "The Child of Nature," *New Idea Woman's Magazine* (September 1904):43, in Box 11: Periodicals, CLC. Lockhart has annotated this copy as "*one* of my first printed stories."

55. See also Lockhart Diary, New Mexico Territory, 1898, Box 17, CLC. Only a few pages are filled.

It is debatable whether MacKenzie was editor of the Sunday edition of the *Post* or the New York *Press*. A clipping dated 19 October 1904 in Agnes Chamberlin's scrapbook indicates that MacKenzie worked for the New York *Press;* but a clipping from the Billings *Gazette,* 7 February 1960, headed "Cody Life Appeals to Writer," says that he was editor of the Boston *Post.*

56. Lockhart Diary, New Mexico Territory, 1898, Box 17, CLC.

57. Ibid.

58. Ibid. See also Lockhart, "The Child of Nature," *New Idea Woman's Magazine* (September 1904):43, Box 11, CLC.

59. "The Child of Nature," p. 43, Box 11, CLC.

60. Ibid.

61. Ibid.

62. Caroline Lockhart, "The Sign That Failed," *Home and Art*, 2 pp., n.d., copy in Box 11: Periodicals, CLC.

63. Ibid.

64. Suzette [Caroline Lockhart], "A Girl in the Rockies," *Lippincott's Monthly Magazine* (August 1902):177–91, Box 5: Periodicals, CLC.

65. Ibid. See also "Autobiographical Draft," Box 9, CLC; and Dominick, "An Introduction to Caroline Lockhart," pp. 14–22, which includes extensive excerpts from the Lockhart autobiography, Box 9, CLC.

66. See handwritten notation, bottom of p. 15, in Dominick, "An Introduction to Caroline Lockhart," Box 9, CLC; "Autobiographical Draft," Box 9, CLC.

67. Lockhart, "A Girl in the Rockies," p. 186.

68. "Autobiographical Draft," Box 9, CLC. See the published version in "A Girl in the Rockies," pp. 188–91.

69. Lockhart, "A Girl in the Rockies," p. 178.

70. Ibid., 181–82.

71. "Autobiographical Draft," Box 9, CLC; also quoted in Dominick, "An Introduction to Caroline Lockhart," pp. 19–20, Box 9, CLC.

72. Dominick, "An Introduction to Caroline Lockhart," p. 21.

73. Ibid., pp. 21–22.

74. See Caroline Lockhart, "In the White Man's Way," *Popular Magazine* (20 March 1925):125–34; and Lockhart, "The Spirit That Talked from a Box," *Popular Magazine* (7 July 1922):59–67. Both items in Box 6: Periodicals, CLC.

75. Caroline Lockhart, "The Pin-Head," *Lippincott's Monthly Magazine* (October 1908):452–59, Box 5: Periodicals, CLC.

76. Ibid., 452.

77. Ibid., 459.

78. Caroline Lockhart, "The Woman Who Gave No Quarter," *Lippincott's Monthly Magazine* (February 1907):262–69, Box 11: Periodicals, CLC.

79. Ibid., 262.

80. Ibid., 263–64.

81. Ibid., 266.

82. Ibid., 268–69.

83. Caroline Lockhart, "A Treasure of the Humble," *Smith's Magazine* (December 1917):329–40, Box 6: Periodicals, CLC.

84. Caroline Lockhart, "The Qualities of Leadership," *Smith's Magazine* (March 1920):872, Box 6: Periodicals, CLC.

85. Caroline Lockhart, "His Own Medicine," *Lippincott's Monthly Magazine* (October 1905):473–79, Box 5: Periodicals, CLC.

86. Ibid., 477.

87. Ibid., 478–79.

88. Caroline Lockhart, "The Tango Lizard," *Smith's Magazine* (November 1917): 215–16, Box 11, CLC.

89. Ibid., 216.

90. Dominick, "An Introduction to Caroline Lockhart," p. 13, Box 9, CLC; Nell B. Kelley, "Cody Life Appeals to Writer: Caroline Lockhart Deserted Career in East for Western Atmosphere," Billings *Gazette*, 7 February 1960, n.p. News article provided by Eloise Stock.

THE NOVELIST

1. "Local Notes," [Cody *Enterprise?*], 19 October 1904. Interviewees and reporters commented on Lockhart's good looks. Cody residents interviewed also noted that Lockhart, in her younger years especially, was an attractive woman. See also "Young Wyoming Girl Is Creator of *Me-Smith*," Denver *Times*, 18 May 1912.

2. Lockhart Diary (hereafter, Diary), New Mexico Territory, 1898, Box 17, CLC. See entries 7 April–19 June 1898. MacKenzie had problems with his eyes and suffered from rheumatism. After Stephen Watts Kearney's takeover of Santa Fe in 1846, New Mexico formally became a part of the United States with the signing of the Treaty of Guadalupe Hidalgo in 1848, but it did not achieve statehood until 6 January 1912.

3. Diary, 13 February 1929, records that Johnson drove the stage taking her to Cody from the station. See Diary, 4 August 1928 to 31 January 1930, Box 2, CLC; Lucille Patrick Hicks, *The Best Little Town by a Dam Site* (Cheyenne: Flintlock Publishing, 1968), pp. 21–24.

4. Lucille Patrick Hicks, *Best Little Town*, pp. 25, 32, 46, 56, 63, 69, 70, 73, citing Wyoming *Stockgrower and Farmer*, 9 February 1904, and 23 February 1904, in Park County Public Library, Cody, Wyoming.

5. Microfilm copies of the Cody *Enterprise* for 1904, housed at the Park County Public Library, give a good picture of Cody at the turn of the century. See also Ray Allan Billington, "The Frontier and American Culture," in his *America's Frontier Culture* (College Station: Texas A & M Press, 1977), p. 52. Billington speaks of the "cultural fault" apparent as one proceeds west.

6. Various authors stress the need for a macrocosmic world view before one can understand the workings of society in microcosm. See, for example, Willa Cather's quote in *Not Under Forty* (New York: Knopf, 1936), p. 88: "You must know the world before you know the village." So it was with Caroline Lockhart, who had seen much of the world before her arrival in Cody in 1904.

"Autobiographical Draft," Box 9, CLC; "Young Wyoming Girl Is Creator of *Me-Smith*," interview in Denver *Times*, 18 May 1912, Denver *Post* Archives, Denver, Colorado; Mary Shivers Culpin, Lockhart Manuscript, pp. 7–8, Buffalo Bill Historical Center, Cody, Wyoming.

7. J. Berg Essenwein, *Writing the Short Story* (New York: Hinds, Nobel and Eldridge, n.d.), p. 54, in Box 13: Booklets and Pamphlets, CLC.

8. Ibid.

9. "Young Wyoming Girl is Creator of *Me-Smith*," Denver *Times*, 18 May 1912, Denver *Post* Archives, Denver, Colorado.

10. Cody historian Lucille Patrick Hicks indicates that the house on Rumsey Avenue was purchased in 1905 from Harry Weston; the deed for this property, however, was recorded at the Park County District Courthouse, 14 May 1914, and lists the seller as John Peter. My appreciation to Paul Fees for researching this information. Dr. Fees indicates that "there were two or three other houses in the neighborhood identical to Caroline's which were built in 1914; [therefore], I suspect that she either had the house built or was the first occupant." Letter, Fees to author, 28 August 1984. Caroline Lockhart eventually owned rental homes as well. See also the following articles, provided to the author courtesy of Eloise Stock: Carole Legg, "Lockhart House Must Go; City Needs Parking Lot," Cody *Enterprise*, 16 February 1983; Frank Boyett, "Lockhart Home Auction Set for the End of This Month," Cody *Enterprise*, 21 September 1983, p. 1; "Lockhart House to Move to West Strip Tomorrow," Cody *Enterprise*, 21 March 1984, Buffalo Bill Historical Center, Cody, Wyoming.

11. Paul R. Eldridge, "Woman on Horseback," pp. 4, 8, 10, Box 7, CLC, discusses this schism.

12. Caroline Lockhart, "Suzette Tells of Manhunt and Holdup in Cody," Box 11: Periodicals, Articles, Clippings, and Copies, CLC. In Caroline's version the date is given as 1 October 1904; the newspapers, however, list the date as 1 November. See "Murder Most Foul Committed at Cody," Meeteetse *News*, 2 November 1904. The news story is quoted in Lucille Patrick Hicks, *Best Little Town*, pp. 78–79, 81. The newspaper indicates that Middaugh was shot through the neck, but otherwise provides minimal detail.

13. Ibid.

14. Ibid.

15. Ibid.

16. Eldridge, "Woman on Horseback," p. 9, CLC.

17. Essenwein, *Writing the Short Story*, p. 316, Box 13, CLC, quoting Frederic Van Rensselaer Day in *The Magic Story*. Brackets are mine.

18. Lucille Patrick Hicks, *Best Little Town*, p. 113. In reality, the population count was closer to 210; the 1,800 may have been a typesetting error.

19. Ibid., p. 114, quoting Lockhart's article in the Wyoming *Stockgrower*.

20. Ibid.

21. Ibid., pp. 70, 75, 80, 84, 88.

22. Caroline Lockhart, "When the Automobile Struck Town," originally printed in the Philadelphia *North American* in 1905 and reprinted in the Cody *Enterprise*, n.d., p. 4, Box 13, CLC.

23. Ibid.

24. See Essenwein, *Writing the Short Story*, marginal notation, p. 60, Box 13, CLC.

25. See Lucille Patrick Hicks, *Best Little Town*, pp. 116, 124–25.

26. Lockhart Scrapbook, Box 7, accession no. 177, CLC.

27. Ibid., "Wedding Bells—Marriage of Mr. Thurston and Miss Goodman Makes a Gay Week in Cody," Cody *Enterprise*, 28 June 1906.

28. Interview, Electa and Ray Prante, 7 July 1982.

29. Caroline Lockhart, *Me-Smith* (Philadelphia: J. B. Lippincott, 1911), 315 pp. See publisher's front-matter.

30. Francis Wayne, "Man of Mistery [sic], Immortalized by Writer, Slain in Gambling Den for Refusing to Cheat," Denver *Post*, 21 December 1921, n.p., Denver *Post* Archives, Denver, Colorado.

31. Lockhart, *Me-Smith*, p. 315. See also review, "*Me-Smith* by Caroline Lockhart," in *American Review of Reviews* 43 (11 June 1911):758.

32. Review, "*Me-Smith* by Caroline Lockhart," *Book Review Digest, 1911*, New York *Times* 16 (19 March 1911):155. See excerpts from reviews in addenda to *The Lady Doc* (Philadelphia: Lippincott, 1912), 339 pp.

33. Letter, Albert Payson Terhune to Lockhart, 17 February 1935, Box 5, CLC.

34. Bertha M[uzzey] Bower was a Montana ranchwife and prolific writer of Western novels of the same period. See *Chip, of the Flying U* (New York: G. W. Dillingham, 1906); Roy W. Meyer, "B. M. Bower: The Poor Man's Wister," *Journal of Popular Culture* 7 (Winter 1973):667–79; and Orrin A. Engen, *Writer of the Plains* (Culver City, Calif.: Pontine Press, 1973).

Lockhart did not regard B. M. Bower highly, perhaps in part because an editor, declining a Lockhart novel, praised Bower "as a shining example of what a western novel and what western humor should be." Lockhart termed Bower a "humorless" writer "who's [sic] characters are of the screen." See Diary, 28 June [1918], Box 3, CLC.

35. See Lucille Patrick Hicks, *Best Little Town*, p. 18, and addendum 4, p. 171.

36. Interviews: E. J. Goppert, Sr., 12 July 1982; Ray and Electa Prante, 7 July 1982; Margaret Sylvester Martin, 12 July 1982.

Marian Sweeney, author of *Gold at Dixie Gulch* (Kamiah, Idaho: Clearwater Valley Publishing, 1982), pp. 107–8, tells of the Caroline Lockhart/J.R. Painter romance. In a letter to the author, 10 June 1984, she shares a transcript from a taped interview with Jo Patterson, granddaughter of the second Mrs. Painter, Ellen Galbraith Jones. Correspondence with Bill Painter, the grandson of J.R., confirms that the Lockhart/Painter relationship was well known among family members. See letters to author from Bill Painter, 21 November 1982, 13 February 1983, 1 April 1983, 31 May 1984. Mr. Painter has also shared information and suggested source material relating to the topic.

37. Interviews: E. J. Goppert, Jr., 30 June 1982; Dick Frost, 6 July 1982; Ray Prante, 7 July 1982; Lucille Patrick Hicks, 8 July 1982; and E. J. Goppert, Sr., 12 July 1982.

For description as quoted, see "Autobiographical Draft," Box 9, CLC, and Dominick, "An Introduction to Caroline Lockhart," p. 33, Box 9, CLC. Dominick's article references affidavits provided him by Lockhart.

38. Interviews: Dick Frost, 6 July 1982; Ray Prante, 7 July 1982.

39. "Autobiographical Draft," Box 9, CLC; Dominick, "An Introduction to Caroline Lockhart," p. 33, Box 9, CLC.

40. See note 39, above.

41. Dominick, "An Introduction to Caroline Lockhart," p. 34, Box 9, CLC.

42. Ibid., pp. 34–37; "Autobiographical Draft," Box 9, CLC.

43. Ibid.

44. Dominick, "An Introduction to Caroline Lockhart," pp. 37–38, marginal notes. See also Box 9: Affidavits, CLC. The catalogue to the Lockhart Collection contains the following note: "It is entirely possible that the following listed documents are manuscripts." This does not appear to be the case, however. Attorney David Dominick, who was given the affidavits by Lockhart, later donated them to the American Heritage Center at the University of Wyoming, Laramie. Dominick maintains that the documents "appeared to be carbon copies to original affidavits taken from patients in the Frances Lane Hospital. . . . I also recollect that on those blue carbon copies, Caroline Lockhart had made a number of penciled notations which appeared to be for the purpose of editing the affidavits directly into her book." Letter, David Dominick to author, 21 November 1984. The list of affidavits, in Box 9, CLC, includes: Houx, F. L., testimony; Keyes, J. T., affidavit, sworn before W. H. Brundage, Justice of the Peace, 18 December 1907; McDonal, Raynald, deposition, sworn before Fred C. Barnett, 16 November 1907, State of Wyoming, Bighorn County; Oleson, John, deposition, sworn before Fred C. Barnett, 12 November 1907, State of Wyoming, Bighorn County; two loose pages . . . regarding—Claude Humphrey, undertaker; Doctor Frances Lane; Cody Trading Company; Dr. Ainsworth, coroner; the hospital; and the cemetery.

45. Raines affidavit is noted in text of Dominick, "An Introduction to Caroline Lockhart," pp. 37–38.

46. Ibid., p. 38.

47. Ibid., p. 39, Oleson affidavit.

48. Ibid., pp. 40–41, McDonal affidavit.

49. Ibid.

50. Ibid., Keyes affidavit.

51. Ibid., p. 36; "Autobiographical Draft," Box 9, CLC. See also Cora M. Beach, *Women of Wyoming* (Casper: S. E. Boyer, 1927), pp. 392, 394, which records that Dr. Lane received "her college education at the University of Chicago and graduated in 1900 from Hering Medical College." She moved to Cody in 1902 and, as president of the Women's Club of Cody in 1912, helped acquire an appropriation from Andrew Carnegie to build the Park County Public Library.

52. *Flexner Report*, American Medical Association (AMA), 1912; telephone interview, N. Sullivan, research librarian, AMA Library, History and Archives Division, Chicago, Illinois, 8 August 1984.

53. Dominick, "An Introduction to Caroline Lockhart," pp. 41–44. See also two loose sheets containing what appear to be drafts for a news story or article telling the particulars of Claude Humphrey's career as undertaker, Box 9, CLC.

54. Dominick, p. 40.

55. Ibid., pp. 43–44.

56. Ibid., p. 44.

57. Ibid., pp. 44–45.

58. Ibid., p. 45.

59. Ibid., quoting Lockhart.

60. Ibid., pp. 44–45.

61. The Billings *Gazette* article is mentioned in Lucille Patrick Hicks, *Best Little Town*, p. 118.

62. Letter, John E. Wilkie to Caroline Lockhart, 19 February 1908, Box 7, CLC.

63. Ibid.

64. Ibid. The letter implies that a cursory investigation took place and that Wilkie shared the report with Caroline.

65. David Dominick notes Larson's quote on pp. 47–48 of his "An Introduction to Caroline Lockhart." See also Caroline Lockhart, *The Lady Doc* (New York: Lippincott, 1912); T. A. Larson, *History of Wyoming* (Lincoln: University of Nebraska Press, 1965), p. 355.

66. Excerpt from review of *The Lady Doc* in the Chicago *Tribune*, quoted in publisher's front-matter in Caroline Lockhart's *The Full of the Moon* (Philadelphia: Lippincott, 1914), 267 pp.

67. Interview, Francis Hayden, 15 July 1982.

68. "Darling," a review of *The Lady Doc* in the New York *Times*, 27 October 1912.

69. Francis Hayden showed the author this list. See also Dominick, "An Introduction to Caroline Lockhart," p. 49.

70. Philadelphia *Bulletin*, 5 April 1914. See also Culpin, Lockhart Manuscript, Buffalo Bill Historical Center, Cody, Wyoming, p. 13.

71. Philadelphia *Bulletin*, 5 April 1914.

72. The petitioners protesting *The Lady Doc* were: J. D. Waters, William M.

Beck, Francis W. Frank, Earle Conilogue, John J. Vondewrit, Phil House, George Honeycutt, Jr., M. G. Crook, and M. B. Henderson. See Box 7, CLC. It is interesting that Lane's and Ross's names were not on this list. Francis Hayden, whose father, Charles E. Hayden, conducted the survey laying out the town of Cody, provided information on petitioners and characters in the book. Interview, Francis Hayden, 15 July 1982. See also "Author Caroline Lockhart Dies in Cody at 91 Years," Billings *Gazette*, 26 July 1962.

73. Lucille Patrick Hicks, *Best Little Town*, pp. 113, 118–97; and Dominick, "An Introduction to Caroline Lockhart," p. 49, have Lockhart moving to Denver after publication of *The Lady Doc*, but records of the Denver *Post* show her arriving in the city in 1918. See A. K. Stone, "Boy Howdy! Meet Caroline Lockhart! Famous Woman Novelist of West joins *Post* staff," Denver *Post*, 3 December 1918, front page. The assumption that Lockhart moved to Denver in 1912 may have been based upon the fact that she submitted occasional articles to the *Post* during this period.

74. Letters, Bill Painter to author, 21 November 1982, 1 April 1983, 30 April 1984; Marian Sweeney, *Gold at Dixie Gulch*, pp. 107–8; Dominick, "An Introduction to Caroline Lockhart," recalls this autobiographical excerpt and discusses it in a handwritten notation (back of p. 3), Box 9, CLC.

75. "Autobiographical Draft." Box 9, CLC, in which she discusses her trip down the river; and "The Wildest Boat Ride in America," *Outing Magazine* (February 1912), pp. 515–24, Box 6, CLC, in which she published the story of her experience.

76. Caroline Lockhart, *The Full of the Moon* (Philadelphia: Lippincott, 1914), 267 pp.; Diary, 2 June 1918, Box 3, CLC.

77. Lockhart, *The Full of the Moon*, pp. 25–27.

78. Ibid., pp. 7–10.

79. Ibid., pp. 11–12. In Lockhart's case, it was her father (rather than her grandfather) who married the "sempstress."

80. Ibid., pp. 12–13.

81. Ibid., pp. 15, 19–20.

82. Ibid., pp. 26, 58, 83–84, 138.

83. See the following reviews of *The Full of the Moon*: New York *Times* 19 (1 March 1914):101; *Publisher's Weekly* 85 (21 March 1914):1060; and *Nation* 98 (7 May 1914):529.

84. Lockhart, *The Full of the Moon*, pp. 201–2. Publisher's front-matter in *The Man from the Bitter Roots* (Philadelphia: Lippincott, 1915) quotes review from the *Globe*.

85. "Autobiographical Data," Box 10, Folder 5, CLC. See also newspaper photographs from Cody *Enterprise*, n.d., showing Caroline Lockhart and Dave Good placing a memorial tablet on Other Buffalo's grave "as a token of her sincere friendship for the Mandan princess," Box 10, Folder 5, CLC.

86. Lockhart, *The Full of the Moon*, pp. 43, 61–62, 74–81. Also, see Diary,

17 April 1898, telling of New Mexico trip, which became basis for Lockhart's article titled "A Child of Nature," Box 17, CLC.

87. Lockhart, *The Full of the Moon*, p. 43; see also reviews cited in note 83, above.

88. John R. Milton, "The Western Novel: Whence and What?" in *Interpretive Approaches to Western American Literature*, ed. by Daniel Alkofer, et al. (Pocatello: Idaho State University Press, 1972), pp. 20–21, compares the symbolism in Walter van Tilburg Clark's *The Track of the Cat* (1949; reprinted, University of Nebraska Press, 1981) with the symbolism of the non-Western novel, *Moby Dick*. "In the Western novel," Milton maintains, "the testing is constant, endless, part of a long-range search or quest." Testing, he notes, pits common folk "against nature, against their environment, and against each other."

89. Lockhart, *The Full of the Moon*, pp. 144, 163–68.

90. Ibid., p. 218.

91. Census records for Bighorn City, Wyoming, show J.R. and family in residence in the Sunlight Valley in 1900, while Gospil's *Philadelphia City Directory* lists J.R. as manager of a music store at 1225 Chestnut Street, indicating a dual residency to that date.

92. Since Henry Villard died in 1900, it is possible—as his grandson Bill Painter writes—that J.R. by that time could personally afford the luxury of travel in a private railroad car, or perhaps his close relations with the Villard family continued. Later, Painter's financial situation worsened.

I am indebted to Bill Painter for his generous assistance in trying to uncover the facts of his grandfather's background and the Lockhart relationship, which continued on a friendly basis until J.R.'s death in August 1936. Bill Painter, who is writing a biography of his grandfather, contributed background information on the Painter family in response to an inquiry in the New York *Times Book Review* of 7 November 1982. See letters from Bill Painter to author, 1982–85.

Mr. Painter also shared information gathered from an interview with Elizabeth Hart, formerly of Dixie, Idaho, whose husband hauled freight for J.R. Elizabeth Hart has considerable interest in history of the area and also provided information for Marian Sweeney's *Gold at Dixie Gulch*. See Sweeney, *Gold at Dixie Gulch*, pp. 106–9; and letters, Sweeney to author, 21 June 1983, 21 July 1983, and 12 October 1984.

93. Diary, 20 September [1918], Box 3, CLC.

94. Ibid., 10 October 1919, Box 1, CLC.

95. Interview, Margaret Martin, 1 July 1982.

96. Bill Painter: interviews with Monroe Wagoman, an employee on the Sunlight Ranch, and with Mary Riddle, a resident of the area; recorded in letter, Painter to author, 31 May 1984. See also Lucille Patrick Hicks, *Caroline Lockhart: Liberated Lady*, pp. 575–77.

97. Sweeney, *Gold at Dixie Gulch*, p. 107. For descriptions of the Salmon River

country, see Robert G. Bailey, *River of No Return* (Lewiston, Idaho: R.G. Bailey Print Co., 1948), pp. 627–37; Johnny Carrey and Cort Conley, *River of No Return* (Cambridge, Idaho: Backeddy Books, 1978), pp. 30–44, 174–77.

98. Bill Painter: interviews with Monroe Wagoman and Mary Riddle, cited in note 96, above. According to Mary Riddle, "the Painter Mine at the Sunlight Mining District was very rich." Wagoman confirmed this with his recollection of the shipment of ore to Belfry.

99. Letter, Bill Painter to author, 5 November 1984; Sweeney, *Gold at Dixie Gulch*, p. 107.

100. Caroline Lockhart, "The Wildest Boat Ride in America," *Outing Magazine* 59 (February 1912):515–24, Box 6, CLC; "Miscellaneous Autobiographical Material," Box 5, CLC; Carrey and Conley, *River of No Return*, pp. 30–34. My gratitude to Cort Conley for locating an article placing Lockhart with Painter around May 1911. The article verifies Lockhart's presence on this trip. See article headed "Among the Mines of Lemhi County, Salmon River Mining Company Sends Fleet of Freight Boats Down the River: Nine Vessels Carrying Machinery and Supplies to the Camp of This Company Near Dixie—A Lady to Accompany the Party Through the Salmon River Canyon," Salmon Lemhi County *Idaho News*, 11 May 1911.

101. In her autobiography, written in later life, Lockhart claims she rode with Sandiland; however, in the article for *Outing Magazine*, written in February 1912 shortly after the event took place, she claims she rode with Guleke.

102. Lockhart, "The Wildest Boat Ride," pp. 518–19; "Miscellaneous Autobiographical Material," pp. 49–50 (two of the few numbered pages), Box 5, CLC.

103. See note 102, above. The autobiographical draft telling of the adventure reads better than the published version.

104. Lockhart, "The Wildest Boat Ride," pp. 519–24.

105. Ibid., p. 515.

106. Letter, Bill Painter to author, 13 February 1983. Sweeney, *Gold at Dixie Gulch*, p. 108, says that the mine itself burned.

107. Caroline Lockhart, *The Man from the Bitter Roots* (Philadelphia: Lippincott, 1915), 327 pp.

108. Letter, D. Engelstoft to Caroline Lockhart, 17 March 1922, Box 5: "Miscellaneous," CLC. Engelstoft sent Lockhart two copies of the foreign edition of *The Man from the Bitter Roots*, issued in shortened form. He also included quotes from foreign reviewers of the book.

109. Under the general heading, "The News of Elk City," in the Idaho County *Free Press*, 14 November 1912, p. 103 [microfilm], appear the following social items: "J.R. Painter, manager of the Salmon River Placer Miners, is in town on business." And "Miss Caroline Lockhart, author of *Me-Smith* and *Lady Doc*, who has spent the summer on Salmon River, passed through Elk City this week for her home in Philadelphia."

My appreciation to Dr. Paul Fees for acquiring this information from microfilm provided by the Idaho Historical Society.

110. *The Full of the Moon*, under copyright by 1913, was published by J. B. Lippin-cott in 1914. The Elk City *News*, 17 July 1913, p. 105 [microfilm], records that "Miss Caroline Lockhart, author of *Me, Smith* [*sic*] is in town on her way to the Salmon River to spend the summer."

111. "Miss Lockhart in Search of Material," in Park County *Enterprise*, 24 December 1913. The copy of this article, as well as others, was provided courtesy of the Park County Public Library, Cody, Wyoming.

112. Ibid.; letter, Bill Painter to author, 9 January 1985. An old-timer of the Salmon River country, Miles Patterson, in an interview with Marian Sweeney, supports the contention that J.R. and Caroline were in South America. Letter, Sweeney to author, 12 October 1984, provides excerpts from taped interview with Patterson.

113. "Autobiographical Draft," Box 10, CLC. This version was rewritten for her by her good friend and professor at the University of Nevada, Paul Eldridge; therefore, there are two drafts, one of which is written on the back of university stationery, ostensibly by Eldridge. Several of these autobiographical drafts, which read like adventure stories, are catalogued under the deceptive title: "Manu-scripts—Typewritten," and are located in Box 10, CLC. Other drafts are located in Box 9, CLC.

114. "Autobiographical Draft," Box 10, CLC, p. 70; "Suzette Loses Novel in Ocean," Philadelphia *Bulletin*, 5 April 1914, recorded in Culpin, Lockhart Manu-script, p. 29, and in letter, Bill Painter to author, 5 November 1984, located in Buffalo Bill Historical Center, Cody, Wyoming.

115. Interview, Electa Prante, 7 July 1982. Electa Prante, daughter of Anna (Mrs. Louis) Howe, recalls that Caroline and her mother had an "intellectual rap-port." When Caroline came to visit, "she had everyone laughing before she left."

116. Interview, Dorothea Nebel, 8 July 1982. Caroline Lockhart's caregiver in later years, Thelma Hinton, also recalled that "some people said she was a greedy person, but I never thought she was." Interview, Thelma Hinton, 9 July 1982.

117. Diary, 17 August 1924, Box 1, CLC.

118. Diary, 21 August 1918, Box 3, CLC. The inventory does not give a year for this section of the Lockhart Diary (May 15 [1918]–November 27 [1918]), but internal evidence shows it to be 1918. A Western Union telegram to Lockhart at the Hotel Calumet in New York, dated 15 July 1918, is included in this file. (Note that these undated entries are to be found out of sequence in the collection and are misfiled with Box 3 rather than Box 1.)

119. Diary, 27 February 1919, Box 1, CLC.

120. Diary, 2 February 1937, Box 3, CLC.

121. Diary, 14 January 1919, Box 1, CLC. Lockhart was not being entirely truthful. At one point, she decided she wanted to marry O.B. Mann, but he surprised her by marrying someone else. See Diary, 27 June 1919, Box 3, CLC.

122. Diary, 8 July [1918], Box 3, CLC.

123. "Autobiographical Draft," Box 9, CLC. This portion of the draft constitutes one of the few numbered sections. The Sheep Queen episode is recorded on pp. 92–99.

124. Ibid., p. 92.

125. Ibid., pp. 92–93.

126. Ibid., pp. 93–94.

127. Ibid., pp. 94–95.

128. Ibid., pp. 95–98.

129. Ibid., p. 96.

130. Ibid., pp. 97–98.

131. Olga (Mrs. Hugh) Von Krosigk, newspaper interview, "Descendant of 'Sheep Queen' is Meeteetse Resident," clipping in Box 5: "Miscellaneous," CLC. (Newspaper name has been cut off.)

132. "Autobiographical Draft," pp. 98–99, Box 9, CLC.

133. Ibid.

134. Caroline Lockhart, *The Fighting Shepherdess* (Boston: Small, Maynard & Co., 1919), 353 pp.; Diary, 28 June–13 July [1918], Box 3, CLC.

135. "Caroline Lockhart's Best Novel," newspaper clipping in Hebard Collection, B-L811-C, Western History Research Center, University of Wyoming, Laramie. See also review of *The Fighting Shepherdess* in the New York *Times* 24 (1 May 1919):271.

136. Lockhart originally tried to market the manuscript of *The Fighting Shepherdess* under the title "The Daughter of Jezebel." See Diary, 30 May [1918], Box 3, CLC.

137. Quoted from advertising copy in front-matter of *The Fighting Shepherdess*.

138. Mary Jester Allen, "Colonel Cody's Dream of Pioneer Center—A Reality," *Annals of Wyoming* 14 (January 1942):21–22. Allen credits Caroline Lockhart, whom she calls "a brilliant writer and publicity person," for promoting the idea of a statue of Cody in his hometown. According to Allen, Lockhart insisted she go to New York to talk with sculptor Gertrude Vanderbilt Whitney. As Caroline admitted: "I am keen on having this statue for Cody by Mrs. Whitney." See letter, Lockhart to Allen [written as president of the Cody Stampede], Buffalo Bill Historical Center, Cody, Wyoming.

139. Lockhart, *The Fighting Shepherdess*, p. 16. Caroline was only slightly more direct in her Diary in expressing her mixed feelings about her "friend," Buffalo Bill Cody.

140. See also Wallace Stegner, "History, Myth, and the Western Writer," *The American West* (May 1967):77; also by Stegner, "The Provincial Consciousness," *University of Toronto Quarterly* 43 (Summer 1974):299–310.

DENVER DAYS

1. Digby Whitman, "Making Headlines," *The RAGAN Report: A Weekly Survey of Ideas and Methods for Communication Executives* (22 November 1982):1.

2. A. K. Stone, "Boy Howdy! Meet Caroline Lockhart!" Denver *Post*, 3 December 1918, pp. 1–2, in Denver *Post* Archives, Denver, Colorado. World War I had just ended.

3. Ibid.

4. Ibid.

5. Ibid.

6. Ibid.

7. Lockhart Diary (hereafter, Diary), 15–21 May [1918], 20 June [1918], in Box 3, CLC. (Undated entries misfiled with Box 3 rather than with Box 1.)

8. Ibid. See also Lucille Patrick Hicks, *Caroline Lockhart: Liberated Lady, 1870–1962* (Cheyenne: Pioneer Printing, 1984), pp. 565–66. Her 61-page Introduction describes Lockhart's early life, then includes excerpts from the Lockhart Diaries, starting with May 1918 and proceeding through 15 July 1942.

9. Letter, Sylvia Crowder to author, 25 October 1982.

10. Ibid.

11. Diary, 21–28 May [1918], Box 3, CLC.

12. Ibid.

13. Diary, 29 May [1918], 2–12 June [1918], Box 3, CLC.

14. Diary, 13 June [1918], Box 3, CLC.

15. Diary, 17 June [1918], Box 3, CLC. By 1924 Mencken and his co-editor, Norman Jean Jeffries, were editors for the *American Mercury*.

16. Diary, 21, 26, 28 June [1918], Box 3, CLC.

17. Diary, 28 June [1918], Box 3, CLC.

18. Ibid.

19. Ibid.

20. Diary, 11 November [1918], Box 3, CLC.

21. Diary, 1 July [1918], Box 3, CLC.

22. Diary, 5 July [1918], Box 3, CLC.

23. Diary, 19 December 1939, Shelf, CLC.

24. Diary, 5, 7 July [1918], Box 3, CLC.

25. Diary, 8 July [1918], Box 3, CLC.

26. Diary, 9 July [1918], Box 3, CLC.

27. Diary, 7–9, 16 July [1918], Box 3, CLC.

28. Diary, 9, 13, 17, 18 July [1918], Box 3, CLC.

29. Diary, 19–20 July [1918], Box 3, CLC.

30. [Caroline Lockhart], "Philadelphia in June," by an Exile, *Lippincott's Monthly Magazine* (June 1905):727, Box 5, CLC.

31. Ibid.; Caroline Lockhart, "From Billings to Broadway," unpublished manuscript, Box 7, CLC.

32. Lockhart, "From Billings to Broadway"; [Lockhart], "When I Came Back to Philadelphia," by Suzette, clipping from Boston *Post,* Box 7, CLC.

33. Lockhart, "From Billings to Broadway," Box 7, CLC.

34. Ibid.

35. Ibid.

36. Diary, entry noted as "Saturday," apparently 27 July [1918]. See also entries for 8, 9, 15 September [1918], Box 3, CLC.

37. Diary, 30 July [1918], Box 3, CLC.

38. Diary, 6 November 1918, Box 3, CLC.

39. Diary, 6 February, 2 March 1919, Box 1, CLC.

40. Diary, 22 January 1919, Box 1, CLC.

41. See articles by Caroline Lockhart such as "Regulate Packers to Protect Stock Industry Is Urged," 27 January 1919; "*Post* Plays Santa to Needy Family, Plea Is Answered," 25 December 1918; "Real Heart Throbs Supplied at Depot As Yanks Return," 9 January 1919, all in Denver *Post,* located in Denver *Post* Archives, Denver, Colorado. See also Diary, 11 February 1919, Box 1, CLC.

42. Lockhart, "After Saving on Grub, Wouldn't President's 50 Chefs Bump You?" Denver *Post,* n.d., Denver *Post* Archives, Denver, Colorado.

43. Diary, 6, 19 February–10 March 1919, Box 1, CLC.

44. Lockhart, "Why Fuss Over Kaiser? Send Him to Cody, Wyoming, to Expiate His Crimes," Denver *Post,* 29 December 1918, Denver *Post* Archives, Denver, Colorado.

45. Lockhart, "Adhere to Rules and Story Writing Becomes a Cinch," Denver *Post,* 27 February 1919, Denver *Post* Archives, Denver, Colorado.

46. Lockhart, "Where Are They, the Best Sellers of By-Gone Days?" Denver *Post,* 31 January 1919, Denver *Post* Archives, Denver, Colorado.

47. Diary, 9 March 1919, Box 1, CLC; 19 December 1939, Box 3, CLC.

48. Diary, 12 March 1919, Box 1, CLC.

49. Diary, 20 March 1919, Box 1, CLC.

50. Diary, 24 March 1919, Box 1, CLC.

51. Diary, 11 February 1919, Box 1, CLC.

52. Ibid.

53. Diary, 31 March 1919, Box 1, CLC.

54. Diary, 4, 5, 9, 10, 12 April 1919, Box 1, CLC.

55. Diary, 15, 16 April 1919, Box 1, CLC.

56. "Autobiographical Draft," Box 9, CLC; see also undated Diary entries between 17 April and 1 May 1919 ("I have no idea what date it is," she writes), Box 1, CLC.

57. See undated references for April–May 1919 cited in note 56, above.

58. Ibid.

59. Ibid.

60. Ibid.

61. Diary, 3 May–18 May 1919, Box 1, CLC.

62. Diary, 25 May 1919, and entries for 1 May–28 May 1919, Box 1, CLC; Lucille Patrick Hicks, *Caroline Lockhart: Liberated Lady*, pp. 152–59.

63. "Drowned in Salt Creek," *The Chief*, n.p., 18 May 1919 (newspaper clipping inserted in Diary, 25 May 1919), Box 1, CLC.

64. In her Diary entry for 25 May 1919, Caroline wrote: "I didn't want my name mixed up in it because of Grace and Roy." The rationale, however, may have been to protect her own identity.

65. Ibid.

66. Diary, 28-30 May 1919, Box 1, CLC.

67. Diary, 2–6 June, 1919, Box 1, CLC.

68. Mary Jester Allen, "Colonel Cody's Dream of Pioneer Center—A Reality," *Annals of Wyoming* 14 (January 1942):20–24. Allen writes: "On January 10, 1917, Uncle Will rode away on that last long ride, not to return" (p. 21).

69. Diary, 3 July 1919, Box 1, CLC.

70. "Noted Cody Authoress Receives Big Offer from Douglas Fairbanks," Park County *Enterprise*, 23 July 1919, p. 1, Box 13, CLC.

71. "Big Audiences See 'The Fighting Shepherdess'—Caroline Lockhart, Well-Known Author, Witnesses Movie, Suffers in Silence," Park County *Enterprise*, 21 July 1920, p. 1, Box 13, CLC.

72. "Filmmakers Unfair to Wyoming People," Park County *Enterprise*, 18 August 1920, p. 6, Box 13, CLC.

73. See note 71, above.

74. Diary entry for 16 January 1920 notes Newton's reaction. Box 1, CLC.

75. Lawrence R. Bourne, *Dude Ranching: A Complete History* (Albuquerque: University of New Mexico Press, 1983), pp. ix, x, 4–6, 213.

76. Lawrence R. Bourne, *Welcome to My West: I. H. Larom—Dude Rancher, Conservationist, Collector,* with Preface by Michael Kelly and Paul Fees (Cody: Buffalo Bill Historical Center, 1982), pp. 1–23.

77. Caroline Lockhart, *The Dude Wrangler* (Garden City: Doubleday, Page, 1921), 319 pp.

78. Ibid., p. 168.

79. Ibid., p. 170.

80. Fred Erisman, "Western Regional Writers and the Uses of Place," in *The American Literary West*, edited by Richard Etulain (Manhattan, Kansas: Sunflower University Press, 1980), p. 38.

81. Lockhart, *The Dude Wrangler*, pp. 234–36.

82. Ibid., pp. 243, 255.

83. Ibid., pp. 270–74.

84. Ibid., pp. 318–19.

85. Erisman, "Western Regional Writers," p. 38.

THE ICONOCLAST

1. Diary, 4 March, 3 April 1920, Box 1, CLC.

2. "Autobiographical Draft," p. 103, Box 9, CLC. See also Diary, 29 April 1920, Box 1, CLC.

3. "Autobiographical Draft," p. 103, Box 9, CLC.

4. Ibid., p. 104; Diary, 30 April 1920, Box 1, CLC.

5. "Announcement," Park County *Enterprise*, 12 May 1920, p. 4, Park County Public Library, Cody, Wyoming (hereafter PCL). See also Diary entries for 29–30 April 1920, Box 1, CLC. The entry for 6 May 1920 indicates that John Chapman from Red Lodge and 'Judge' Walls were also present "to close the deal for the *Enterprise*." Lockhart confides that she will "enjoy helping on it. It will give me a little power and prestige."

6. Mary Shivers Culpin, "Lockhart Manuscript," p. 8, Buffalo Bill Historical Center, Cody, Wyoming.

7. "From the Start the Cody Stampede Was a Success," Cody *Enterprise*, n.d., news clipping provided by Paul Fees, Buffalo Bill Historical Center. In 1946 the Stampede Association voted to move the affair to the top of the hill, where a new grandstand was constructed using materials provided by the oil industry.

8. Caroline Lockhart, "Cody Boosters Plan Annual Frontier Event, Spirit of Old West to be Preserved and the Yip of the Cowboy to Drown the Honk of the Tin Lizzie for Three Whole Days," subheaded: "Cody Stampede Association Formed," Park County *Enterprise*, 5 May 1920, PCL.

9. Interview, Ernest J. Goppert, Sr., 12 July 1982.

10. Park County *Enterprise*, 5 May 1920, PCL.

11. Ibid.; Diary, 27 April 1920, Box 1, CLC.

12. Park County *Enterprise*, 5 May 1920, PCL.

13. [Caroline Lockhart], "Plenty of Thrills at the Cody Stampede," Park County *Enterprise*, 23 June 1920, PCL.

14. Interview, Ernest J. Goppert, Sr., 12 July 1982.

15. "From the Start the Cody Stampede Was a Success," Cody *Enterprise*, n.d.,

clipping, Buffalo Bill Historical Center. By 1923 headlines in the *Enterprise* read: "1923 Cody Stampede Smashes All Records—Receipts Above $11,000—Great Ride Puts Frankie Lasater Among Champions," 11 July 1923, Box 13, CLC.

16. Interview, Ernest J. Goppert, Sr., 12 July 1982; see also "For County and Prosecuting Attorney Republican Party," Park County *Enterprise*, 14 July 1920, PCL.

17. "Billings Must Hand It to Little Old Cody, Pinkie Gist, Champion Bull-Dogger of the World, Tells Montana Stockmen that We Know How to Get Out and Step," Park County *Enterprise*, 26 May 1920, p. 1, PCL. See also in same issue, "Stampede Program as Good as the Best."

18. "Its-Be-Che-Loti to Organize Indians," Park County *Herald*, 4 June 1924, PCL; "Plenticoos, Crow Chief, Planning to Attend Stampede Ball October 28," Park County *Enterprise*, 20 October 1920, PCL; "We All Come to the Cody Stampede," Cody *Enterprise*, 24 May 1922, Box 13, CLC.

19. [Lockhart], "Josh Tells How to Barbecue," Cody *Enterprise*, 24 August 1921, Box 13, CLC; "Fair Board Doing Good Team Work . . . Josh Deane's Barbecue a Drawing Card," Cody *Enterprise*, 21 August 1921, Box 13, CLC.

20. Nell B. Kelley, "Caroline Lockhart, Writer and Rodeo Sponsor, Is Living Example of Wonderful Cody Pioneers," Northern Wyoming *Daily News* (Worland), 28 August 1958, p. 2, clipping in Box 9: Biographical File (B-L811-C), CLC.

21. "Stampede Officers Elected for 1922," Cody *Enterprise*, 22 February 1922, Box 13, CLC.

22. Caroline Lockhart, "As Seen from the Water Wagon" (hereafter "Water Wagon"), Cody *Enterprise*, 1 March 1922, Box 13, CLC.

23. Ibid.

24. Caroline Lockhart, "Water Wagon," Cody *Enterprise*, 2 January 1924, Box 13, CLC.

25. Ibid.

26. Caroline Lockhart, draft of protest letter to Montana Fish and Game Department, Box 9: "Correspondence," CLC.

27. [Caroline Lockhart], "Caroline's Bobcat Cures Rheumatism," Cody *Enterprise*, 23 January 1924, Box 13, CLC.

28. Caroline Lockhart, "Never a Redeeming Trait," *Popular Magazine* 98 (20 December 1929):88–96, Box 6, CLC; interview, Lucille Patrick Hicks, 3 July 1982; interview, Caroline Buckingham, 12 July 1982.

29. Letter, Caroline Lockhart to Montana Fish and Game Department, Box 9: "Correspondence," CLC.

30. Caroline Lockhart, "Plenticoos, Crow Chief, Planning to Attend Stampede Ball October 28th," Park County *Enterprise*, 20 October 1920, PCL.

31. Caroline Lockhart, "Baby Wrangler to Be Provided," Park County *Enter-*

prise, 3 November 1920, PCL; ———— [report on the success of the Stampede Ball], Park County *Enterprise*, 3 November 1920, PCL.

32. June Little, "Cowboys and Big Hats; Let's Keep Cody as It Used to Be," Cody *Enterprise*, 14 February 1923, pp. 4, 15, Box 13, CLC.

33. "History of Cody Stampede," in Cody Stampede *Program*, 1984, Buffalo Bill Historical Center, Cody, Wyoming.

34. Lockhart had completed *The Dude Wrangler* manuscript by 25 April 1920. She sent it to the publisher on 20 July. In her Diary she refers to the occasion as "historic . . . since I sent off my sixth book." In May 1920 she wrote: "Am sore as a crab at Eldred again over an obituary on the front page after my telling him. . . . Larom is displeased with the paper also." See Diary entries for these dates, Box 1, CLC.

Lucille Patrick Hicks, in *Caroline Lockhart: Liberated Lady*, transcribes entries from the Lockhart Diaries through 1919, at which point she indicates that "the diaries stop," noting that Lockhart had burned some of them. Hicks takes up the transcription of the Diaries in 1921. Many of the Diaries for 1920, however, do in fact exist and can be found in Box 1 of the Lockhart Collection (CLC) at the University of Wyoming. The first entry therein is dated "Christmas Day 1919" and is somewhat misleading, but the following entries extend through 23 August 1920. The next folder in Box 1 picks up with 24 December 1920 and includes entries through 17 September 1921.

35. "Autobiographical Draft," n.p., Box 9, CLC.

36. Ibid.

37. "Caroline Lockhart and Charles M. Conger—Owners and Publishers," Cody *Enterprise*, 10 August 1921, p. 4, with subhead, "S. A. Nock Becomes Editor of *Enterprise*," PCL. The 28 December issue is the first included in the Lockhart Collection at the University of Wyoming, but the actual buying out of the other partners occurred earlier.

38. "Jackson Hole to Be Ruled by Women," Park County *Enterprise*, 19 May 1920, PCL.

39. David Dominick, "An Introduction to Caroline Lockhart," pp. 54–55, Box 9, CLC. Catherine Buckingham (interview, 12 July 1982) recalled that Lockhart "always took up for the underdog; she didn't cater to the 'upper crust'."

40. Dominick, "An Introduction to Caroline Lockhart," p. 57, Box 9, CLC.

41. Caroline Lockhart, "The Story of Poker Nell," Rocky Mountain *Empire*, Magazine Section, 25 May 1947, p. 8; "Poker Nell's Husband to Hang at Rawlins for Killing 'Slim' Smith," Cody *Enterprise*, 15 March 1922, Box 13, CLC.

42. Caroline Lockhart, "As Seen from the Water Wagon," Cody *Enterprise*, 23 January 1924, Box 13, CLC.

43. "Autobiographical Draft," p. 104, Box 9, CLC.

44. "Caroline Lockhart and Charles M. Conger—Owners and Publishers," Cody *Enterprise*, 10 August 1921, p. 4. The first Lockhart-Conger issue of the *Enterprise* appeared 22 June 1921. My appreciation to Paul Fees and his staff at the Buffalo Bill Historical Center for their research support in determining certain dates.

45. "Autobiographical Draft," p. 106, Box 9, CLC. See also the seven-paragraph editorial criticizing Prohibition and the Volstead Act in the 24 August 1921 issue of the *Enterprise*, p. 4, PCL.

46. Dominick, "An Introduction to Caroline Lockhart," p. 52, Box 9, CLC.

47. Caroline Lockhart, "Water Wagon," Cody *Enterprise*, 17 August 1921, PCL.

48. Dominick, "An Introduction to Caroline Lockhart," quoting Lockhart, "Where Is Our Wandering Boy Tonight?" p. 54, Box 9, CLC. See also "Hairbreadth Harry Among the Missing," Cody *Enterprise*, 21 September 1921, p. 1, Box 13, CLC; Dominick interview with Caroline Lockhart, recorded in "An Introduction to Caroline Lockhart," p. 54, Box 9, CLC.

49. Caroline Lockhart, "Water Wagon," Cody *Enterprise*, 31 May 1922, Box 13, CLC.

50. Ibid., 20 May 1925, Box 13, CLC.

51. "Woodrow Wilson Is Dead," Cody *Enterprise*, 6 February 1924, p. 1; "Train Drops into River Near Casper When Bridge Breaks," 3 October 1923; "Big Gas Well Blows in Here," 4 February 1925; all articles in Cody *Enterprise*, Box 13, CLC.

52. See coverage of case in Cody *Enterprise* for 18 February 1925 and additional coverage in "Marston Frees Mrs. Strand," 25 March 1925, Box 13, CLC.

53. "Autobiographical Draft," pp. 104–6, Box 9, CLC.

54. Ibid.

55. "U.S. Is Falling off Water Wagon," Cody *Enterprise*, 4 January 1922, Box 13, CLC.

56. Caroline Lockhart, "Water Wagon," Cody *Enterprise*, 19 November 1924, p. 1, Box 13, CLC.

57. Eldridge, "Woman on Horseback," p. 4, Box 7, CLC.

58. "Sage Ticks," Cody *Enterprise*, 17 August 1921, p. 4, Box 13, CLC; Caroline Lockhart, "Water Wagon," Cody *Enterprise*, 31 August 1921, Box 13, CLC.

59. Cody *Enterprise*, 24 August 1921, p. 4, Box 13, CLC.

60. Caroline Lockhart, "Water Wagon," Cody *Enterprise*, 27 September 1922; ibid., 5 April 1922; ibid., 3 June 1925; all in Box 13, CLC.

61. Cody *Enterprise*, 16 November 1921, p. 8, Box 13, CLC.

62. "Sage Ticks," Cody *Enterprise*, 31 August 1921, p. 4, Box 13, CLC.

63. Ibid.

64. Quoted by Dominick in "An Introduction to Caroline Lockhart," p. 52, Box 9, CLC.

65. Caroline Lockhart, "Water Wagon," Cody *Enterprise*, 16 August 1922, p. 1, Box 13, CLC.

66. Ibid., 24 October 1923, Cody *Enterprise*, p. 1, Box 13, CLC.

67. Caroline Lockhart, "Enemies of the Home," Cody *Enterprise*, 9 November 1921, p. 4, Box 13, CLC.

68. [Caroline Lockhart], "Costs $1.00 to Kick an Editor," Cody *Enterprise*, 2 May 1923, p. 1, Box 13, CLC.

69. Caroline Lockhart, "Water Wagon," Cody *Enterprise*, 30 May 1923, p. 1, Box 13, CLC.

70. Ibid., 5 September 1923, p. 1, Box 13, CLC.

71. [Caroline Lockhart], "Local News Items: Following the Ponies," Cody *Enterprise*, 9 November 1921, p. 8, Box 13, CLC.

72. [Caroline Lockhart], "Editor Ralph Smith Compares *Enterprise* and the *Herald*, Hears the Rustle of Wings in One Shop, Smells Brimstone in the Other—But Feels Quite at Home," Cody *Enterprise*, 5 October 1921, p. 19, Box 13, CLC.

73. Ibid.

74. Caroline Lockhart, "Water Wagon," Cody *Enterprise*, 3 October 1923, p. 1, Box 13, CLC.

75. Ibid. A favorite tactic of Lockhart was to quote her critics verbatim, then launch her counterattack.

76. "New York *Evening Post* Praises *Enterprise*," Cody *Enterprise*, 22 February 1922, p. 1, Box 13, CLC.

77. " 'Dude Wrangler' Will Be Filmed," Cody *Enterprise*, 31 May 1922, Box 13, CLC.

78. See reference cited in note 76 above, in which Lockhart quotes Christopher Morley.

79. Ibid.

80. Mary Jester Allen, "Colonel Cody's Dream of a Pioneer Center—A Reality," *Annals of Wyoming*, 14 (January 1942):20–21.

81. Ibid., p. 21.

82. Ibid., p. 22; letter, Lockhart to Mary Jester Allen, on letterhead stationery imprinted "Cody Stampede, July 4, 5, 6, 1921" with photo-print of Lockhart on rearing horse, n.d. Copy provided by Buffalo Bill Historical Center, Cody, Wyoming.

83. [Caroline Lockhart], "Statue of Buffalo Bill by Mrs. Harry Payne Whitney Appeals to Cody," Cody *Enterprise*, 15 February 1922, p. 1, Box 13, CLC.

84. Mary Jester Allen, see note 80, above, p. 22.

85. "Sammy Girls Launch Campaign for Buffalo Bill Statue by Mrs. Harry Payne Whitney, Famous Sculptor," Cody *Enterprise*, 10 May 1922, p. 1, Box 13, CLC.

86. "Design for Statue Is Being Prepared," Cody *Enterprise*, 4 October 1922, p. 1, Box 13, CLC.

87. Article quoted in "Miss Lockhart's Western Gang Due for a Surprise in New York," Cody *Enterprise*, 15 August 1923, p. 4, Box 13, CLC.

88. "Plans for Unveiling Statue of Buffalo Bill Now Being Made," Cody *Enterprise*, 21 May 1924, p. 1, Box 13, CLC.

89. "Statue of Colonel Cody to Start on Journey Westward in Week," Cody *Enterprise*, 28 May 1924, p. 1, Box 13, CLC.

90. "Buffalo Bill Memorial Is an Expression of American Life Well Interpreted by Gertrude Vanderbilt Whitney, the Sculptor," 2 April 1924; "More Than Ten Thousand People Witness Unveiling," 4 July 1924, both articles in Park County *Herald*, p. 1, PCL. (The Park County *Herald* was the successor to the Northern Wyoming *Herald*.) See also "Statue of Buffalo Bill Triumph of Mrs. Harry Payne Whitney's Career," Cody *Enterprise*, 16 January 1924, Box 13, CLC.

91. Diary, 24 January 1921, Box 1, CLC.

92. Ibid., 23 October 1920, 18 November 1920, 18 February 1921, Box 1, CLC.

93. Ibid., 9–18 February 1921, Box 1, CLC.

94. Ibid., 23 October 1920, 23 January 1920, 9 February 1921, 16–24 March 1921, 13 April 1921, Box 1, CLC.

95. Ibid., 30 March 1921, Box 1, CLC.

96. Ibid., 8 August 1921, 9–16 October 1921, 1 September 1921, Box 1, CLC.

97. Ibid., 26–27 September 1921, 2–5 January 1922, Box 1, CLC.

98. Ibid., 14 November–8 December 1921, 2–5 January 1922, Box 1, CLC.

99. Ibid., 12 January 1922, Box 1, CLC.

100. Records for the case of C. M. *Conger* v. *Caroline Lockhart* can be found in File 890, Park County District Courthouse, Cody, Wyoming. See also Conger's "Reply and Answer to Cross Petition," filed by attorneys Donley and Greever on 20 February 1922, Civil Appearance Docket 43, File 885–1204, p. 7, Park County District Courthouse, Cody, Wyoming.

101. C. Lockhart's "Answer and Cross Petition" (including copy of "Memorandum of Agreement," dated 22 November 1921) witnessed by F. M. McGee and D. E. Hollister before F. F. McGee, dated 11 February 1922, Park County District Courthouse, Cody, Wyoming.

102. C. M. *Conger* v. *Caroline Lockhart*, Civil Appearance Docket 3, File 885–1204, p. 7, Park County District Courthouse, Cody, Wyoming. See also Diary, 23 March 1923, Box 1, CLC.

103. "*Enterprise* Moves into New Home," Cody *Enterprise*, 14 February 1923, p. 1, Box 13, CLC.

104. Ibid.

105. See note 102 above.

106. "Couldn't Convince the Judge Blanche Gokel Is Dangerous—Pugilistic Cook Goes on Rampage—Out to Whip Editor of *Enterprise*, City Attorney, and W. L. Simpson," Cody *Enterprise*, 23 May 1923, Box 13, CLC.

107. Ibid.

108. Ibid.

109. "Autobiographical Draft," n.p., Box 9, CLC.

110. Caroline Lockhart, "Carey Tells Story of the Killing of 'Scotty' Sirrine by Two Deputies," Cody Enterprise, 5 March 1924, p. 1, PCL.

111. Caroline Lockhart, "Greybull Man Is Killed by Cody Prohibition Officers; Companion Badly Wounded," Cody Enterprise, 27 June 1923, p. 1, Box 13, CLC. Note that clippings are removed from the library copy, but this clipping is cited by title and in full in the petition filed by Goppert against Lockhart (Section 3) before Paul R. Greever on 9 July 1923 in Park County District Court, Cody, Wyoming.

112. Ibid.; Caroline Lockhart, "Goppert Objects to Enterprise Story of Killing," 4 July 1923, Box 13, CLC; [Lockhart], "Goppert Sues Caroline Lockhart and the Cody Enterprise for $30,000," Cody Enterprise, 11 July 1923, p.1, Box 13, CLC. The Denver Post also covered the case; see "Caroline Lockhart Is Sued for Libel," 27 April 1926, n.p., Denver Post Archives, Denver, Colorado.

113. Interview, E. J. Goppert, Sr., 12 July 1982.

114. Ibid.

115. Caroline Lockhart, "Gop Gets Pop in Raid on Car," Cody Enterprise, 11 July 1923, Box 13, CLC.

116. Caroline Lockhart, "Water Wagon," Cody Enterprise, 21 November 1923, Box 13, CLC.

117. Ibid., 12 September 1923, PCL. The similarity in names was called to my attention by Annette Kolodny.

118. "Here's Chance for Goppert to Sue Casper Oil Index," Cody Enterprise, 18 July 1923, Box 13, CLC.

119. Caroline Lockhart, "Water Wagon," Cody Enterprise, 14 November 1923, Box 13, CLC.

120. Caroline Lockhart, "Jury Finds Carey Guilty on 4 Counts; Fined $2750, 11 Months, Loses Car," Cody Enterprise, 27 February 1924, p. 1, Box 13, CLC. See also Lockhart, "Water Wagon," Cody Enterprise, 12 September 1923, Box 13, CLC.

121. Caroline Lockhart, "Water Wagon," Cody Enterprise, 20 February 1924, p. 1, PCL. The Park County District Court Journal 3:407, order 1061, relating to Goppert v. Lockhart, shows that Judge Percy Metz on 26 January 1924 granted a change of venue for the case to Washakie County, Wyoming.

122. "Goppert-Lockhart Case Is Postponed," Cody Enterprise, 15 April 1925, PCL.

123. "Autobiographical Draft," n.p., Box 9, CLC; Dominick, "An Introduction to Caroline Lockhart," p. 52, Box 9, CLC, notes that the trial was held in Basin.

124. "Autobiographical Draft," n.p., Box 9, CLC. See last page.

125. Ibid.; Ernest J. Goppert v. Caroline Lockhart, District Court of Washakie County, Wyoming, 29 April 1926, Judgment 436. The jury found in favor of the defendant and ordered that Goppert reimburse Lockhart for court costs in the amount of $356.70.

126. "Caroline Lockhart Found Not Guilty of Libel on Lawyer," Denver *Post*, 29 April 1926, n.p., Denver *Post* Archives, Denver, Colorado.

127. " 'Gop' Has Another Tantrum; Demands $50 Damages from the Cody *Enterprise*," 22 April 1925, p. 1, Box 13, CLC.

128. "Gop's Troubles to Be Heard Next Term of District Court," Cody *Enterprise*, 27 April 1925, p. 1, Box 13, CLC; Park County District Court *Journal* 4:163, Park County District Courthouse, Case 1212, E. J. *Goppert* v. *Caroline Lockhart, George Huss, and the Cody Enterprise*, 17 August 1927, by Bryan S. Comer, Judge.

129. "Newton Sells Cody *Herald* to Partner," Cody *Enterprise*, 5 March 1924, Box 13, CLC.

130. "V. H. Abrahamson Buys Cody *Enterprise*," 4 October 1925, Box 13, CLC.

131. "Caroline Lockhart Retires," miscellaneous clipping dated October 1925; see also "Caroline Lockhart Quits Cody *Enterprise*," miscellaneous clipping dated October 1925; both clippings in Hebard Collection, B-L811-C, Western History Research Center, University of Wyoming, Laramie.

132. Eldridge, "Woman on Horseback," pp. 9–10, Box 7, CLC.

133. Dominick, "An Introduction to Caroline Lockhart," p. 49, Box 9, CLC.

134. Ibid., quoted on p. 50.

135. "Prohibition, Thy Name Is Failure," Cody *Enterprise*, 25 February 1925, PCL.

136. Sarah Fritjofson, "Tough People Made the Cody *Enterprise*," n.d., n.p., miscellaneous clipping provided by Buffalo Bill Historical Center, Cody, Wyoming.

THE CATTLE QUEEN

1. "Ranch Work Delays Author in Completing New Book," Casper *Herald*, 16 February 1928, Box 2, CLC.

2. Final Certificate, Homestead, James Wasson, 19 February 1926, Record Group 49, Serial Patent 980527, National Archives.

Final Proof Certificate, Stock Raising Homestead, Caroline Lockhart, 7 July 1931, Record Group 49, Serial Patent 027323, National Archives. Among Lockhart's earliest acquisitions were: purchase of land from William Howe, 26 January 1926, T8 R28, Section 2; purchase from Josephine Caldwell, 8 March 1927; and purchase from Lou Erickson, 22 June 1927, T8 R28.

See also "Writer and Her Housekeeper Win in Homestead Disputes," Billings *Gazette*, 29 March 1936, brought to my attention by Mary Shivers Culpin in her Lockhart Manuscript.

3. Lockhart Diary (hereafter, Diary), 20 July, 19 August 1924, 21 September 1925, Box 1, CLC. After returning to Cody from her second trip, she wrote: "Back again to hell." And later, "After the peace and healthy outdoor life of the last two months in the Dryhead, [it] is dull!"

4. Paul R. Eldridge visited Caroline on the Dryhead each summer for many years. His biographical article, "Woman on Horseback," contains the best firsthand documentation describing the area as it was during Lockhart's residence there. See Eldridge manuscript, dated 21 December 1977, in Box 7, CLC.

5. Ibid.; Diary, 16 October 1926, 9 May 1927, 12–16 August 1927, Box 1, CLC. On 23 February 1926, Caroline wrote in her Diary that she had received a heartbroken letter from Edith Barry saying that Ruth had run away and married. "I do not know what foundation there is, if any for the tales they tell . . . of Mrs. Barry's cruelty, but at any rate she is a brilliant, well-bred woman and I am sorry for her." By August 1927, the Barrys were allowing their cattle to run on Lockhart's pasture. Relations deteriorated, and Caroline changed her initially favorable impression.

6. Diary, 13 November 1925, 21 September 1925, 6 October 1925, Box 1, CLC.

7. Diary, 7 October–12 November 1925, Box 1, CLC.

8. Diary, 20 November 1925, Box 1, CLC.

9. Ibid.

10. Transcript of Testimony at Consolidation of Hearings (1933, Federal Land Office, Billings, Montana), Record Group 49, National Archives.

11. Diary, 18 December 1925, Box 1, CLC.

12. Diary, 26 December 1925, Box 1, CLC.

13. Diary, 27 December, 30 December 1925, Box 1, CLC.

14. Diary, 11 December 1925, Box 1, CLC.

15. On 1 May 1926, Caroline wrote in her Diary: "We took Gop to a Cleaning. . . . The jury brought in a verdict after a short deliberation and he pays the costs—several hundred dollars." And on 18 June she recorded: "Consented to the consolidating of the *Enterprise* and *Herald.*"

16. Diary, 19 June 1926, Box 1, CLC.

17. Diary, 19 June, 23–28 June, 16 July, and 5 September 1926.

18. See note 10 above; see also Diary, 18 June 1927, Box 1, CLC.

19. Diary, 13 June–3 July 1927, Box 1, CLC. The reference to "Old Satan" is found in the entry for 24 April 1927. See also note 10 above.

20. "Autobiographical Notes," pp. 3–4, Folder 5, Box 10, CLC.

21. Ibid.; Diary, 23–29 March, 14 October 1928, Box 2, CLC; 30 July 1927, Box 1, CLC. Later, Lockhart would add the wife of Chief Plenty Coups to her list of women she cared for.

22. Marie Louise visited her at the ranch on several occasions. See "Autobiographical Notes," Box 10, CLC.

23. Diary, 28 March, 7 April 1928, Box 2, CLC.

24. Diary, 14 June–12 July 1928, Box 2, CLC.

25. Diary, 16 October–27 December 1928, Box 2, CLC.

26. Diary, 2 January 1929, Box 2, CLC.

27. Ibid.

28. Diary, 23 January–23 February 1929, Box 2, CLC.

29. Diary, 23–24 February 1929, Box 2, CLC.

30. Diary, 29 June 1929, Box 2, CLC.

31. Diary, 3–6 October, 26 October 1929, Box 2, CLC.

32. Diary, 26 May–19 July 1930, 20 June 1933, Box 2, CLC.

33. Diary, 30 December 1931, Box 2, CLC.

34. Diary, 15 October–18 November 1931 (see especially entries for 2–18 November), Box 2, CLC.

35. Diary, 11 February 1930, Box 2, CLC.

36. Diary, 25 April 1930, Box 2, CLC.

37. Diary, 11 February 1933, Shelf (not in box), CLC. See also "Notice for Publication," 14 May 1931, signed by C. R. Giddings, Acting Register, Federal Land Office, Billings, Montana, indicating that Lockhart filed proof of final claim for 7 July 1931 on the land in question; also letter, Assistant Commissioner to Caroline Lockhart, 7 July 1931, stating "that entrywoman did not establish residence in the land as alleged in her final proof, nor was residence thereon maintained in the manner and for the period stated in the said proof"; also letter, Giddings to Caroline Lockhart, 20 July 1931; all in Record Group 49, Serial Patent File 1085616, National Archives.

38. Diary, 12 February 1933, Shelf (not in box), CLC. See also Petition, signed by Philip Snell, Joe Smith, E. C. Hulbert, Ervin Howard, E. G. Barry, C. G. St. John, Clarence A. Curen, F. W. Blythe, to Federal Land Office, Billings, Montana, in Record Group 49, Serial Patent File 1085616, National Archives.

39. Letter, Joe LeFors to Fred Johnson, 21 May 1934, in Record Group 49, Serial Patent File 1085616, National Archives.

40. Letter, Caroline Lockhart to Fred H. Johnson, 15 May 1934; letter, F. T. McGee to Fred H. Johnson, 21 May 1934; letter, J. W. Hay to Fred H. Johnson, 22 May 1934; letter, John F. Cook to Fred H. Johnson, 23 May 1934; letter, Fred H. Johnson to Joe LeFors, 2 June 1934; letter, Fred H. Johnson to Caroline Lockhart, 4 June 1934; letter, Fred H. Johnson to Joseph C. O'Mahoney, 2 July 1934; all in Record Group 49, Serial Patent File 1085616, National Archives.

41. Letter, F. T. McGee to Fred H. Johnson, 21 May 1934, in Record Group 49, Serial Patent File 1085616, National Archives.

42. Letter, Caroline Lockhart to Fred H. Johnson, 15 May 1934, in Record Group 49, Serial Patent File 1085616, National Archives.

43. Ibid.; see also "Stipulation for Consolidation of Hearings," 16 September 1933, *United States of America* v. *Caroline Lockhart, Clay Jolly, and Lou Ketcham,* Dept. of Interior, Federal Land Office, Billings, Montana; "Transcript of Testimony at Consolidation of Hearings," October 1933; "Brief on Appeal, *History of Case,*" 3 July 1935, Guy C. Perry, Attorney, U.S. Dept. of Interior; in Record Group 49, National Archives.

44. Re: "Closing Case—Promulgating Departmental Decision of March 12, 1936," D. K. Parrott to Register, Federal Land Office, Billings, Montana; in Record Group 49, National Archives.

45. "Tops Steer Market," Lovell *Chronicle,* 12 September 1935, in Box 11: Periodicals, Articles, Clippings, and Copies, Hebard Collection, B-L811-C, Western History Research Center, University of Wyoming, Laramie.

46. Diary, 1 March–30 April 1932, 7 June 1932, Shelf, CLC.

47. Caroline Lockhart, *Old West and New* (Garden City: Doubleday, Doran, 1933) 357 pp. Reviewed ("Changing West") in New York *Times Literary Supplement,* 9 November 1933, p. 776.

48. Caroline Lockhart, *Old West and New,* pp. 10–11.

49. Ibid., p. 36.

50. Ibid., p. 64.

51. Ibid., pp. 23–24, 225, 314–15.

52. Ibid., p. 331.

53. Ibid., pp. 230–33. See also Diary, 1 November 1926, 22 January, 24 March, 22 April 1927, in Box 1, CLC; Diary, 1 July 1929, 16 March 1931, in Box 2, CLC.

54. Caroline Lockhart, *Old West and New,* pp. 28–29.

55. Ibid., p. 354.

56. "Caroline Lockhart Puts Stamp of Individuality on *Old West and New,*" Cody *Enterprise,* 19 April 1932, Box 11: Wyoming Clippings Folder, CLC; Review ("Changing West"), New York *Times Literary Supplement,* 9 November 1933, p. 776.

57. Diary, 29–30 May 1933, Shelf, CLC.

58. Caroline Lockhart, "That Wicked Woman," 333-page manuscript, Box 9: Folder 3, CLC. See also rewrite by Eleanor Shoemaker, entitled "Black Widow," 330-page manuscript, Box 11: Folder 7, CLC.

59. Eldridge, "Woman on Horseback," p. 21, Box 7, CLC. See also Diary, 2 July–21 August 1933, Box 2, CLC; "Local Ranch Woman Announce [sic] Engagement of Her Employees," Cody *Enterprise,* 1944, copy in CLC.

60. Eldridge, "Woman on Horseback," p. 28, Box 7, CLC.

61. Ibid.; letter, Paul Eldridge to Caroline Lockhart, 19 September 1948, Box 9: Correspondence, CLC; letters, Eleanor Shoemaker to Caroline Lockhart, 24 March, 31 March, 21 May, 9 July 1948, Box 9: Correspondence, CLC.

62. Letter, Eleanor Shoemaker to Caroline Lockhart, 9 July 1948, Box 9: Correspondence, CLC; letters, Ellan McIlvaine to Miss Lockhart, 30 July 1948, Box 10: Folder 5, CLC. Lockhart also sent McIlvaine short stories, such as "No Grounds for Divorce."

63. Letter, Agnes M. Reeve to Miss Lockhart, 23 March 1953, Box 10: Folder 5, CLC.

64. Letter, Caroline Lockhart to Dorothea Nebel, 4 November 1948, Box 3, CLC.

65. Eldridge, "Woman on Horseback," pp. 22–23, Box 7, CLC.

66. Ibid.; Caroline Lockhart, "Not a Redeeming Trait," *Popular Magazine* 98, no. 3 (December 1929):88–96, Box 6, CLC; republished in *Western Stories*, edited by William McLeod Raine (New York: Dell, 1949), pp. 137–92, Box 9, CLC.

67. Eldridge, "Woman on Horseback," p. 25, Box 7, CLC.

68. Ibid., p. 26.

69. Caroline Lockhart, "Nothin'll Ever Happen to Me" (assorted autobiographical pieces), Box 9, CLC.

70. Diary, 10 June 1938, Box 3, CLC; letter, Caroline Lockhart to Dorothea Nebel, 11 June 1950, copy provided to author by D. Nebel.

EPILOGUE: THE LAST LEAF ON THE TREE

1. Letter, Caroline Lockhart to Dorothea Nebel, 11 June 1950, copy provided by D. Nebel.

2. Interview, Dorothea Nebel, 1 July 1982.

3. Letters, Caroline Lockhart to Dorothea Nebel, 23 September, 22 November, 31 December 1948, 29 March, 28 August 1950, copies provided by D. Nebel.

4. Letter, Caroline Lockhart to Dorothea Nebel, 21 June 1952, copy provided by D. Nebel.

5. "Dave Good, Cody Old-Timer, Dies Monday," Cody *Enterprise*, 15 April 1965, Park County Public Library, Cody, Wyoming. Lockhart's year of birth, 1870 or 1871, remains in question. She contradicts her year of birth in various Diary entries.

6. Letter, Caroline Lockhart to "Dottie-Runs-at-the-Nose," 13 June 1951; "Noted Cody Authors: Caroline Lockhart—Eloise Jensen," newspaper clipping, n.d., n.p.; provided by D. Nebel.

7. Interview, Eloise Stock, 1 July 1982.

8. Letter, Caroline Lockhart to Dorothea Nebel, 8 July 1951.

9. Letters, Caroline Lockhart to Dorothea Nebel, 21 August, 22 August 1951, 18 January 1952; "Noted Cody Authors," newspaper clipping; provided by D. Nebel.

10. Interviews, Dorothea Nebel and Eloise Stock, 1 July 1982.

11. Interview, Dorothea Nebel, 1 July 1982.

12. Letter, Sylvia Crowder to author, 25 October 1982, in which she quotes from a letter to her mother, Grace (Lockhart's sister), dated 6 October 1954.

13. Letter, Caroline Lockhart to Vernon Spencer, 25 January 1960, CLC; Kathryn Wright, "Author Caroline Lockhart Dies in Cody at 91 Years," Cody *Enterprise*, n.d., n.p., CLC.

14. Letter, Dorothea Nebel to author, 12 July 1982.

15. Ibid.; Telephone interview, Sylvia Crowder, n.d. (record of note on type-written letter from Crowder to author, 15 July 1982).

16. Interviews: Bill De Maris, 17 July 1982; Dick Frost, 6 July 1982.

17. "Caroline Lockhart Among Who's Who," Lander *Evening Post,* n.p., 24 November 1930, Box 11, CLC; Caroline Lockhart, "Last Will and Testament," Park County District Courthouse, Cody, Wyoming, 1 October 1953, with codicils, Box 17, CLC.

Bibliography

Archival Depositories

American Heritage Center (Caroline Lockhart Collection), University of Wyoming, Laramie, Wyoming
Buffalo Bill Historical Center, Cody, Wyoming
Denver *Post* Microfilm Archives, Denver, Colorado
Denver Public Library, Denver, Colorado
Idaho State Historical Society, Boise, Idaho
Lovell County Courthouse, Lovell, Wyoming
National Archives and Records Administration, Washington, D.C.
Park County District Courthouse, Cody, Wyoming
Park County Public Library, Cody, Wyoming
Western History Research Center (Hebard Collection), University of Wyoming, Laramie, Wyoming

Primary Sources

WORKS BY CAROLINE LOCKHART

Books

Me-Smith. Philadelphia: J. B. Lippincott, 1911.
The Lady Doc. New York: J. B. Lippincott, 1912.
The Full of the Moon. Philadelphia: J. B. Lippincott, 1914.
The Man from the Bitter Roots. Philadelphia: J. B. Lippincott, 1915.
The Fighting Shepherdess. Boston: Small, Maynard, and Co., 1919.
The Dude Wrangler. New York: Doubleday, Page, and Co., 1921.
Old West and New. Garden City: Doubleday, Doran, and Co., 1933.

Short Stories and Magazine Articles

"The Greengrocery Man." *The Orphan's Bouquet,* 1 June 1893.
"A Girl in the Rockies" [by Suzette]. *Lippincott's Monthly Magazine,* August 1902.
"The Child of Nature." *New Idea Woman's Magazine,* September 1904.
"Philadelphia in June" [by an Exile]. *Lippincott's Monthly Magazine,* June 1905.

"His Own Medicine." *Lippincott's Monthly Magazine,* October 1905.

"The Woman Who Gave No Quarter." *Lippincott's Monthly Magazine,* February 1907.

"The Pin-Head." *Lippincott's Monthly Magazine,* October 1908.

"The Wildest Boat Ride in America." *The Outing Magazine,* February 1912.

"The Tango Lizard." *Smith's Magazine,* November 1917.

"A Treasure of the Humble." *Smith's Magazine,* December 1917.

"The Qualities of Leadership." *Smith's Magazine,* March 1920.

"The Spirit that Talked from a Box." *The Popular Magazine,* 7 July 1922.

"In the White Man's Way." *The Popular Magazine,* 20 March 1925.

"Not a Redeeming Trait." *The Popular Magazine,* 20 December 1929.

"The Sign that Failed." *Home and Art,* n.d.

Newspaper Articles

"Suzette Tells of Manhunt and Holdup in Cody." N.p., 1 November 1904. Caroline Lockhart Collection. Box 11.

"Murder Most Foul Committed at Cody." Meeteetse *News,* 2 November 1904.

"When the Automobile Struck Town." Philadelphia *North American,* 1905.

"Post Plays Santa to Needy Family, Plea Is Answered." Denver *Post,* 25 December 1918.

"Why Fuss Over Kaiser? Send Him to Cody, Wyoming to Expiate His Crimes." Denver *Post,* 29 December 1918.

"Real Heart Throbs Supplied at Depot as Yanks Return." Denver *Post,* 9 January 1919.

"Regulate Packers to Protect Stock Industry Is Urged." Denver *Post,* 27 January 1919.

"Where Are They, the Best Sellers of By-Gone Days?" Denver *Post,* 31 January 1919.

"Adhere to Rules and Story Writing Becomes a Cinch." Denver *Post,* 27 February 1919.

"Cody Boosters Plan Annual Frontier Event; Spirit of Old West to Be Preserved and the Yip of the Cowboy to Drown the Honk of the Tin Lizzie for Three Whole Days—Cody Stampede Organization Is Formed." Park County *Enterprise,* 5 May 1920.

"Plenty of Thrills at the Cody Stampede." Park County *Enterprise,* 23 June 1920.

"Plenticoos, Crow Chief, Planning to Attend Stampede Ball October 28th." Park County *Enterprise,* 20 October 1920.

"Report on the Success of Stampede Ball." Park County *Enterprise,* 3 November 1920.

"As Seen from the Water Wagon." Cody *Enterprise,* 17 August, 31 August 1921.

"Editor Ralph Smith Compares *Enterprise* and the *Herald*, Hears the Rustle of Wings in One Shop, Smells Brimstone in the Other—but Feels Quite at Home." Cody *Enterprise*, 5 October 1921.

"Local News Items—Following the Ponies." Cody *Enterprise*, 9 November 1921.

"Enemies of the Home." Cody *Enterprise*, 9 November 1921.

"As Seen from the Water Wagon." Cody *Enterprise*, 16 November 1921.

"Statue of Buffalo Bill by Mrs. Harry Payne Whitney Appeals to Cody." Cody *Enterprise*, 15 February 1922.

"As Seen from the Water Wagon." Cody *Enterprise*, 1 March, 31 May, 16 August, 27 September 1922.

"*Enterprise* Moves into New Home." Cody *Enterprise*, 14 February 1923.

"Costs $1.00 to Kick an Editor." Cody *Enterprise*, 2 May 1923.

"Couldn't Convince the Judge Blanche Gokel Is Dangerous—Pugilistic Cook Goes on Rampage—Out to Whip Editor of the *Enterprise*, City Attorney, and W. L. Simpson." Cody *Enterprise*, 23 May 1923.

"As Seen from the Water Wagon." Cody *Enterprise*, 30 May 1923.

"Greybull Man Is Killed by Cody Prohibition Officers; Companion Badly Wounded." Cody *Enterprise*, 27 June 1923.

"Goppert Objects to *Enterprise* Story of Killing." Cody *Enterprise*, 4 July 1923.

"Gop Gets Pop in Raid on Car." Cody *Enterprise*, 11 June 1923.

"Here's Chance for Goppert to Sue Casper *Oil Index.*" Cody *Enterprise*, 11 July 1923.

"Goppert Sues Caroline Lockhart and the Cody *Enterprise* for $30,000." Cody *Enterprise*, 18 July 1923.

"As Seen from the Water Wagon." Cody *Enterprise*, 5 September, 12 September, 3 October, 14 November, 21 November 1923; 2 January, 23 January, 20 February 1924.

"Jury Finds Carey Guilty on 4 Counts; Fined $2750, 11 Months, Loses Car." Cody *Enterprise*, 27 February 1924.

"Carey Tells Story of the Killing of 'Scotty' Sirrine by Two Deputies." Cody *Enterprise*, 5 March 1924.

"As Seen from the Water Wagon." Cody *Enterprise*, 19 November 1924.

[*State* v. *A. Strand*]. Cody *Enterprise*, 18 February 1925.

"The Story of Poker Nell." Rocky Mountain *Empire Magazine*, 25 May 1947.

"Cody Author Recalls Pleasant Interview with Famed Financier." Billings *Gazette*, 7 August 1955.

"Cody Writer Recalls Meeting with Former Heavyweight Champion." Billings *Gazette*, 20 October 1955.

"After Saving on Grub, Wouldn't President's 50 Chefs Bump You?" Denver *Post*, n.d.

"When I Came Back to Philadelphia" [by Suzette]. Boston *Post*, n.d.

"Cody Writer Tells of Meeting Buffalo Bill." Cody *Enterprise,* n.d.

"Incident of Childhood Makes Lincoln Birthday Memorable to Writer." N.p., n.d. Caroline Lockhart Collection. Box 9.

"Suzette Sees Machine that Can Level Cities, End Wars." Philadelphia, n.d. Denver *Post* Archives.

Unpublished Personal Documents and Manuscripts

Album and Scrapbook. Box 7. Accession No. 177. Caroline Lockhart Collection. American Heritage Center. Laramie, Wyoming.

Autobiographical Drafts. Boxes 9, 10. Caroline Lockhart Collection. American Heritage Center. Laramie, Wyoming.

Autobiographical Miscellany. Boxes 5, 7, 9, and 10. Caroline Lockhart Collection. American Heritage Center. Laramie, Wyoming.

Diary: New Mexico Territory, 1898. Box 17. Caroline Lockhart Collection. American Heritage Center. Laramie, Wyoming.

Diaries and Journals: Cody, Wyoming, 1918–38. Boxes 1, 2, 3, and Shelf Storage. Caroline Lockhart Collection. American Heritage Center. Laramie, Wyoming.

Manuscript. "That Wicked Woman." [Revised version by Eleanor Shoemaker entitled "The Black Widow.] Caroline Lockhart Collection. Box 9, folder 3.

Manuscript. "From Billings to Broadway." Caroline Lockhart Collection. Box 6.

BOOK REVIEWS

Review of *Me-Smith* by Caroline Lockhart. New York *Times* 16(19 March 1911).

Review of *Me-Smith* by Caroline Lockhart. *American Review of Reviews* 43 (11 June 1911).

"Young Wyoming Girl Is Creator of *Me-Smith.*" Review of *Me-Smith* by Caroline Lockhart. Denver *Times,* 18 May 1912.

"Darling." Review of *The Lady Doc* by Caroline Lockhart. New York *Times* 98 (27 October 1912).

Review of *The Lady Doc* by Caroline Lockhart. Chicago *Tribune.* N.d.

Review of *The Full of the Moon* by Caroline Lockhart. New York *Times* 19 (1 March 1914).

Review of *The Full of the Moon* by Caroline Lockhart. New York *Times Book Review,* 1 March 1914.

Review of *The Full of the Moon* by Caroline Lockhart. *Publishers Weekly* 85 (21 March 1914).

Review of *The Full of the Moon* by Caroline Lockhart. *Nation* 98(7 May 1914).

Review of *The Fighting Shepherdess* by Caroline Lockhart. New York *Times* 24 (1 May 1919).

"Caroline Lockhart Puts Stamp of Individuality on 'Old West and New.'" Review of *Old West and New* by Caroline Lockhart. Cody *Enterprise*, 19 April 1932.

"Changing West." Review of *Old West and New* by Caroline Lockhart. New York *Times Literary Supplement*, 9 November 1933.

CORRESPONDENCE

Andrews, E. E., to author. Ponca City, Oklahoma. 1 November 1982.

Commissioner, Asst. U.S. Land, to Caroline Lockhart. Billings, Montana. 7 July 1931.

Cook, John F., to Fred Johnson. Cody, Wyoming. 23 May 1934.

Crowder, Sylvia, to author. Tonkawa, Oklahoma. 15 July, 25 October 1982.

Dominick, David, to author. Denver, Colorado. 21 November 1984.

Dominick, Elizabeth P. (Mrs. Dewey), to author. Cody, Wyoming. 11 November 1982.

Eldridge, Paul, to Caroline Lockhart. Reno, Nevada. 19 September 1948.

Engelstoft, D., to Caroline Lockhart. Copenhagen, Denmark. 17 March 1922.

Fees, Paul, to author. Cody, Wyoming. 8 May, 28 August 1984.

Giddings, C. R., to Caroline Lockhart. Billings, Montana. 20 July 1931.

Hay, J. W., to Fred Johnson. Rock Springs, Wyoming. 22 May 1934.

Johnson, Fred, to Joe LeFors. Washington, D.C. 2 June 1934.

———, to Caroline Lockhart. Washington, D.C. 4 June 1934.

———, to Joseph C. O'Mahoney. Washington, D.C. 2 July 1934.

LeFors, Joe, to Fred Johnson. Buffalo, Wyoming. 21 May 1934.

Link, Betty, to author. Park Ridge, Illinois. 5 April 1984.

Lockhart, Caroline, to Fred Johnson. Dryhead, Montana. 15 May 1934.

———, to Dorothea Nebel. Dryhead, Montana. 4 November 1948.

———, to Dorothea Nebel. Kane, Wyoming. 23 September, 31 December 1948; 29 March, 11 June, 28 August 1950; 21 June 1952.

———, to Betty (—). Cody, Wyoming. 2 January 1951.

———, to Dottie-Runs-at-the-Nose. Kane, Wyoming. 13 June 1951.

———, to Dorothea Nebel. Cody, Wyoming. 8 July, 21 August, 22 August 1951; 18 January 1952.

———, to Vernon Spencer. Cody, Wyoming. 25 January 1960.

———, to Mary Jester Allen. Cody, Wyoming. N.d.

———, to Montana Fish and Game Department. Cody, Wyoming. N.d.

McGee, F. T., to Fred Johnson. Cody, Wyoming. 21 May 1934.

McIlvaine, Ellan, to Caroline Lockhart. New York City, New York. 30 July 1948.

Nebel, Dorothea, to author. Lovell, Wyoming. 12 July 1982.

Painter, Bill, to author. Millis, Massachusetts. 21 November 1982; 13 February,

1 April 1983; 30 April, 31 May, 26 June, 10 October, 5 November, December
    1984; 9 January 1985.
Reeve, Agnes M., to Caroline Lockhart. Franklin, Ohio. 23 March 1953.
Shoemaker, Eleanor, to Caroline Lockhart. New York City, New York. 24 March,
    31 March, 21 May, 28 May, 9 July 1948.
Sutton, Elizabeth, to author. Tonkawa, Oklahoma. 14 July 1984.
Sweeney, Marian, to author. Hamilton, Montana. 21 June, 21 July 1983; 10 June,
    12 October 1984.
Terhune, Albert Payson, to Caroline Lockhart. Pompton Lakes, New Jersey. 17 Feb-
    ruary 1935.
Wilkie, John E., to Caroline Lockhart. Washington, D.C. 19 February, 5 June
    1908.

COURT DOCUMENTS AND CENSUS RECORDS

Census records. Bighorn City, Wyoming. 1900.
Conger, C. M. "Reply and Answer to Cross Petition." Civil Appearance Docket
    43. File 885-1204. Park County District Courthouse. Cody, Wyoming. 20 Feb-
    ruary 1922.
C. M. Conger v. Caroline Lockhart. Civil Appearance Docket 3. File 885-1204 and
    File 890. Park County District Courthouse. Cody, Wyoming. 23 March 1923.
Department of Commerce, United States. Bureau of the Census. Twelfth Census of
    the United States, 1900: volume 179, E.D.
Giddings, C. R., Acting Registrar. Department of the Interior. U.S. Land Office.
    Billings, Montana. 14 May 1931.
E. J. Goppert v. Caroline Lockhart. Judgment 436. District Court of Washakie
    County, Wyoming. 29 April 1926.
E. J. Goppert v. Caroline Lockhart, George Huss and the Cody Enterprise. District
    Court of Washakie County, Wyoming. 29 April 1926.
Houx, F. L. Testimony. American Heritage Center. Caroline Lockhart Collection.
    Laramie, Wyoming.
Keyes, J. T. Affidavit sworn before W. H. Brundage, Justice of the Peace. 18 Decem-
    ber 1907. American Heritage Center. Caroline Lockhart Collection. Laramie,
    Wyoming.
Lockhart, Caroline. "Answer and Cross Petition," including copy of "Memoran-
    dum of Agreement" (dated 22 November 1921). 11 February 1922. Park County
    District Courthouse. Cody, Wyoming.
———. "Stock Raising Homestead Final Proof Certificate." 7 July 1931.
———. "Last Will and Testament." Park County District Courthouse. Cody,
    Wyoming.
McDonal, Raynald. Deposition sworn before Fred C. Barrett, Notary Public. Big-

horn County. State of Wyoming. 16 November 1907. American Heritage Center. Caroline Lockhart Collection. Laramie, Wyoming.

Oleson, John. Deposition sworn before Fred C. Barrett, Notary Public. Bighorn County. State of Wyoming. 12 November 1907. American Heritage Center. Caroline Lockhart Collection, Laramie, Wyoming.

Parrott, D. K., to Registrar. Re: "Closing Case: Promulgating Departmental Decision of March 12, 1936." U.S. Department of the Interior. General Land Office. Billings, Montana.

Perry, Guy C., Attorney. "Brief on Appeal." *History of Case.* U.S. Department of the Interior. N.d.

Petition, signed by Philip Snell, Joe Smith, E. C. Hulbert, Ervin Howard, E. G. Barry, C. G. St. John, Clarence A. Curen, and F. W. Blythe to Federal Land Office. Billings, Montana. N.d.

"Transcript of Testimony at Consolidation of Hearings." Department of the Interior in the U.S. Land Office. Billings, Montana.

United States of America v. *Caroline Lockhart, Clay Jolly, and Lou Ketcham.* "Stipulation for Consolidation of Hearings." Department of the Interior in the U.S. Land Office. Billings, Montana. 16 September 1933.

Wasson, James. Final Certificate, Homestead. 19 February 1926.

INTERVIEWS WITH THE AUTHOR

Buckingham, Catherine. Cody, Wyoming. 12 July 1982.
Crowder, Sylvia. Albuquerque, New Mexico. N.d.
De Maris, Bill. Cody, Wyoming. 17 July 1982.
Edgar, Bob and Terry. Cody, Wyoming. 9 July 1982.
Frost, Dick. Cody, Wyoming. 6 July, 8 July 1982.
Garlow, Fred. Cody, Wyoming. 30 June 1982.
Goppert, Ernest J., Jr. Cody, Wyoming. 30 June 1982.
Goppert, Ernest J., Sr. Cody, Wyoming. 12 July 1982.
Greever, William. Cody, Wyoming. 19 July 1982.
Hall, Lucylle. Cody, Wyoming. 8 July 1982.
Hayden, Francis. Cody, Wyoming. 15 July 1982.
Hicks, Lucille Patrick. Cody, Wyoming. 8 July 1982.
Hinton, Thelma. Cody, Wyoming. 9 July 1982.
Martin, Margaret Sylvester. Cody, Wyoming. 1 July, 12 July 1982.
Nebel, Dorothea. Cody, Wyoming. 1 July, 8 July, 9 July 1982.
Prante, Ray and Electa. Cody, Wyoming. 7 July 1982.
Roes, K. T. Cody, Wyoming. 8 July 1982.
Simpson, Milward. Cody, Wyoming. 13 July 1982.
Spencer, Mrs. Clifford. Cody, Wyoming. 8 July 1982.

Spencer, Helen. Cody, Wyoming. 17 July 1982.

Steffens, Ron. Cody, Wyoming. 9 July 1982.

Stock, Eloise. Cody, Wyoming. 1 July 1982.

Sullivan, N. Chicago, Illinois. 8 August 1984.

Sutton, Elizabeth. Tonkawa, Oklahoma. 5 July, 24 October 1984.

Todd, Audrey. Cody, Wyoming. 14 July 1982.

Secondary Sources

BOOKS

Alkofer, Daniel, Richard Etulain, William A. Gibson, and Cornelius A. Hoffman, editors. *Interpretive Approaches to Western American Literature.* Pocatello: Idaho State University Press, 1972.

Armitage, Susan, and Elizabeth Jameson, editors. *The Women's West.* Norman: University of Oklahoma Press, 1987.

Backus, Truman J. *Shaw's New History of English and American Literature.* New York: Thelden and Company, 1884.

Bailey, Robert G. *River of No Return.* Lewiston, Idaho: R. G. Bailey Print Co., 1948.

Beach, Cora M. *Women of Wyoming.* Casper, Wyo.: S. E. Boyer and Company, 1927.

Billington, Ray Allen. *America's Frontier Culture.* College Station: Texas A&M Press, 1977.

Bourne, Lawrence R. *Welcome to My West: I. H. Larom, Dude Rancher, Conservationist, Collector.* Cody: Buffalo Bill Historical Center, 1982.

————. *Dude Ranching: A Complete History.* Albuquerque: University of New Mexico Press, 1983.

Bower, Bertha M. *Chip of the Flying U.* New York: G. W. Dillingham, 1906.

Brown, Dee. *The Gentle Tamers: Women of the Old Wild West.* Lincoln: University of Nebraska Press, 1958.

Cather, Willa. *Not Under Forty.* New York: Alfred A. Knopf, 1936.

Carrey, Johnny, and Cort Conley. *River of No Return.* Cambridge, Idaho: Backeddy Books, 1978.

Connelly, William A. *A Standard History of Kansas and Kansans.* Volume 3. Chicago: Lewis Publishing, 1918.

Duke, Maurice, Jackson R. Bryer, and M. Thomas Inge, editors. *American Women Writers: Bibliographical Essays.* Westport, Conn.: Greenwood Press, 1983.

Engen, Orrin A. *A Writer of the Plains: The Biography of B. M. Bower.* Culver City, Ca.: Pontine Press, 1973.

Etulain, Richard W., editor. *The American Literary West*. Manhattan, Kansas: Sunflower University Press, 1980.

Essenwein, J. Berg. *Writing the Short Story*. New York: Hinds, Nobel, and Eldridge, n.d.

Faust, Langdon Lynne, editor. *American Women Writers: A Critical Reference Guide from Colonial Times to the Present*. New York: Continuum, 1983.

Fink, Augusta. *I-Mary: A Biography of Mary Austin*. Tucson: University of Arizona Press, 1983.

Fischer, Christiane, editor. *Let Them Speak for Themselves: Women in the American West. 1849–1900*. New York: E. P. Dutton, 1978.

Furman, Necah Stewart. *Walter Prescott Webb: His Life and Impact*. Albuquerque: University of New Mexico Press, 1976.

Hicks, Lucille Nichols Patrick. *The Best Little Town by a Dam Site*. Cheyenne: Flintlock Publishers, 1968.

——— . *Caroline Lockhart: Liberated Lady, 1870–1962*. Cheyenne: Pioneer Printing and Stationery Company, 1984.

James, Edward T., Janet Wilson James, and Paul S. Boyer, editors. *Notable American Women, 1607–1950: A Biographical Dictionary*. Volume 2. Cambridge: Harvard University Press, 1971.

Jeffrey, Julie Roy. *Frontier Women: The Trans-Mississippi West, 1840–1880*. New York: Hill and Wang, 1979.

Jensen, Joan M., and Darlis A. Miller, editors. *New Mexico Women: Intercultural Perspectives*. Albuquerque: University of New Mexico Press, 1986.

Larson, T. A. *History of Wyoming*. Lincoln: University of Nebraska Press, 1965.

Limerick, Patricia Nelson. *The Legacy of Conquest: The Unbroken Past of the American West*. New York: W. W. Norton, 1987.

Myres, Sandra. *Westering Women and the Frontier Experience, 1800–1915*. Albuquerque: University of New Mexico Press, 1982.

Rascoe, Burton. *Belle Starr: The Bandit Queen*. New York: Random House, 1941.

Ray, Grace Ernestine. *Wily Women of the West*. San Antonio: Naylor Company, 1972.

Riley, Glenda. *The Female Frontier: A Comparative View of Women on the Prairie and the Plains*. Lawrence: University of Kansas Press, 1988.

Schlissel, Lillian, Vicki L. Ruiz, and Janice Monk, editors. *Western Women: Their Land, Their Lives*. Albuquerque: University of New Mexico Press, 1988.

Stauffer, Helen Winter. *Mari Sandoz: Story Catcher of the Plains*. Lincoln: University of Nebraska Press, 1982.

Steffen, Jerome O. *Comparative Frontiers*. Norman: University of Oklahoma Press, 1980.

Sweeney, Marian. *Gold at Dixie Gulch*. Kamiah, Idaho: Clearwater Valley Publishing Company, 1982.

Webb, Walter Prescott. *The Great Frontier*. Austin: University of Texas Press, 1951.

JOURNAL ARTICLES, ESSAYS, AND REPORTS

Allen, Mary Jester. "Colonel Cody's Dream of Pioneer Center—A Reality." *Annals of Wyoming* 14 (January 1942): 20–22.

Armitage, Susan. "19th-Century Western Women Beginning to Come into Focus." *Montana: The Magazine of Western History* (Summer 1982): 2–7.

Billington, Ray Allen. "Cowboys, Indians, and the Land of Promise." In *America's Frontier Culture: Three Essays*. College Station: Texas A&M Press, 1977.

Campbell, D'Ann. "Was the West Different? Values and Attitudes of Young Women in 1943." *Pacific Historical Review* 47, no. 3 (1978):453–63.

"Caroline Lockhart's Best Novel." Hebard Collection. Western History Research Center. Laramie, Wyoming.

Dominick, Dewey. "Caroline Lockhart." *Dude Rancher Magazine* (Spring/Summer 1982):8–9.

Flexner Report. American Medical Association. 1912.

Griswold, Robert L. "Anglo Women and Domestic Ideology in the American West in the Nineteenth and Early Twentieth Centuries." In *Western Women: Their Land, Their Lives*, Lillian Schlissel, Vicki Ruiz, and Janice Monk, editors. Albuquerque: University of New Mexico Press, 1988.

"History of Cody Stampede." [Cody Stampede Program]. Buffalo Bill Historical Center. Cody, Wyoming. 1984.

Huseboe, Arthur R., and William Geyer. "Herbert Krause and the Western Experience." In *Where the West Begins: Essays on Middle Border and Siouxland Writing*, Huseboe and Geyer, editors. Sioux Falls, S.D.: Center for Western Studies Press, 1978.

Jameson, Elizabeth. "We Always Knew We Were Here: Women as Workers and Civilizers in the American West." In *The Women's West*, Armitage and Jameson, editors. Norman: University of Oklahoma Press, 1987.

Jensen, Joan M., and Darlis A. Miller. "The Gentle Tamers Revisited: New Approaches to the History of Women in the American West." *Pacific Historical Review* 49, no. 2 (May 1980):173–212.

Krauthammer, Charles. "Smithsonian Exhibit Takes Revisionism Back to the Frontier." Albuquerque *Journal*, 4 June 1991, A-3.

Matsuda, Mari J. "The West and the Legal State of Women: Explanations of Frontier Feminism." *Journal of the West* 24 (January 1985):45–55.

Meyer, Roy W. "Bertha M. Bower: The Poor Man's Wister." *Journal of Popular Culture* 7 (Winter 1973): 667–79.

Milton, John R. "The Western Novel: Whence and What?" In *Interpretive*

Approaches to Western American Literature, Daniel Alkofer, Richard Etulain, William A. Gibson, Cornelius A. Hoffman, editors. Pocatello: Idaho State University Press, 1972.

Norward, Vera. "Women's Place: Continuity and Change in Response to Western Landscapes." In *Western Women: Their Land, Their Lives*, L. Schlissel et al., editors. Albuquerque: University of New Mexico Press, 1988.

Petrick, Paula. "The Gentle Tamers in Transition: Women in the Trans-Mississippi West." *Feminist Studies* 11, no. 3(1985):677–94.

Robbins, Peggy. "Calamity Jane! Hellcat in Leather Britches." *American History Illustrated* 10 (June 1975):12–21.

Stegner, Wallace. "History, Myth, and the Western Writer." *The American West* (May 1967):77.

———. "The Provincial Consciousness." *University of Toronto Quarterly* 43 (Summer 1974).

Trulio, Beverly. "Anglo-American Attitudes toward New Mexico Women." *Journal of the West* 12 (1973):229–39.

Turner, Frederick Jackson. "The Significance of the Frontier in American History." *American Historical Association Annual Report for the Year 1893*.

Welter, Barbara. "The Cult of True Womanhood: 1820–1860." *American Quarterly* 18 (1966): 151–74.

Whitman, Digby. "Making Headlines." *The RAGAN Report: A Weekly Survey of Ideas and Methods for Communication Executives*, 22 November 1982.

MANUSCRIPTS

Culpin, Mary Shivers. Lockhart Manuscript. Buffalo Bill Historical Center. Cody, Wyoming.

Dominick, David. "An Introduction to Caroline Lockhart." Box 9. Caroline Lockhart Collection. American Heritage Center. Laramie, Wyoming.

Eldridge, Paul R. "Woman on Horseback." Box 7. Caroline Lockhart Collection. American Heritage Center. Laramie, Wyoming.

NEWSPAPER ARTICLES

"Local Notes." Cody *Enterprise*, 19 October 1904.

"Wedding Bells—Marriage of Mr. Thurston and Miss Goodman Makes a Gay Week in Cody." Park County *Enterprise*, 28 June 1906.

"The News of Elk City." Idaho County *Free Press*, 14 November 1912.

"Miss Caroline Lockhart, Author of 'Me, Smith' [sic], Is in Town on Her Way to Salmon River to Spend the Summer." Elk City *News*, 17 July 1913.

"Miss Lockhart in Search of Material." Park County *Enterprise*, 24 December 1913.

"Suzette Loses Novel in Ocean." Philadelphia *Bulletin*, 5 April 1914.

Stone, A. K. "Boy Howdy! Meet Caroline Lockhart! Famous Woman Novelist of West Joins *Post* Staff: Writer of Range Stories Has Known Adventure in Many Parts of World, but West Is Her First and Last Love and *Post* Her Choice of Newspapers." Denver *Post*. 3 December 1918.

"Drowned in Salt Creek." *The Chief*, n.p., 18 May 1919.

"Noted Cody Authoress Receives Big Offer from Douglas Fairbanks." Park County *Enterprise*, 23 July 1919.

"Announcement." Park County *Enterprise*, 12 May 1920.

"Jackson Hole to Be Ruled by Women." Park County *Enterprise*, 19 May 1920.

"Billings Must Hand It to Little Old Cody: Pinkie Gist, Champion Bull-Dogger of the World, Tells Montana Stockmen That We Know How to Get Out and Step." Park County *Enterprise*. 26 May 1920.

"For County and Prosecuting Attorney Republican Party." Park County *Enterprise*, 14 July 1920.

"Big Audiences See 'The Fighting Shepherdess'—Caroline Lockhart, Well-Known Author, Witnesses Movie, Suffers in Silence." Park County *Enterprise*, 21 July 1920.

"Filmmakers Unfair to Wyoming People." Park County *Enterprise*, 18 August 1920.

"Baby Wrangler to Be Provided So Mothers May Dance—Mary Quilico with Accordeen [*sic*]." Park County *Enterprise*, 20 October 1920.

"Caroline Lockhart and Charles M. Conger Owners and Publishers." Cody *Enterprise*, 10 August 1921.

"Fair Board Doing Good Team Work . . . Josh Deane's Barbecue a Drawing Card." Cody *Enterprise*, 21 August 1921.

"Josh Tells How to Barbecue." Cody *Enterprise*, 24 August 1921.

"Sage Ticks." Cody *Enterprise*, 31 August 1921.

"Hairbreadth Harry among the Missing." Cody *Enterprise*, 21 September 1921.

Wayne, Francis. "Man of Mistery [*sic*], Immortalized by Writer, Slain in Gambling Den for Refusing to Cheat." Denver *Post*, 21 December 1921.

"U.S. Is Falling Off Water Wagon." Cody *Enterprise*, 4 January 1922.

"Stampede Officers Elected for 1922." Cody *Enterprise*, 22 February 1922.

"New York *Evening Post* Praises *Enterprise.*" Cody *Enterprise*, 22 February 1922.

"Poker Nell's Husband to Hang at Rawlins for Killing 'Slim' Smith." Cody *Enterprise*, 15 March 1922.

"Sammy Girls Launch Campaign for Buffalo Bill Statue by Mrs. Harry Payne Whitney, Famous Sculptor." Cody *Enterprise*, 10 May 1922.

"We All Come to the Cody Stampede." Cody *Enterprise*, 24 May 1922.

"'Dude Wrangler' Will Be Filmed." Cody *Enterprise*, 31 May 1922.

"Design for Statue Is Being Prepared." Cody *Enterprise*, 4 October 1922.

"Enterprise Moves into New Home." Cody *Enterprise*, 14 February 1923.

Little, June. "Cowboys and Big Hats: Let's Keep Cody as It Used to Be." Cody *Enterprise*, 14 February 1923.

"1923 Cody Stampede Smashes All Records—Receipts Above $11,000—Great Ride Puts Frankie Lasater Among Champions." Cody *Enterprise*, 11 July 1923.

"Here's Chance for Goppert to Sue Casper *Oil Index*." Cody *Enterprise*, 18 July 1923.

"Miss Lockhart's Western Gang Due for a Surprise in New York." Cody *Enterprise*, 15 August 1923.

"Train Drops into River near Casper when Bridge Breaks." Cody *Enterprise*, 3 October 1923.

"Statue of Buffalo Bill Triumph of Mrs. Harry Payne Whitney's Career." Cody *Enterprise*, 16 January 1924.

"Caroline's Bobcat Cures Rheumatism." Cody *Enterprise*, 23 January 1924.

"Woodrow Wilson Is Dead." Cody *Enterprise*, 6 February 1924.

"Newton Sells Cody *Herald* to Partner." Cody *Enterprise*, 5 March 1924.

"Buffalo Bill Memorial Is an Expression of American Life Well Interpreted by Gertrude Vanderbilt Whitney, the Sculptor." Park County *Herald*, 2 April 1924.

"Plans for Unveiling Statue of Buffalo Bill Now Being Made." Cody *Enterprise*, 21 May 1924.

"Statue of Colonel Cody to Start on Journey Westward in Week." Cody *Enterprise*, 28 May 1924.

"Its-Be-Che-Loti to Organize Indians." Park County *Herald*, 4 June 1924.

"More than Ten Thousand People Witness Unveiling." Park County *Herald*, 4 July 1924.

"Big Gas Well Blows in Here." Cody *Enterprise*, 4 February 1925.

"Prohibition, Thy Name is Failure." Cody *Enterprise*, 25 February 1925.

"Marston Frees Mrs. Strand." Cody *Enterprise*, 25 March 1925.

"Goppert Lockhart Case Is Postponed." Cody *Enterprise*, 15 April 1925.

"Gop Has Another Tantrum; Demands $50 Damages from the Cody *Enterprise*." Cody *Enterprise*, 22 April 1925.

"Gop's Troubles to Be Heard Next Term of District Court." Cody *Enterprise*, 27 April 1925.

"Caroline Lockhart Quits Cody *Enterprise*." October 1925, B-L811-C, Hebard Collection.

"Caroline Lockhart Retires." October 1925, B-L811-C, Hebard Collection.

"V. H. Abrahamson Buys Cody *Enterprise*." 14 October 1925, Box 13, Caroline Lockhart Collection.

"Caroline Lockhart Is Sued for Libel." Denver *Post*, 27 April 1926.

"Caroline Lockhart Found Not Guilty of Libel on Lawyer." Denver *Post*, 29 April 1926.

"Ranch Work Delays Author in Completing New Book." Casper *Herald,* 16 February 1928.

"Caroline Lockhart Among Who's Who." Lander *Evening Post,* 24 November 1930.

"Tops Steer Market." Lovell *Chronicle,* 12 September 1935.

"Writer and Her Housekeeper Win in Homestead Disputes." Billings *Gazette,* 29 March 1936.

"Caroline Lockhart, Dryhead Rancher and Author, Has Had Life as Colorful as Any of Her Books." Billings *Gazette,* 25 April 1943.

"Local Ranch Woman Announce [sic] Engagement of Her Employees." Cody *Enterprise,* 1944.

Kelley, Nell B. "Caroline Lockhart, Writer and Rodeo Sponsor, Is Living Example of Wonderful Cody Pioneers." Northern Wyoming *Daily News,* 28 August 1958.

"Cody Life Appeals to Writer: Caroline Lockhart Deserted Career in East for Western Atmosphere." Billings *Gazette,* 7 February 1960.

"Author Caroline Lockhart Dies in Cody at 91 Years." Billings *Gazette,* 26 July 1962.

"Dave Good, Cody Oldtimer, Dies Monday." Cody *Enterprise,* 15 April 1965.

Legg, Carole. "Lockhart House Must Go; City Needs Parking Lot." Cody *Enterprise,* 16 February 1983.

Boyett, Frank. "Lockhart Home Auction Set for the End of this Month." Cody *Enterprise,* 21 September 1983.

"Lockhart House to Move to West Strip Tomorrow." Cody *Enterprise,* 21 March 1984.

"From the Start the Cody Stampede Was a Success." Cody *Enterprise,* n.d.

"Noted Cody Authors: Caroline Lockhart—Eloise Jensen." Cody *Enterprise,* n.d.

Fritjofson, Sarah. "Tough People Made the Cody Enterprise." N.p., n.d.

"Joseph C. Lockhart Is Dead." N.p., n.d.

Von Krosigk, Olga (Mrs. Hugh). "Descendant of Sheep Queen Is Meeteetse Resident." N.p., n.d.

Wright, Kathryn. "Author Caroline Lockhart Dies in Cody at 91 Years." Cody *Enterprise,* n.d.

PERSONALITY EVALUATION

Link, Betty. "Personality Evaluation of Caroline Lockhart." Professional Handwriting Analysts, Inc. Park Ridge, Illinois, 5 April 1984. Buffalo Bill Historical Center. Cody, Wyoming.

Index

All literary works are by Caroline Lockhart, unless otherwise indicated.